Global Institutions and the HIV/AIDS Epidemic

Written by a leading expert in the field, this book provides a clear and incisive analysis of the different perspectives of the global response to HIV/AIDS, and the role of the different global institutions involved. The text highlights HIV/AIDS as an exceptional global epidemic in terms of the severity of its impact as a humanitarian tragedy of unprecedented proportion, its multidimensional characteristics, and its continuous evolution over more than two decades.

The careful analysis in this volume critically reviews key issues in the global response, including:

- HIV/AIDS as a development challenge;
- North–South power relationships and tensions;
- international and regional partnerships between donor governments and recipient countries;
- governance of global institutions and impact on the capacity of developing countries to respond effectively to the epidemic;
- prevention versus treatment as options in HIV/AIDS services;
- how to make the money work in support of effective AIDS financing.

Providing a comprehensive but easy to read and compact overview of history, trends, and impacts of HIV/AIDS and the global efforts to respond effectively, this book is essential reading for all students of international relations, health studies, and international organizations.

Franklyn Lisk is Professorial Research Fellow at the Centre for the Study of Globalisation and Regionalisation (CSGR), University of Warwick, and was a Professor at the Africa Centre for HIV/AIDS Management at Stellenbosch University, South Africa, 2005–6. Prior to that he was the founding Director of the ILO Programme on HIV/AIDS and the World of Work in Geneva, as well as the ILO Global Coordinator for UNAIDS, 2001–5. He is co-editor (with Sophie Harman) of *Governance of HIV/AIDS: Making Participation and Accountability Count* (2009).

Routledge Global Institutions

Edited by Thomas G. Weiss
The CUNY Graduate Center, New York, USA
and Rorden Wilkinson
University of Manchester, UK

About the Series

The "Global Institutions Series" is designed to provide readers with comprehensive, accessible, and informative guides to the history, structure, and activities of key international organizations. Every volume stands on its own as a thorough and insightful treatment of a particular topic, but the series as a whole contributes to a coherent and complementary portrait of the phenomenon of global institutions at the dawn of the millennium.

Books are written by recognized experts, conform to a similar structure, and cover a range of themes and debates common to the series. These areas of shared concern include the general purpose and rationale for organizations, developments over time, membership, structure, decision-making procedures, and key functions. Moreover, current debates are placed in historical perspective alongside informed analysis and critique. Each book also contains an annotated bibliography and guide to electronic information as well as any annexes appropriate to the subject matter at hand.

The volumes currently published include:

37 Global Institutions and the HIV/AIDS Epidemic (2009)
Responding to an international crisis
by Franklyn Lisk (University of Warwick)

36 Regional Security (2009)
The capacity of international organizations
by Rodrigo Tavares (United Nations University)

35 The Organisation for Economic Co-operation and Development (2009)
by Richard Woodward (University of Hull)

34 Transnational Organized Crime (2009)
by Frank G. Madsen (University of Cambridge)

Books currently under contract include:

African Economic Institutions
by Kwame Akonor (Seton Hall University)

International Law, International Relations, and Global Governance
by Charlotte Ku (University of Illinois, College of Law)

Preventive Human Rights Strategies in a World of New Threats and Challenges
by Bertrand G. Ramcharan (Geneva Graduate Institute of International and Development Studies)

Humanitarianism Contested
by Michael Barnett (University of Minnesota) and Thomas G. Weiss (The CUNY Graduate Center)

Forum on China–Africa Cooperation (FOCAC)
by Ian Taylor (University of St. Andrews)

The Bank of International Settlements
The politics of global financing supervision in the age of high finance
by Kevin Ozgercin (SUNY College at Old Westbury)

For further information regarding the series, please contact:

Craig Fowlie, Senior Publisher, Politics & International Studies
Taylor & Francis
2 Park Square, Milton Park, Abingdon
Oxford OX14 4RN, UK

+44 (0)207 842 2057 Tel
+44 (0)207 842 2302 Fax

Craig.Fowlie@tandf.co.uk
www.routledge.com

Global Institutions and the HIV/AIDS Epidemic

Responding to an international crisis

Franklyn Lisk

Routledge
Taylor & Francis Group

LONDON AND NEW YORK

First published 2010
by Routledge
2 Park Square, Milton Park, Abingdon, Oxon OX14 4RN

Simultaneously published in the USA and Canada
by Routledge
270 Madison Avenue, New York, NY 10016

Routledge is an imprint of the Taylor & Francis Group, an informa business

© 2010 Franklyn Lisk

Typeset in Times New Roman by
Taylor & Francis Books
Printed and bound in Great Britain by
TJ International Ltd, Padstow, Cornwall

British Library Cataloguing in Publication Data
A catalogue record for this book is available from the British Library

Library of Congress Cataloging in Publication Data
Global institutions and the HIV/AIDS epidemic : responding to an international crisis / Franklyn Lisk.
   p. cm.
Includes bibliographical references and indexes.
1. AIDS (Disease)–Prevention–International cooperation. 2. AIDS (Disease)–International cooperation. 3. HIV-positive persons–Services for–International cooperation. 4. AIDS (Disease)–Patients–Services for–International cooperation. I. Title.
   RA643.8.L63 2009
   362.196'9792–dc22
              2009010894

ISBN 13: 978-0-415-44496-5 (hbk)
ISBN 13: 978-0-415-44497-2 (pbk)
ISBN 13: 978-0-203-87038-9 (ebk)

Contents

Illustrations

Table

Figures

Foreword

The current volume is the thirty-seventh in a dynamic series on "global institutions." The series strives to provide readers with definitive guides to the most visible aspects of what we know as "global governance." Remarkable as it may seem, there exist relatively few books that offer in-depth treatments of prominent global bodies, processes, and associated issues, much less an entire series of concise and complementary volumes. Those that do exist are either out of date, inaccessible to the non-specialist reader, or seek to develop a specialized understanding of particular aspects of an institution or process rather than offer an overall account of its functioning. Similarly, existing books have often been written in highly technical language or have been crafted "in-house" and are notoriously self-serving and narrow.

The advent of electronic media has helped by making information, documents, and resolutions of international organizations more widely available, but it has also complicated matters. The growing reliance on the Internet and other electronic methods of finding information about key international organizations and processes has served, ironically, to limit the educational materials to which most readers have ready access—namely, books. Public relations documents, raw data, and loosely refereed web sites do not make for intelligent analysis. Official publications compete with a vast amount of electronically available information, much of which is suspect because of its ideological or self-promoting slant. Paradoxically, the growing range of purportedly independent web sites offering analyses of the activities of particular organizations has emerged, but one inadvertent consequence has been to frustrate access to basic, authoritative, critical, and well researched texts. The market for such has actually been reduced by the ready availability of varying quality electronic materials.

For those of us who teach, research, and practice in the area, this access to information has been particularly frustrating. We were

delighted when Routledge saw the value of a series that bucks t
and provides key reference points to the most significant glob
tutions. They know that serious students and professionals want
analyses. We have assembled a first-rate line-up of authors to a⸳ₐress
that market. Our intention is to provide one-stop shopping for all
readers—students (both undergraduate and postgraduate), negotiators,
diplomats, practitioners from nongovernmental and intergovernmental
organizations, and interested parties alike—seeking information about
the most prominent institutional aspects of global governance.

Global institutions and the HIV/AIDS epidemic

Few diseases have punctured public consciousness like HIV/AIDS.
Fewer still have been entwined with and been used as vehicles for social
prejudices to be aired, cemented, and perpetuated. Prejudices have
certainly been expressed about the global South as a harbinger of Ebola,
dengue fever, river blindness, yellow fever, typhoid, and malaria,
among many other diseases. But the emergence and spread of HIV/AIDS
has become entangled with and reinforced prejudices about sexuality,
public morality, development, and civilization. These prejudices have,
in turn, frustrated both the medical response to HIV/AIDS as well as
the acknowledgment of the disease's "exceptionality" and its hidden
costs. They have also proven to be significant obstacles in developing a
coherent and robust global response to this deadly pandemic.

The first diagnoses of HIV/AIDS were embedded in a discourse that
associated the disease with immorality, played on social prejudices, and
served as an easy vehicle for blame. The initial discovery of AIDS by
American scientists treating gay men in New York and California in
the early 1980s led to crude monikers that reflected prejudices about
what was seen as socially problematic sexual activity. Among the names
by which HIV/AIDS was first known were "Gay-related Immune
Deficiency" (GRID) and "Gay Cancer." The discovery of the disease's
transmission among intravenous drug users sharing needles served only
to reinforce prejudicial ideas about the disease, its spread, and cause. For
far too many, deviant behavior was seen as the cause of the disease and
its contraction a harrowing form of natural justice. Indeed, only hemophiliacs that had caught the disease through contaminated blood transfusions were seen to be "innocents."

With the acceleration of the HIV/AIDS pandemic came a thickening
of the mythology about its cause and spread. Popular misconceptions
ranged from unclean or contaminated toilet seats, sharing cups and
glasses, sneezing, and the like. Gay men were heavily blamed for the

disease's spread and became social pariahs. Drug users were similarly demonized. Even "innocent" hemophiliacs were discriminated against for fear that they might inadvertently infect "healthy" populations.

Social knowledge about the disease did not, however, keep apace with the development of research into the causes and consequences of HIV/AIDS. Indeed, the research itself took many years to cast aside these prejudices, albeit in some quarters they continue to prevail. The discovery of HIV/AIDS in heterosexual women and men reinforced, rather than attenuated, social prejudices about gay men and intravenous drug users. Moreover, the location of the root of HIV/AIDS genesis in Africa, among primates, played into popular prejudices and misconceptions about the continent, the sexual morality of its populations, and development therein.

One consequence of these prejudices has been to frustrate international efforts to combat the spread of the disease as well as to help those living with its ravages. The emergence of a global HIV/AIDS architecture, the establishment of a World AIDS Day (1 December of each year), and other initiatives have been frustrated by the persistence of social myths about the disease as well as their mutation into other forms of "knowledge." One example of the latter has been the claim, prevalent in too many sub-Saharan African societies, that by having sexual intercourse with a virgin, men can "cure" themselves of the disease—though the only result has been to dramatically increase the number of rapes of young girls as well as the infection rates in this vulnerable section of the world population. As such, one of the first goals of these initiatives has been to correct public misconceptions about the disease and its impact and consequences. A second goal has been to highlight the hidden consequences of HIV/AIDS that often go unacknowledged—the disproportionately greater impact of the disease on women and girls, its effects on communities and development, the relationship between HIV/AIDS and poverty, and so on. But the challenge has not just been education and knowledge correction; it has also been to navigate the special interests of other powerful actors that, through the perpetuation of other social myths, have sought to frustrate global HIV/AIDS campaigns. Here, religious groups have proven to be particularly problematic. The Catholic Church's stand on condom usage has been particularly problematic; so too has been the suspect advice given to poor and marginal communities by non-state donors and other religious groups.

The story of this book, then, is not just about an institutional architecture designed to combat a particularly nasty disease. It is also about a struggle over knowledge, prejudice, and special interests. It is at one and the same time a harrowing and compelling account that relays to readers the qualities that all of the books in the Global Institutions series have—clear concise analysis, accurate factual information about aspects of global governance, and authority, clarity, and compunction of argument—as well as the political turbulence that has surrounded the disease and the international response that its spread has engendered.

Franklyn Lisk is the perfect person to write this book. We were delighted when he accepted our invitation. Franklyn is currently a visiting professorial research fellow in the Centre for the Study of Globalisation and Regionalisation at the University of Warwick working on a joint project with UNDP on Governance and HIV/AIDS Responses. Previously he was a professor at the African Centre for HIV/AIDS Management at Stellenbosch University in South Africa; and from 1974 until 2005 he was with the International Labour Organization (ILO) where he was, among other things, foundation director of the Global ILO Programme on HIV/AIDS and the World of Work. In addition, he was a global coordinator in the Committee of Co-sponsoring Organization (CCO) of UNAIDS and represented the CCO on the executive board of the Global Fund to Fight AIDS, Tuberculosis, and Malaria.

Franklyn's knowledge of HIV/AIDS and the governance response is second to none; the breadth and extent of his expertise is evident on every page of this fine book. This book is essential and compelling reading. We heartily recommend it; and we welcome comments from readers.

Thomas G. Weiss, the CUNY Graduate Center, New York, USA
Rorden Wilkinson, University of Manchester, UK
August 2009

Acknowledgments

The idea to write a book about *global* institutions and the *global* response to the *global* HIV/AIDS epidemic was suggested to me by Rorden Wilkinson, one of the two editors of the Routledge Global Institutions series, following a presentation that I made on global governance architecture for responding to HIV/AIDS at a conference in 2007. This book has been written while I am at the Centre for the Study of Globalisation and Regionalisation (CSGR) at the University of Warwick, which is an ideal setting from which to carry out research and sound out colleagues on my thinking and ideas on various issues covered in the book. I am grateful to the director and colleagues at CSGR for their support. I am particularly indebted to Sophie Harman, now at City University, who was a research fellow at CSGR when most of the work on this book was done; she read the draft chapters and gave me valuable comments. I would also like to express my gratitude to Annamarie Bindenagel Sehovic, a researcher in political economy and philosophy at the University of Kiel in Germany, and a collaborator of mine, who also read and commented on the manuscript and helped with ensuring that it met with the guidelines provided by the publishers. Sharifah Seakala, a Warwick Law School Ph.D. student working on HIV/AIDS issues and Jessica Owens, a former colleague at ILO/AIDS, Geneva, both provided research assistance at various stages in the writing of this book, and I appreciate their support.

Outside the academic community, I am especially grateful to Peter Piot, who as executive director of UNAIDS, Geneva, not only granted me interviews but also put his colleagues at my disposal to respond to requests for information and materials. Peter's deputy, Michel Sidibe, who has now succeeded him as UNAIDS executive director, was particularly supportive and found time on a number of occasions to discuss the "project" with me. Former colleagues from UN organizations that make up the UNAIDS co-sponsorship and from the Global Fund to Fight AIDS, Tuberculosis, and Malaria in Geneva also met with my requests for information and reports, and I am grateful to all of them. Finally, within my own family, the greatest thanks go to my wife, Janet, who missed out on a number of social events that I could not make myself available for because of "the book" but nevertheless supported me throughout and shared my passion for this work. My older daughter, Lynette, who also had her own writing project, a School of Oriental and African Studies (SOAS) Ph.D., was good at keeping in touch, comparing notes on our respective progress, and encouraging me to make it to the finish line.

Franklyn Lisk, CSGR, University of Warwick
February 2009

Abbreviations

AAAS	American Association for the Advancement of Science
ACT	AIDS Campaign Team for Africa
AIDS	Acquired Immune Deficiency Syndrome
ART	Antiretroviral Therapy
ARV	Antiretroviral
ASO	AIDS Support Organization
AU	African Union
CARICOM	Caribbean Community
CCM	Country Coordinating Mechanism
CCO	Committee of Co-sponsoring Organizations
CDC	U.S. Centers for Disease Control
CGD	Center for Global Development
CHGA	Commission on HIV/AIDS and Governance in Africa
CIS	Commonwealth of Independent States
CMH	WHO Commission on Macroeconomics and Health
DAC	OECD's Development Assistance Committee
DPKO	UN Department of Peace Keeping Operations
ECA	UN Economic Commission for Africa
ECOSOC	United Nations Economic and Social Council
ERC	External Review Committee
FHI	Family Health International
Global Fund	Global Fund to Fight HIV/AIDS, Tuberculosis and Malaria
GHWA	Global Health Workforce Alliance
GIPA	Greater Involvement of People Living with AIDS
GMC	General Management Committee
GPA	Global Programme on HIV/AIDS
GRID	Gay-Related Immune Deficiency Syndrome
GTT	Global Task Team
HIPC	Heavily Indebted Poor Country Initiative

HIV	Human Immune-deficiency Virus
HRH	Human Resources for Health
IAAG	Inter-Agency Advisory Group
IAS	International AIDS Society
IASC	United Nations Inter-Agency Standing Committee
IDA	International Development Agency
IFIs	International Financial Institutions
ILO	International Labour Organization
IMF	International Monetary Fund
IPRs	Intellectual Property Rights
IOM	International Organization for Migration
LFA	Local Fund Agent
MAP	Multi-Country AIDS Programme
MDG	Millennium Development Goal
MOU	Memorandum of Understanding
NAC	National AIDS Council
NGO	Non-governmental Organization
NIC	U.S. National Intelligence Council
NORAD	Norwegian aid agency
NPI	PEPFAR's New Partner Initiative
ODA	Official Development Assistance
OECD	Organisation for Economic Cooperation and Development
OGAC	U.S. Global AIDS Coordinator
OHCHR	Office of the High Commissioner for Human Rights
OVC	Orphans and Vulnerable Children
PCB	Programme Coordinating Board
PEPFAR	President's Emergency Plan for HIV/AIDS Relief
PLWHA	People Living With HIV/AIDS
PMTCT	Prevention of Mother to Child Transmission
PRSP	Poverty Reduction Strategy Paper
RP	Principal Recipient
SSA	Sub-Saharan Africa
TAC	Treatment Action Campaign
TB	Tuberculosis
TRP	Technical Review Panel
TRIPS	Trade-related Intellectual Property Rights
TTR	WHO's Treat, Train and Retain Initiative
UBW	Unified Budget and Workplan
UN	United Nations
UNAIDS	Joint United Nations Programme on HIV/AIDS
UNDP	United Nations Development Programme

UNESCO	United Nations Educational, Scientific and Cultural Organization
UNFPA	United Nations Population Fund
UNGASS	United Nations General Assembly Special Session on HIV/AIDS
UNHCR	Office of the United Nations High Commissioner for Refugees
UNICEF	United Nations Children's Fund
UNIFEM	United Nations Fund for Women
UNODC	United Nations Office on Drugs and Crime
USAID	United States Agency for International Development
VCCT	Voluntary Confidential Counseling and Testing
WFP	World Food Programme
WHA	World Health Assembly of the World Health Organization
WHO	World Health Organization
WPRO	WHO Regional Office for the Western Pacific
WSSD	World Summit on Sustainable Development
WTO	World Trade Organization

Introduction

This book presents different perspectives of the global response to the HIV/AIDS epidemic and the role of international institutions involved in this response. It focuses on the functions and governance structures of relevant global institutions and specifically analyzes the impact of decisions and actions of those institutions on the capacity of countries, communities, and individuals to respond to threats and challenges of the global HIV/AIDS epidemic. Looking at the HIV/AIDS epidemic as an international crisis, the analysis of the global response highlights the power relationships and tensions between the global South and the global North. The former is made up of the developing regions, mostly poor countries, where the epidemic is concentrated but with limited resources to deal with the problem, in contrast to the developed and rich industrialized countries that have the resources and knowledge to ensure an effective global response but are less affected by HIV/AIDS.

The book is organized to reflect the "exceptionality" of HIV/AIDS as a global crisis and to trace the "internationalization" of the response to this crisis. Key issues and actors involved in the global response to the epidemic are highlighted and analyzed in the various chapters, starting with the evolution of HIV/AIDS as a global epidemic and ending with a review of unresolved and emerging issues and challenges of critical importance to the response. In between, the individual chapters cover early efforts at global coordination of the response and at putting and keeping HIV/AIDS on the international agenda; the establishment of the special inter-agency institutional partnership established within the UN system to coordinate the global response; the challenges presented by the impact of the epidemic on human resource capacity and development prospect; the threat posed by HIV/AIDS to human rights and national security; the complexity of the financing of the global response; and concerns about imbalances in the governance structures of global institutions and the adverse effects on the response.

The book is also structured to show the significance of the evolution and impact of the HIV/AIDS epidemic as an exceptional global crisis in the context of current and emerging global health and international development concerns and policies. In this regard, it elaborates on the competing claims made by HIV/AIDS on health sector and overall developmental resources, as well as analyzing the threats posed by the epidemic to social and economic objectives of development, including the achievement of the Millennium Development Goals (MDGs). With respect to its focus on global institutions, the analysis of the global response examines the significance and relevance of new global institutions set up to deal exclusively with HIV/AIDS, and supports the need for change in the governance structures and decision-making processes of major global institutions in favor of an effective response to the epidemic at all levels. There is also recognition of the importance of international cooperation in the global HIV/AIDS response, which is reflected in the application of the concept of "global public goods" to the operational framework of the response and its emphasis on the universality of benefits from an effective global response. This is particularly relevant to the concluding discussion of critical and emerging issues in the global response, such as the feasibility of "universal access" to HIV/AIDS prevention, treatment and care, and the search for a successful vaccine against HIV infection, which undoubtedly require increased collaboration and solidarity between the North and the South and improved global governance.

The "exceptionality" of HIV/AIDS

Since AIDS was first diagnosed in the early 1980s, HIV—the virus that causes AIDS—has been identified and reported in every continent. It is now evident that HIV/AIDS can spread quickly and relatively easily within countries and across national borders. According to the latest annual *AIDS Epidemic Update*[1] published by the Joint United Nations Programme on HIV/AIDS (UNAIDS) and the World Health Organization (WHO), an estimated 33.2 million people globally were living with HIV at the end of 2007. In that year alone, there were 2.5 million new infections worldwide. The majority of those infected are in the developing regions and particularly in sub-Saharan Africa (SSA) where some of the poorest countries are to be found.[2] An estimated 25 million lives have been lost to AIDS so far, and the number of deaths from AIDS-related illnesses in 2007 was reported as 2.1 million, of which 1.6 million occurred in SSA. The global nature of the HIV/AIDS epidemic today is reflected in recent UNAIDS and WHO global HIV/

AIDS surveillance reports which indicate that, outside SSA, the disease is spreading in parts of Asia and in some countries in Eastern and Central Europe, and that HIV prevalence rates in parts of Latin America and the Caribbean are approaching 10 percent of the adult population. These reports also point to a resurgence of HIV infections among vulnerable groups in North America and Western Europe. Without doubt, HIV/AIDS is a global epidemic, or a "pandemic" in the sense of a series of epidemics of worldwide proportions (Figure I.1).

HIV/AIDS, however, is not the first global epidemic that has resulted in loss of lives in extremely large numbers and with significant demographic and social consequences. The bubonic plague in the Middle Ages killed tens of millions among the general population in a large swathe of Europe stretching from the Mediterranean to Scandinavia, and this consequently changed the course of European history on account of massive depopulation and labor scarcity in several existing "growth" centers and subsequent demographic changes and socio-economic adjustments. The Great Influenza of 1918–20 killed as many as 100 million people on both sides of the Atlantic over a very short period, making it the deadliest plague in history.[3] What then makes HIV/AIDS exceptional and different from previous global epidemics or more threatening than recent outbreaks of deadly infectious diseases with the potential of a global epidemic, such as Ebola fever, the SARS epidemic and the avian flu?[4]

The "exceptionality" of HIV/AIDS is linked first and foremost to the unique and specific biomedical characteristics of the disease, especially in terms of the modes and speed of the transmission of the virus and

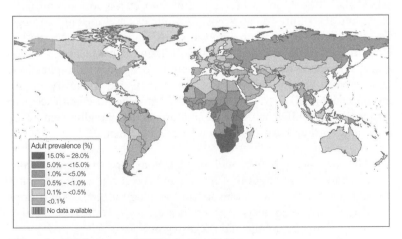

Figure 1. *A global view of HIV infection, 2007*

also on account of the fact that as yet there is no known cure for AIDS or an effective vaccine against HIV. Next, HIV/AIDS has profound and lasting non-health implications of the epidemic which include negative impact on development and threat to human and national security. In addition, the impact of HIV/AIDS on individuals and societies has given rise to complex legal and ethical issues that are linked to the stigma and discrimination directed at sufferers of the disease and consequent violations of fundamental human rights principles.

Unlike other past and recent global epidemics, HIV/AIDS has been around as a visible epidemic for nearly three decades without interruption. This is a considerably long period for the persistence of a single epidemic condition, and one with no sign of being brought under control, despite the unprecedented international attention and substantial financial resources that HIV/AIDS prevention and treatment have received and continue to attract. As already noted, there is no known cure for the disease or a successful vaccine against the infection, even though hundreds of millions of dollars have gone into scientific research and field trials worldwide. Human behavior plays an exceptionally important role in the spread of HIV/AIDS compared to other health problems or medical conditions. In the absence of a cure or a vaccine, the prevention of HIV and the control of its spread depend crucially on the responsibility of individuals not to put themselves or others at risk of infection.

A "long-wave" humanitarian tragedy

HIV/AIDS is exceptional because of its impact now on human well-being and the future threat it poses to human development. Through the immediate impact on mortality, expectancy, and population growth, HIV/AIDS has negative and profound consequences for economic and social development and serious demographic implications that threaten future generations. The severity and longevity of the impact of HIV/AIDS was emphasized by Peter Piot, the first executive director of UNAIDS, at a public lecture at the London School of Economics in February 2005, when he observed that:

> The key factor here would be the cumulative weakening from generation to generation of human and social capital: the severing of connections between one generation and another ... Apart from chronic armed conflicts, ... there is arguably no other cause today of such utter economic and social regress.[5]

The reality of HIV/AIDS as a continuing crisis has been described in terms of a "long wave" event whose path and outcome is not easy to predict.[6] This stands the HIV/AIDS epidemic apart from other recent epidemics like SARS and the avian flu or other humanitarian tragedies caused by natural disasters such as the tsunami, cyclones and earthquakes.

HIV/AIDS has killed at least 25 million people worldwide since it was diagnosed as a generalized epidemic in the early 1980s. While in terms of a humanitarian tragedy more people have died from other epidemics in the past, the continuation of a killer epidemic for more than a quarter century and with no sign of abating is without precedence in the history of global public health. Many millions already infected with HIV and who do not have access to adequate treatment and care will certainly die from AIDS-related illnesses within the next 10 years, even if a cure for the disease is found now. Although there is now treatment for AIDS that can prolong the lives of those infected with the virus, access to adequate and sustainable treatment and care is still beyond the reach of the vast majority of HIV-positive people who live in low-income countries in sub-Saharan Africa and other developing regions.[7]

Unlike other infectious diseases or major health problems such as tuberculosis and malaria, HIV/AIDS is exceptional in that most of those infected are from the working-age population. The disease disproportionately affects those in the prime of their productive lives who have critical economic and social roles in society. According to the International Labour Organization (ILO), over two-thirds of those who were infected with HIV worldwide in 2005 were workers in formal or informal employment or unemployed persons of working age.[8] Given the very high mortality rates associated with HIV infection in developing countries, the economic and social consequences of AIDS-related deaths at household and national levels are bound to affect the progress and sustainability of human development.

Human rights and gender equality concerns

One of the most disturbing features of the HIV/AIDS epidemic is the stigma and discrimination directed at HIV-positive persons. It is now widely acknowledged that HIV-related discrimination is a violation of basic human rights and a breach of the fundamental principle of non-discrimination and the equality of all people, as enshrined in the Universal Declaration of Human Rights of 1948 and other international human rights instruments which have been ratified by most member states of the UN. Human rights violations linked to HIV/AIDS are particularly serious in the context of the world of work in terms of access to employment and income-earning opportunities, as discussed later in Chapter 4, but there are also human rights implications with respect to the impact of the epidemic on vulnerable groups such as women, children and migrants which compound existing problems of discrimination, xenophobia, and gender inequality.

The gender dimension of HIV/AIDS is a particularly worrying feature of the impact of the epidemic. No other global epidemic or health problem has highlighted gender imbalances as much as in the context of the transmission, treatment and care of HIV/AIDS. The vulnerability of women and girls to the disease is reflected in the assertion that a woman of child-bearing age is two to three times more likely to be infected with HIV than her male peer in sub-Saharan Africa, which gives the epidemic a different status in terms of its strong link with gender inequality.[9] In addition, women are known to bear the brunt of the burden of care for HIV/AIDS victims in poor households in the developing regions, often at the expense of their own needs and interests, which further highlights the issue of the "feminization" of the epidemic as a matter of concern and principle.

Development challenge

The impact of HIV/AIDS on socio-economic development is seriously affecting some of the poorest countries in the world. This has transformed the fight against the epidemic into a major development challenge for those countries. There is already evidence from highly affected countries that the impact of HIV/AIDS is a factor in slowing down the pace of economic growth and in reversing past development gains.[10] This is undermining efforts to reduce poverty within countries and contributing to an increase in international inequalities through a widening of the gap between rich and poor countries. The impact of the HIV/AIDS epidemic in developing countries is now seen by the UN and the international donor community as a major obstacle to the attainment of the Millennium Development Goals (MDGs) set by the United Nations in 2000 with the overall aim of reducing extreme poverty significantly by 2015.[11]

Another feature of HIV/AIDS that warrants attention from a development perspective is its link with poverty. This is a two-way causative relationship: HIV/AIDS causing poverty at the household level through its negative impact on earnings and productive capacity and also through spending on AIDS treatment; and poverty being a factor in sustaining and spreading the existence of HIV infection, especially among high-risk groups.[12] In low-income countries, poor households are likely to become even poorer due to the impact of AIDS on their income, and poverty can contribute to greater exposure to the risk of being infected with HIV such as through the need to earn an income through commercial sex activities. Thus the epidemic is a manifestation of poverty conditions which are themselves the outcome of unsustainable livelihoods. At the macro level, resource-poor countries are likely to be less effective in responding to the threat posed by the epidemic, due to lack of basic healthcare services and facilities for preventing HIV and treating AIDS.

The "internationalization" of HIV/AIDS

The substantial attention given to HIV/AIDS on the international agenda in recent years has resulted in some of the biggest vertical programs in the history of public health and healthcare focused on a single disease. Over the past decade, two well resourced, specialized global institutions, UNAIDS and the Global Fund to Fight AIDS, Tuberculosis and Malaria (Global Fund), have been established to bolster the global effort against HIV/AIDS. International partnerships involving private sector organizations and philanthropic foundations, such as the Global Business Coalition on HIV/AIDS and the Bill and Melinda Gates Foundation, are major contributors to the global HIV/AIDS efforts,[13] and global advocacy bodies, such as the International AIDS Society and the International AIDS Alliance, have been created to promote and coordinate HIV/AIDS policy and action programs. The World Health Organization (WHO), which has the mandate for global health policy within the UN system, has launched a number of high profile HIV/AIDS initiatives including the Global Programme on AIDS (GPA) in the 1980s, and more recently the "3 by 5" Initiative in 2003 which was aimed at providing treatment to 3 million people in low- and middle-income countries by the end of 2005. Other UN agencies with non-health mandates, such as the United Nations Development Programme (UNDP), the United Nations Educational, Scientific and Cultural Organization (UNESCO), the United Nations High Commissioner for Refugees (UNHCR), the United Nations Office on Drugs and Crime (UNODC) and the International Labour Organization (ILO), are co-sponsors of UNAIDS and also allocate some of their own budgetary resources toward the global effort to combat HIV/AIDS. The World Bank has created special flexible and concessionary facilities to increase access of poor countries to financial resources for addressing HIV/AIDS. Since 2001, the United Nations

General Assembly has convened a number of special sessions and high-level meetings in New York devoted exclusively to HIV/AIDS.

HIV/AIDS is today prominent on the international agenda. This is reflected in declarations by the UN and the international community to take action against the epidemic, such as the Millennium Declaration (2000), the UNGASS Declaration of Commitment (2001),[14] the Political Declaration of the UN High-level Meeting (2006) and recent G8 summit communiqués (2005, 2007, 2008). In addition, a number of initiatives and partnerships have emerged on the international scene specifically to help mobilize resources and provide technical assistance to countries for a strengthened and effective HIV/AIDS response. Funding from various sources for the global HIV/AIDS response has skyrocketed from US$300 million in 1996 to US$8.9 billion in 2006. No other single global health problem or humanitarian concern has received so much attention or financial resources from the world community.

The UN and the international donor community are largely in agreement on the need for more resources to address the daunting multiple challenges of the global HIV/AIDS epidemic. There has been an upsurge in international cooperation among rich and poor countries to support the global HIV/AIDS response. This has resulted in external transfers and subsidies from richer countries to fund HIV/AIDS responses in resource-poor countries, primarily because the epidemic is seen as a global threat. The application of the concept of "global public goods" to the global HIV/AIDS response in this manner is founded on the thinking that it is in everyone's interest to act collectively against the epidemic and that lack of action can have consequences for all. Mobilizing international support to control the spread of the global HIV/AIDS epidemic is seen as a cost-effective investment on the part of rich countries, while at the same time could yield benefits to those poor countries facing deep and intractable development challenges due to the impact of HIV/AIDS.

1 The evolution of HIV/AIDS as a global epidemic and early global response

This chapter traces the evolution of HIV/AIDS from an unknown health condition as recently as the early 1980s to one of the most notorious diseases of our time, and outlines the initial response at the international level to a global epidemic. The notoriety of the HIV/AIDS epidemic can be attributed to many factors, ranging from its origin as a disease that primarily affected gay men in the United States and other rich countries and the identification of sex, both homosexual and heterosexual, as a means of HIV transmission to the vast numbers infected with the virus worldwide and the millions of deaths that it has caused so far, and the long-term impact on economic well-being and human development in poor countries. Following initial doubts about the generalized nature of the disease and its potential as a global epidemic, growing awareness of the negative impacts of HIV/AIDS contributed to early efforts by the United Nations, mainly through its health agency the World Health Organization (WHO), toward a coordinated global response.

The origin of AIDS

HIV/AIDS was first recognized as a medical condition in the early 1980s, although it is now known that symptoms resembling the "Human Immunodeficiency Virus" (HIV) that causes the "Acquired Immune Deficiency Syndrome" (AIDS) had been recorded by researchers as early as the 1950s.[1] Many uncertainties and conspiracy theories surround the origin of HIV/AIDS and the evolution of the disease into a global epidemic.[2]

The earliest cases of AIDS were reported in the United States in 1981 when doctors noticed cases of an extremely rare disease linked to immune deficiency syndrome among homosexual men mainly in New York and San Francisco. The first official report of this particular health condition was recorded in the weekly journal of the U.S. Centers for Disease Control (CDC) in June 1981.[3] Similar cases were later identified by U.S. doctors among other groups, mainly hemophiliacs and recipients of blood transfusions, and later among injecting drug users who shared needles.[4] By then, it was apparent that the immune deficiency syndrome was not restricted to "gay" men; previously labeled "Gay-Related Immune Deficiency Syndrome" (GRID), the disease was renamed "Acquired Immunodeficiency Syndrome" (AIDS) by the CDC in 1982. In 1983 the human immunodeficiency virus (HIV) was identified as the possible cause of AIDS, and by the mid-1980s it was already possible to test for the virus with reasonable accuracy.

Upon reading the June 1981 CDC report, some doctors in Belgium and France realized that they had encountered similar conditions among patients in central and western African countries since the mid-1970s. It was in Zaire (now Democratic Republic of the Congo) in the early 1980s that the epidemiology of heterosexual HIV/AIDS was first determined, laying the foundation for a pattern of the epidemic whose main features were to spread throughout sub-Saharan Africa with devastating effects.[5] It took quite some time before Western medical institutions endorsed the heterosexual-based diagnosis of HIV/AIDS, which had been observed and documented in Africa by both local and visiting physicians and epidemiologists. The disease did not attract international attention as a global public health problem of epidemic potential when it was first diagnosed, apparently, because it was originally linked to small and specific groups in rich countries which had the means to deal with the problem. It was much later that the international health and donor communities began to respond to HIV/AIDS as a generalized epidemic of potential crisis proportions.

Two Western medical scientists who later went on to head major global AIDS programs were associated with the earliest investigations of the epidemic in the developing world by Western medical institutions. Peter Piot, then a young Belgian epidemiologist and who later became the first executive director of UNAIDS, was a member of a team of European and American doctors which visited Kinshasa, Zaire, in October 1983 to follow up on reports about an immune dysfunctional disease affecting men and women equally. The team saw AIDS patients at the Mama Yemo Hospital in Kinshasa and reported their observations in the United States and Europe. Initial reactions to reports about the occurrence of AIDS among heterosexuals in Africa ranged from suspicion to disbelief. It took quite some time to convince the Western medical establishments about the validity of the report by

Piot and his colleagues. Eventually, the CDC agreed to fund a research project, "Projet SIDA," which was launched in Kinshasa in June 1984.[6] The project was led by an American public health specialist, Jonathan Mann, who later became the first director of the WHO's Global Programme on AIDS (GPA) in Geneva.

Mann and his team of dedicated workers carried out pioneering research which defined the epidemiology of HIV/AIDS as a global disease and laid the foundation for future biomedical analysis and action which are still applicable and practiced today. Projet SIDA was in effect the first international program on the epidemic, as it involved collaboration between Congolese, American, Belgian and French medical specialists, including Peter Piot.[7] Unfortunately, the project came to an abrupt end in 1991 when its premises were overrun by rioters and looters during political disturbances in the country and the expatriate staff left.

Initial response by the international system

The initial response at the international level to the spread of HIV/AIDS was by the United Nations through its health agency, the World Health Organization (WHO), and this was rather slow. Western medical scientists, including influential advisers to the WHO, were not convinced that the disease was a heterosexual problem, let alone of its potential to become a global epidemic or pandemic. This was despite reports in the early 1980s of HIV infection cases by African member states of the WHO, including statements by health ministers from the region at the annual WHO assembly. WHO continued to acknowledge the existence of HIV/AIDS as a new disease among specific groups in rich countries, and reports of the disease coming from Africa were perceived as cases of sexually transmitted infections and referred to a small unit at its Geneva headquarters that dealt with this condition.[8]

Further pressure from its African constituents led the WHO finally to begin to regard HIV/AIDS as a generalized public health problem. Around 1984, the WHO cautiously endorsed separate research findings by two Western scientists, Dr. Luc Montagnier of the Pasteur Institute in France and Dr. Robert Gallo of the National Institutes of Health in the United States, which confirmed that AIDS was caused by a retrovirus, HIV, and that the main modes of transmission were blood and semen. Even then, little attention and resources were allocated by the global health agency to the fight against HIV/AIDS as a global epidemic. It was felt that the rich countries where most AIDS patients at that time were to be found had the means to deal with the disease in their midst, and that it was not a major public health concern in the developing countries. Hence, at the first meeting on HIV/AIDS called by the WHO in Denmark in October 1983, the main priorities for action were listed as "safeguarding blood supplies and alerting homosexuals."[9] Until the mid-1980s, the WHO's role in addressing HIV/AIDS was essentially that of monitoring developments in member states, reporting and sharing information on outbreaks, and providing guidance to countries on how to minimize the risk of infection.

By continuing to regard HIV/AIDS as a health problem of rich countries which could afford to respond effectively to the disease, the WHO missed the initial opportunity to act against the rapid spread of the epidemic in Africa and also in the Caribbean and to contain its explosion into a global problem. The perception of the WHO at the time of the limited impact of HIV/AIDS in developing countries is reflected in the agency's statistics on reported cases of AIDS issued in September 1985: these indicated that about 15,000 persons were suffering from the disease worldwide, distributed as follows: "13,074 in the United States alone, 1,284 cases in Europe, 103 in Australia, 15 in Asia, and 723 in Latin America. No cases were reported from Africa, although several hundred were suspected there."[10]

Such a limited interpretation of the global spread of HIV/AIDS presumably prompted the WHO's director-general at the time, Dr. Halfdan Mahler, a Danish national, during a visit to Zambia in 1985 to strongly rebut the claim by African member states of the WHO that "AIDS is spreading like a bush fire in Africa."[11] He warned against African countries "making AIDS a front page issue" to the detriment of "malaria and other tropical diseases that are killing millions of children" in the continent.[12] It is significant to note that this view by Mahler was expressed after the first International AIDS Conference had been held in Atlanta in 1985 under the joint co-sponsorship of the CDC and the WHO. This rather slow initial response by the international system to the epidemic was out of line with what was known then about the ease and speed with which the disease was transmitted in several African countries. It unfortunately, and with grave consequence, delayed the emergence of a coordinated global response by the United Nations.

Mahler's judgment on HIV/AIDS reaction and response in Africa did not in any way reflect a bias by the WHO against investment in healthcare by developing countries. In fact, Mahler was a staunch supporter of promoting and improving health standards in the developing countries and had been responsible for launching the WHO's Primary Healthcare initiative in the late 1970s as the priority program of the agency. At the time, Mahler genuinely believed and considered HIV/AIDS as diversion from the objectives of the WHO's "Health for All" programs in the developing regions.[13]

Early efforts at a coordinated global response

Continued increase in the number of AIDS cases worldwide after 1985 triggered the move toward a coordinated global approach to HIV/AIDS response from the WHO. The health agency acknowledged its responsibility to coordinate a global strategy for containing the disease, in addition to promoting and facilitating exchange of information about AIDS among member states in all regions. As part of its new responsibility, the WHO sought to identify antiviral vaccines that might be used against HIV/AIDS.

WHO's Division of Communicable Diseases was headed by Dr. Fakry Assad, a Syrian national, who was given overall responsibility for managing the agency's global HIV/AIDS response. This move marked a change in WHO's perception of and, hence, its response to HIV/AIDS, representing a shift from a disease affecting mainly specific groups in rich countries to increasingly a disease of epidemic proportions affecting developing countries without the means to cope. Coming from a developing country himself, Assad felt that WHO should specifically provide direct support to countries in the developing regions, asserting that, "AIDS is not only an American problem," and pointing out that, "When we began to realize that it is spreading to other countries, we decided we must make sure we have the means available, all the tools for handling it."[14]

Once it was obvious within the WHO hierarchy that HIV/AIDS was fast becoming a global epidemic, action was initiated by Director-General Mahler to mobilize donor funding from rich countries and to provide technical assistance to member states in developing regions as part of the agency's strategy for dealing with the disease. Increasing pressure from African member states led the WHO's executive board in January 1986 to instruct Mahler to develop activities within the framework of the agency's programs to support national AIDS control efforts, especially in Africa. At a meeting called by the WHO Regional Office for Africa in March 1986, it was proposed that WHO should assist member states in the region to develop capacity to carry out epidemiological assessment, maintain an HIV/AIDS surveillance system and provide public education for prevention of the infection. Later, at the World Health Assembly in May that year, health ministers from the African region led the discussions resulting in the adoption of a resolution by the Assembly calling for a "Global Strategy for Prevention and Control of AIDS."

WHO responded to this resolution by setting up the Control Program on AIDS within its Division of Communicable Diseases in the second half of 1986. By then, Mahler had come to realize that AIDS was "a pandemic as mortal as any pandemic there has ever been." The program was renamed the Special Program on AIDS in February 1987 and later became the Global Programme on AIDS (GPA) in January 1988 in recognition of the global characteristic of the epidemic and the more permanent status for addressing the problem within the WHO's structure. Dr. Jonathan Mann, then the director of Projet SIDA in Zaire and already one of the world's leading experts on the epidemic, was appointed as the first director of the GPA.

Conclusion

Following initial hesitation and consequent delay on the part of the United Nations system and the international donor community to recognize and address HIV/AIDS as a global health problem, for reasons outlined in this chapter, the establishment of the GPA in 1987 marked the beginning of awareness at the global level of the scale and potential catastrophe of a global HIV/AIDS crisis. Implicit in this awareness was the need to mobilize international support and resources for a coordinated global response by the United Nations aimed at controlling the spread of the epidemic. The GPA, which is discussed in the next chapter, was seen as a suitable and cost-effective arrangement for collective action by the UN system, coordinated by the WHO, and collaboration within the international community of states. This was based on two considerations. First, that the impact of the HIV/AIDS epidemic has implications beyond the health sector, and therefore required a multi-sectoral response involving inputs from other UN agencies. The second is the notion that the fight against the global HIV/AIDS epidemic was in the common interest of all countries, both rich and poor, in a globalizing world with increasing interdependence between countries. In retrospect, what was not foreseen at the time the GPA was launched by the WHO was the probability of inter-agency rivalry within the UN system that would eventually result in failings of the GPA with respect to its main function of coordinating the global response.

2 The rise and fall of the WHO's Global Programme on AIDS (GPA)

This chapter recounts the earliest effort by the United Nations through its health agency, the WHO, to put in place an institutionalized arrangement for the coordination of the global response to the HIV/AIDS epidemic. It traces the history of the GPA from its establishment as a WHO-led global program in 1987 to its demise in 1992/1993, following a mixed performance which ranged from initial successes in mobilizing what were then massive financial resources and international support for a still relatively unknown epidemic to the challenges and tensions implicit in the inter-agency and intra-WHO rivalries that marked the operation of the program. Noteworthy achievements of the GPA which are still pertinent to the global response included the promotion of a rights-based approach which was aimed at addressing the serious problem of stigma and discrimination associated with the disease, and the need to recognize the non-health and multidimensional characteristics of the epidemic and their impact. Yet, it was on account of failing to respond adequately to this latter need that criticisms were levied against the GPA that contributed to its demise. This first attempt at an inter-agency coordination at the global level to combat HIV/AIDS, or any global infectious disease for that matter, could be seen as the precursor for the model of UN inter-agency collaboration that was to emerge a decade later as the joint program, UNAIDS, which is the subject of Chapter 3.

Early success of the GPA under the leadership of Mann and Mahler

The establishment of the GPA by the WHO at the beginning of 1987 brought the UN health agency to the forefront of the global effort to fight HIV/AIDS, and led to its designation by the UN General Assembly in the autumn as the "lead agency" for coordinating action by the UN system against HIV/AIDS. The GPA could thus be seen as the precursor of a model of UN inter-agency collaboration on HIV/AIDS response that was to emerge a decade later as the Joint United Nations Programme on HIV/AIDS (UNAIDS).[1]

Although the GPA was located in and managed by the WHO, the program was not financed within the framework of the agency's regular budget. It was funded mainly by extra-budgetary contributions from rich donor countries who preferred to provide assistance to the developing countries for HIV/AIDS through a competent multilateral agency rather than bilaterally. At the time, the major bilateral donors either lacked the expertise to cooperate with their development partners at country level on HIV/AIDS projects, and some may have been concerned about political and religious sensitivities associated with the epidemic and the implications of them being directly involved. In the WHO, they found a partner which had the knowledge and capacity to coordinate a global response and the experience of working with national authorities on health issues. The GPA thus provided an ideal mechanism for the mobilization of resources by the international donor community to support a coordinated global response against the HIV/AIDS epidemic.

The GPA grew and blossomed under the leadership of Jonathan Mann, who had succeeded in winning the confidence and support of a once-skeptical Director-General Mahler. The two men complemented each other: as the executive head of WHO, Mahler spared no effort to raise public awareness about the epidemic; as the technical specialist and a competent manager, Mann focused on defining the global strategy for coordinating efforts by the UN and the international donor community and providing technical assistance at national level. At a press conference at the United Nations in New York in November 1986, Mahler described HIV/AIDS as "an unprecedented challenge to global public health," and at the 1987 session of the UN General Assembly he publicly committed the WHO fully to the "urgent, difficult and complex task of global AIDS prevention."[2]

With support from Mahler and substantial funding from bilateral and multilateral donors,[3] Mann built a dynamic team of able and competent staff which numbered over 200 at the peak of the program. The initial priorities of the GPA were exchange of information and provision of guidelines; public education as a means of controlling the spread of the virus; assessment of diagnostic methodology; advice on safe blood and blood products; and coordination of research. Under Mann's leadership, AIDS was not perceived solely as a medical problem. He had defined the "global AIDS strategy"[4] in terms of prevention of

HIV infection, reducing the human and social impact of the epidemic, and harmonization of national and international efforts against AIDS. This broader conceptualization of the global response was reflected in Mahler's address to the UN General Assembly in late 1987, in which he not only seized the opportunity to draw attention to HIV/AIDS as a global health problem, but also referred to the "social, economic, demographic, cultural, and political" impact of the disease.[5] This was probably the first time that HIV/AIDS was publicly recognized at the global level as not merely a biomedical concern, but as a health problem with other important non-health implications. The multi-dimensional characterization of the disease precipitated the adoption of a UN General Assembly resolution in 1987 which acknowledged the pandemic proportions and the wider non-health implications of HIV/AIDS.[6]

The global AIDS strategy had mentioned the need to ensure confidentiality of HIV testing and the provision of counseling and other support services, and this point was again emphasized in an update of the strategy by the WHO in 1992 which drew attention to the stigma attached to the infection and objected to discrimination against HIV-infected persons.[7] Mann had opposed compulsory testing for the purpose of screening, detecting and isolating infected persons, which was then considered a sound public health principle; he argued that discriminatory measures would in fact drive infected persons underground, where they are inaccessible to interventions to control the spread of the disease. Mann was particularly concerned about detecting and excluding HIV-positive persons from employment and other socio-economic opportunities, and in June 1988, the GPA teamed up with the ILO to organize a joint "Consultation on AIDS and the Workplace" in Geneva. The final report of this meeting, which was attended both by representatives of the world of work and health specialists, "Statement from the Consultation on AIDS and the Workplace," made reference to the World Health Assembly resolution entitled "Avoidance of Discrimination in Relation to HIV-infected People and People with AIDS," which, *inter alia*, urged member states to "protect the human rights and dignity" of those affected.[8]

Advocacy by the GPA to counter HIV/AIDS-related stigmatization and discrimination laid the foundation for the incorporation of a rights-based approach in HIV/AIDS responses.[9] In this regard, Mann was visionary, as the issue of HIV-related violation of human rights was hardly on the international AIDS response agenda at the time. Within a few years, the WHO had taken a definitive position on protection of rights: at its annual World Health Assembly in 1992, it adopted a resolution which stated clearly that, "there is no public health rationale for any measures that limit the rights if the individual, notably measures establishing mandatory screening."[10] Other UN agencies such as the ILO, the United Nations Development Programme (UNDP) and the United Nations Children's Fund (UNICEF) were later to embrace a rights-based approach as a central pillar of their own HIV/AIDS initiatives.

Mann was proud of the GPA's contribution to the incorporation of a rights-based approach in HIV/AIDS response, and observed that "For the first time in history, preventing discrimination against infected people became an integral part of a strategy to control an epidemic of infectious disease."[11] However, there were those in the international health community who did not agree with him on the need for a rights-based approach in HIV/AIDS response, arguing that such an approach which excluded screening was not realistic in the context of what was known to be a mass heterosexual epidemic. They evoked the traditional public health approach that calls for action by public authorities to protect society against the spread of epidemics, as opposed to a rights-based approach that seeks to protect human rights in the context of efforts to control the transmission of the disease. The clash between the two diametrically opposed approaches has continued to be a feature of AIDS and human rights debate, and is discussed in detail in Chapter 4.

The existence of the GPA, and the high profile it enjoyed under Mann, encouraged an increasing number of member states to formally request WHO's assistance in the preparation of short- and medium-term country plans to control the spread of HIV/AIDS. By 1989 well over 100 requests for technical assistance from member states had been dealt with by the GPA, and the majority of these concerned the implementation of national AIDS plans which were developed with the assistance of the WHO. The GPA became the conduit for channeling financial assistance from both bilateral and multilateral donors to member states toward the implementation of the plans. The global program was also instrumental in providing guidance for the establishment of HIV/AIDS units within health ministries at national level in the late 1980s and early 1990s.

In addition to working with health ministries at country level, the GPA found it also practicable to involve relevant non-governmental organizations (NGOs) and AIDS Support Organizations (ASOs) in the implementation of the national AIDS plans. Although as an intergovernmental institution, the WHO is obliged to deal primarily with governmental authorities at national level on issues of policy and planning, Mann had nevertheless recognized the importance of partnership with civil society and community-based organizations in HIV/AIDS prevention and care, in view of the nature of the disease and the wider non-health implications of its impact. The GPA therefore encouraged governments in affected member states to recognize and support NGOs and ASOs and their activities as part of their national HIV/AIDS programs.

Although the GPA's global strategy recognized the multiple and non-health sector implications of HIV/AIDS, it was not easy to incorporate these into national HIV/AIDS responses. Most national AIDS plans at the time were prepared by medical doctors and specifically designed to be implemented and managed by medical personnel in the health ministry and sector. Hence the economic and social impact and wider development implications of the epidemic were hardly addressed in those early plans. It was also not easy to get health ministries to accept the need for a broader multi-sectoral response involving other sector ministries, as this would have entailed them sharing available financial resources for combating HIV/AIDS with those ministries. The WHO, through the GPA, therefore did not achieve much initially in terms of promoting a multi-sectoral approach to the global response. It was left to the UNDP, the development planning arm of the United Nations and one of the original sponsors of the GPA within the UN system, to press for the adoption of a multi-sectoral approach at the country level which reflected a broader understanding of the causes and consequences of HIV/AIDS. UNDP teamed up with the GPA to establish a pragmatic alliance, the "WHO/UNDP Alliance to Combat AIDS," which focused mainly on the provision of broader development-oriented support for national AIDS programs.

As the GPA expanded its activities globally, Mahler and Mann sought to ensure that HIV/AIDS attracted international attention beyond the United Nations system. Because of the role of the rich donor countries in funding the GPA through the WHO, the issue of HIV/AIDS had been discussed at the G7 Venice summit of heads of state and government in June 1987. The WHO included HIV/AIDS on the agenda of a world summit of health ministers in London in January 1988, and the "London Declaration on AIDS Prevention"[12] which emerged from that meeting went well beyond the medical dimension of HIV/AIDS to recognize social consequences as well as the need for the protection of human rights. The London Declaration significantly also called for international cooperation between rich and poor countries in the global response to the epidemic, which corresponded to the need for a global public goods approach to the response, as was to emerge much later. In a further attempt to put HIV/AIDS on the international agenda, the WHO set up the Global Commission on AIDS in 1988 to serve as a policy guidance framework for the global response. This commission was made up of international experts and the objective was to provide the WHO/GPA with guidance on the currency and relevance of its policies and strategies for dealing with what was still an evolving global epidemic.

Pressure for change in the status and governance of the GPA: the Nakajima era

The high profile of the GPA and its success raising large amounts of extra-budgetary funding for its activities led to jealousy and friction within the WHO. Some within the agency's senior management felt that the practice by the GPA of working directly with member states instead of going through the WHO's regional structures gave the perception of the program being a separate entity, rather than an integral part of the WHO. This eventually led to pressures both within and outside the WHO for the GPA to be integrated into the regular budget and management structure of the WHO. Until then, the GPA had been run as a relatively autonomous donor-funded program within the wider WHO structure. Significantly, these pressures for change in the status and governance of the GPA coincided with the election in 1988 of a new WHO director-general, Dr. Hiroshi Nakajima, a Japanese scientist and former director of WHO's Regional Office for the Western Pacific (WPRO).

Unlike Mahler, Nakajima was from the start enthusiastic about bringing the GPA within the direct control of the WHO's powerful regional offices, which are headed by elected regional directors, rather than by officials appointed by the director-general as in the case of other UN agencies. Nakajima, who had himself served two five-year terms as the regional director of WPRO immediately before his election as WHO director-general, argued that integrating the activities of the GPA into the regional programs of the WHO was in line with the decentralized structure and work plan of the health agency and consistent with established protocol governing relationships with member states.

Nakajima therefore sought to limit the scope and personality of Mann's authority and to scale down the GPA, which by then had become by far the largest and richest WHO program. Soon after taking office as director-general, Nakajima established a General Management Committee (GMC) to supervise the GPA. The GMC was made up of the UN agencies that had sponsored and supported the establishment of the GPA, UNICEF, UNDP, the United Nations Population Fund (UNFPA), the United Nations Educational and Scientific Organization (UNESCO), and the World Bank, and representatives of donor and recipient countries. The GMC was authorized to oversee the activities of the GPA, including monitoring and evaluation of the program. Furthermore, stemming from his own background and previous experience in the WHO in drug procurement and distribution, Nakajima favored a biomedical approach to HIV/AIDS response by the WHO that emphasized the development and availability of effective antiviral drugs. However, confining the GPA to a mainly biomedical mandate as envisaged by Nakajima, could in effect erode the WHO's overall responsibility for coordination of the global response, which included non-health issues.

In the wider context of the WHO's mandate for global health policy, there were hints from Nakajima's pronouncements and actions that he was of the opinion that HIV/AIDS was getting far too much attention within the overall structure of the agency. In Nakajima's view, the balance had to be redressed sooner rather than later. This tendency to downplay the importance of HIV/AIDS in the WHO's global health agenda, as well as Nakajima's own preference for bringing the GPA under the control of the regional directors, brought him onto a collision course with Mann.[13] It was therefore not surprising when Mann resigned in March 1990, to be replaced by Dr. Michael Merson, previously head of the WHO's Control of Diarrhea program.

The departure of Mann provided an opportunity for Nakajima to introduce measures that effectively limited the autonomy of the GPA and brought it more under the control of WHO's senior management. Merson thus took over as director of a much weakened GPA that was characterized by considerable demoralization among the technical staff, several of whom left the program following the resignation of Mann. After Mann's departure, there was apparently also concern among some of the major donors of the program about the effectiveness of the GPA in its new and weakened format. This was to be reflected in a decline in donors' contributions to the GPA for the first time in 1991.

Criticisms of the GPA as a mechanism for coordination of the global response

The UN agencies which had sponsored and supported the GPA financially became increasingly disillusioned with the mainly medical approach that the program was advocating and practicing during the Nakajima era. Some openly criticized the WHO and observed that presumably the health agency had realized that it was beyond its competence and capacity to coordinate the non-medical aspects of the HIV/AIDS epidemic. WHO, on its part, felt that these criticisms were unfair, as there was evidence of the GPA striving for a broad-based response that reflected the multidimensional nature of the epidemic and its impact, as well as indications of its willingness to work with other UN agencies at the global level and with non-health sector ministries at country level. Merson saw ulterior motives among the main critics within the UN system who, in his opinion, "wanted their agencies to be more prominent in the pandemic and to have more money, and one way of doing this was to accuse the WHO of being more medicalized."[14]

There may have been some truth in Merson's view. By then some agencies, such as UNICEF[15] and UNDP, had already put in place their own HIV/AIDS programs which were vying with the WHO for donor money; also the World Bank was by then committing its own funds to support national AIDS responses.[16] It was felt within the WHO that other UN agencies were more interested in waving their own flags, rather than being content with being part of a joint UN effort coordinated by the WHO. Similarly, some bilateral donors were by then finding it in their interest to be identified directly with specific interventions AIDS on the ground, rather than putting their money into a common pool via the WHO. Interestingly, the UN inter-agency rivalry and flag-waving by bilateral donors which emerged in these early years of the global response has continued to be a feature of the global AIDS response up to the present time.

In trying to respond to criticisms levied at the GPA, the WHO made some practical moves toward promoting and incorporating a multi-sectoral approach to the global HIV/AIDS response. These included attempts to get health ministries to work closely with other sector ministries in national responses. But in so doing, WHO was caught in a dilemma: on the one hand, it recognized the validity of multi-sectoralism, but on the other, realized that this approach would take money and power away from the health sector and from its own constituency, the ministries of health at country level.

With its regional offices now having a greater say in the implementation of the GPA, the bulk of the WHO's resources to fight AIDS at country level was under the control of the health ministries, which were understandably suspicious of multi-sectoralism. They saw this approach as a means of taking away resources from them in favor of non-health sectors to address a problem which they perceived as primarily a health concern. Not surprisingly, the vast majority of health ministries were against adopting a multi-sectoral approach in their national AIDS control programs. Two notable exceptions at the time were the health authorities in Thailand and Uganda, which had favored a multi-sectoral approach in their national response even as early as the beginning of the 1990s in recognition of the wider developmental impact of the epidemic on their societies.

The issue of the country-specificity of HIV/AIDS response was another ground on which criticisms were levied at the WHO. It was alleged that GPA-sponsored national AIDS plans were based on a "one-size-fits-all" blueprint that was strongly influenced by Geneva, and that such a standardized approach did not respond adequately to socio-economic and cultural differences and diversities between countries. This was all the more serious when it later became apparent that HIV/AIDS was now a long-wave epidemic which required sustained interventions grounded on tradition and trend, rather than quick fix solutions associated with shorter-wave infectious disease outbreaks. WHO was cognizant of the shortcomings associated with lack of country-specificity in the earlier national AIDS plans, and sought to rectify this problem in the next set of plans which appeared in the early 1990s. These were inherently more country-specific to accommodate special country circumstances, as well as flexible to allow for the involvement of non-health sector ministries and non-state actors in policy formulation and plan implementation.

Challenge to the WHO's lead agency role

Although the WHO's lead agency role within the UN system in HIV/AIDS response was explicitly recognized in two United Nations Economic and Social Council (ECOSOC) resolutions in successive years, 1987 and 1988,[17] this did not deter criticisms of the GPA by other UN agencies and by donors which argued that the program was failing in its global coordinating function and that it lacked interest and capacity to adopt a multi-sectoral approach. Ironically, these ECOSOC resolutions provided a basis for advocating change in the global coordination of HIV/AIDS response within the UN system. The 1987 ECOSOC resolution, for example, called for an integrated approach to the management of HIV/AIDS within the UN system, and to this end a "Standing Committee" chaired by the UN Under-Secretary-General for Economic and Social Affairs was set up within the UN secretariat. The Standing Committee actually operated through a "Steering Committee" that was made up of representatives or focal points of the New York-based UN agencies. The primary objective of this arrangement was to promote inter-agency cooperation in the implementation of the global AIDS strategy. The WHO for its part responded to this UN secretariat-based initiative and the ECOSOC 1987 resolution by setting up an "Inter-Agency Advisory Group" (IAAG) in April 1988, with the main objective of "coordinating the activities of the entire UN system in support of the WHO Global AIDS Strategy."

The existence of these parallel structures for the purpose of inter-agency coordination represented an unnecessary and possibly costly duplication, and reflected the continuing in-fighting between WHO, on the one hand, and the participating UN agencies, on the other. In the end, neither structure fulfilled its mandate effectively: the Standing Committee met infrequently and lacked authority, while the IAAG initially focused its attention mainly on developing an HIV/AIDS policy aimed at UN personnel.

Failure to achieve any visible measure of inter-agency collaboration, and the perception by major donors that the WHO under the leadership of Nakajima was more interested in addressing HIV/AIDS as only a health sector issue, led to the decision by the General Management Committee of the GPA in late 1989 to commission an independent external review of the program after five years in existence. The terms of reference and membership of the External Review Committee (ERC) which was made up of 10 people of different nationalities and a range of professional backgrounds were agreed upon during 1990. The first meeting of the review committee took place in January 1991, and this was to set in train a process that was to lead eventually to the demise of the GPA and establishment of a new joint UN program in its place.

External review of the GPA and the demise of the program

The ERC carried out its work throughout 1991, during which time its members visited a number of countries as well as the regional offices of the WHO. Interviews were conducted with WHO personnel, including GPA staff, and with representatives of other UN agencies, donors, governments, and NGOs. The ERC produced a draft report by the end of 1991 which was circulated among members of an ad hoc Working Group of the GMC for their observations. The final report was published in June 1992.[18]

The report recognized major achievements of the GPA, particularly in raising public awareness and facilitating exchange of information at global and national levels in what was then an unknown epidemic, and providing advice and technical assistance to well over 100 countries. It also highlighted the non-medical consequences of the epidemic and its impact, including the need for action to protect human rights. The main criticism of the GPA in the report was with respect to its weaknesses and failings in its main function of coordinating inter-agency activities at global and country level, and collaboration with other relevant institutions and organizations outside the health sector. In particular, it noted that inter-agency rivalries led to costly duplication of efforts at country level and weakened the global response to HIV/AIDS.

In addressing one of its terms of reference which concerned the future role and priorities of the GPA, the ERC report was quite clear about the need for "new or alternative mechanisms for ensuring effective coordination of the global efforts to combat AIDS at the country level and adequate collaboration within and beyond the UN system."[19] In this regard, the report went on to outline a number of options. The ERC favored an arrangement involving clearly defined roles and activities of several participating agencies, with a new coordinating structure situated within the UN at a significantly high level but outside the structure of the WHO. While recognizing and endorsing the lead role of the WHO in global health policy within the UN system, the report nevertheless called for a clarification of this role at both international and national levels. Finally, the ERC report recommended that a working group be set up to act on its findings, especially on the issue of UN collaboration and inter-agency coordination. This process was to lead eventually to the establishment of the UNAIDS.

The recommendations of the ERC generated much interest and lively debates and negotiations among key stakeholders. Major donors, including the Scandinavian countries, the U.K., Canada, and the Netherlands, favored a "joint and co-sponsored" program with participating agencies drawn from those who were members of the GPA General Management Committee (GMC)—namely, UNDP, UNICEF, UNFPA, UNESCO, the World Bank, and, of course, WHO. The WHO was rather apprehensive about the prospect of losing control to a new agency on HIV/AIDS, and sought reassurance in the negotiations that it would retain management—and thus control—of the new joint program which would be cosponsored by multiple agencies. To support its claim for some sort of control over the new joint program, the WHO evoked the existing model of the Tropical Diseases Research and Training Programme, which is a joint and co-sponsored program that is based in the health agency, as a workable arrangement for the new joint program on HIV/AIDS.

Key stakeholders, including the UN, major donors and civil society organizations, believed that a successor to the GPA should be a sort of joint program whose ownership would be identified with a broad spectrum of UN agencies rather than a structure dominated by a single or lead agency. This itself was a major challenge for a UN system that is made up of diverse specialized agencies, each with its own identity, mandate, and territorial niche, and each run by its own secretariat and governing body.

Conclusion

The experience and lessons from the GPA clearly indicated that an effective global response had to be grounded on inter-agency collaboration and broad-based cooperative effort involving multiple stakeholders at global and national levels. This reflected the need to respond to HIV/AIDS as a multidimensional task that required the expertise of policy-makers from other sectors in addition to health. The non-medical dimensions of the epidemic included not only social and economic impact but also culture, religion, human rights, and politics. Because of this multidimensional characteristic of HIV/AIDS, it was felt both within and outside the United Nations that no single agency within the UN system was capable of responding adequately to the totality of the multiple problems and possible solutions of HIV/AIDS. The emerging consensus was that coordination of the global response needed collective action by multiple stakeholders, based on the recognition of the multidimensional nature of the epidemic and its impact. As we shall see in the next chapter, the establishment of the new joint and cosponsored program, UNAIDS, was a bold and significant move in this direction that resulted in the creation of one of the most unique experiments in UN inter-agency collaboration.

3 The birth of the Joint United Nations Programme on HIV/AIDS (UNAIDS)

This chapter traces the events leading to the establishment of UNAIDS as a unique institutional partnership within the framework of the UN system, following the demise of the GPA, and outlines the obstacles and challenges that confronted the birth of the new joint program. The structure and governance of UNAIDS is presented and analyzed in the light of the concept and the reality of "co-sponsorship" around which the new program has been modeled, highlighting the trying relationship between the co-sponsoring agencies and the increasingly powerful secretariat, and between the program and the efforts within the higher-level United Nations Organization. The chapter also brings into focus the achievements of UNAIDS in mobilizing global support and resources to combat the epidemic, and in ensuring that the problem of HIV/AIDS has remained prominently on the international agenda in the face of challenge from other pressing global concerns such as poverty, climate change, and terrorism.

The transition from the GPA to a new joint program

As recommended by the External Review Committee (ERC) on the future of the GPA, the WHO established a "working group" made up of government representatives of both donor and recipient countries and the European Commission to act on the findings of the ERC report. The working group which met several times during 1992 proposed new ways to strengthen coordination of HIV/AIDS response at global and country levels. With respect to inter-agency collaboration at the global level, while endorsing the leadership of the WHO in global health policy, the working group favored the establishment of a new program under the "joint ownership" of a number of UN agencies, as opposed to one controlled or dominated by a single agency. It recommended that participating agencies should become "co-sponsors" of the new joint program, and that a new coordinating structure should be situated within the UN at a very high level. However, it was realized that agreement on the structure and functioning of the type of coordinating mechanism favored at the working group would require long consultations and negotiations among the participating agencies and others concerned, and that these would take much more time than the working group had at its disposal. Priority was therefore given to securing the willingness and commitment of the participating agencies to work together and on how to achieve this, while leaving the details on structure and operating modalities of the new program to be worked out later.

A broad-based "Task Force on HIV/AIDS Coordination" made up of representatives of donor and recipient governments, UN agencies, and NGOs was set up and mandated to work closely with the General Management Council of the GPA. The idea of establishing a link between this task force and the WHO, via the GPA, was regarded by the working group as necessary to facilitate the transition of UN-system coordination of the global HIV/AIDS response away from a WHO-led and controlled mechanism and toward a joint, multi-agency co-sponsored program. The activities of the task force precipitated a number of important developments in the process within the UN system that eventually led to the creation of UNAIDS by the Economic and Social Council (ECOSOC).

Concerned about the proposal of the task force to replace the GPA by a new joint program, the WHO at its annual World Health Assembly (WHA) in May 1993 adopted a resolution which called on the director-general of the agency to explore the feasibility of a "joint and co-sponsored" UN program on HIV/AIDS that would address "the social and economic impact of the epidemic" in addition to bio-medical interventions.[1] Action taken by the WHO on the WHA was designed to ensure the continuation of the existing GPA-type coordinating arrangement which left the health agency in control, and ignored the need for a broader response to HIV/AIDS beyond what the GPA was offering. This also overlooked the practical problems of competence and resources implicit in the WHO taking on the additional responsibility of an expanded response on behalf of the entire UN system. It was obvious that the WHO was not going to embrace the idea of surrendering overall responsibility for coordination of the global response to a new independent agency within the UN system, given that it considered HIV/AIDS to be essentially a health problem which falls within its constitutional mandate as the health agency of the UN system.

Notwithstanding the position of the WHO and its interpretation of the May 1993 WHA resolution, developments were unfolding at the United Nations in New York that sounded the death knell for the GPA. The conclusions of the ERC pertaining to the future of the GPA and the different options proposed for the coordination of the global response to the HIV/AIDS epidemic within the UN system were reviewed by ECOSOC, which eventually went ahead and adopted its own resolution in July 1994 that effectively endorsed the establishment of a joint UN program on HIV/AIDS.[2] The ECOSOC resolution called on the five GPA participating agencies, UNDP, UNESCO, UNFPA, UNICEF and the World Bank, to cooperate with the WHO in a consultative process to establish such a joint program. These six agencies established an inter-agency working group to act on the ECOSOC resolution, and they were to become the original co-sponsors of the new joint program.

Prior to the adoption of the July 1994 ECOSOC resolution, UN Secretary-General Boutros Boutros-Ghali, in an attempt to streamline the management of HIV/AIDS response within the UN system, had informed the UN General Assembly on World AIDS Day (1 December) in 1992 that the existing Inter-agency Advisory Group on HIV/AIDS (IAAG) would be reconstituted to become the sole inter-agency coordinating mechanism for HIV/AIDS activities within the UN system. IAAG was strengthened and made more representative and democratic, with an increase in the number of participating agencies and the annual rotation of its chair among the member agencies. It should be noted that IAAG has continued to exist even after the establishment of UNAIDS, and today it constitutes a broader forum for inter-agency cooperation on HIV/AIDS response within the UN system than the UNAIDS co-sponsorship arrangement.[3]

Events leading to the establishment of UNAIDS

While there was interest among the participating agencies in coordination of HIV/AIDS response at the global level, it was apparent that some agencies were not ready to sacrifice their distinct approaches to the response in favor of joint activities at country level. The World Bank, for example, which had integrated HIV/AIDS concerns into its development agenda and lending programs, and by then committed hundreds of millions of dollars for HIV/AIDS-related activities in Africa, was not enthusiastic about any option that would involve giving direct responsibility for project implementation at country level to the new joint program. Other participating agencies like UNESCO, UNFPA and UNICEF, even though at the time they did not have significant HIV/AIDS programs of their own, also had reservations about a joint program whose coordination functions extended beyond the global level to include activities in the field. The consensus that emerged from the participating agencies on the structure and responsibility of the new joint program was in favor of an option that would concentrate on defining a global strategy and coordinating the efforts of UN agencies, but without interfering in the design, planning, and implementation of programs and activities by individual agencies at country level.

This option, however, did not address the need to improve coordination of HIV/AIDS activities by UN agencies at country level, an issue which the report of the ERC had identified as vital to the success of the proposed joint program and one which recipient countries themselves regarded as necessary. The ECOSOC resolution of July 1994, which in effect formally authorized the establishment of a new joint and co-sponsored program and set a timetable for it to become operational by 1 January 1996, unfortunately did not elaborate on coordination arrangements at the country level. The resolution was more concerned about getting the new joint program operational by the target date without clarifying operational details, apparently to forestall any attempt by the WHO to prolong the existence of the GPA.

The 1994 ECOSOC resolution listed six broad objectives of the new joint program, including the provision of global leadership, promoting global consensus on policy and program approaches, strengthening program implementation and monitoring capacity at the national level, advocating and enhancing political commitment at all levels, and promoting wide political and social mobilization. However, the resolution was rather vague on the governance and management structures and on financing of the new joint program, leaving such important matters to be determined later on the basis of inter-agency discussions among the co-sponsors of the new program. The lack of clarity in the 1994 ECOSOC resolution about the management of the new joint program and the modality of inter-agency collaboration was later to become the basis for future misunderstanding and tension between the co-sponsors, on the one hand, and the independent secretariat of UNAIDS. This would also contribute in the future to the uncertainty at times among members of the UNAIDS governing body and its major donors about the division of responsibilities between the joint program's secretariat and the co-sponsoring agencies.

The concept of "co-sponsorship" and the central role of the Committee of Co-sponsoring Organizations (CCO)

The 1994 ECOSOC resolution called for the establishment of a "Committee of Co-Sponsoring Organizations" (CCO), made up of representatives of the original six participating agencies. In order to avoid the problem of inter-agency rivalry which plagued the GPA, the resolution stressed the importance of the concept of "co-sponsorship" and indicated that the new joint program would be operated on "the basis of co-ownership, collaborative planning and execution, and an equitable sharing of responsibility" among the co-sponsors. The ECOSOC resolution also implicitly gave the CCO responsibility to act as the transition team to supervise the development and establishment of the new joint program, including defining its strategic and policy directions. The involvement of the co-sponsors in the establishment of the new program in this manner was perceived as vital for ensuring cooperation among the different participating agencies and harmonization of their respective HIV/AIDS activities at global and, hopefully, country level. The CCO was later to become the main organ for coordination of inter-agency activities including the implementation of a unified UNAIDS budget and work plan (UBW) involving all of the co-sponsors, as well as the mechanism for liaison between the co-sponsoring agencies and the secretariat of the joint program.

The CCO met for the first time in the autumn of 1994, and it decided that the new joint program would operate with administrative support from the WHO and that co-sponsoring agencies should assign professional staff to the secretariat of the joint program. Acting as the transition team for the establishment of the new joint program, the CCO prepared a report with details on the purpose, staffing requirements, resource mobilization strategy and proposed budget for the new program, and presented it to ECOSOC in May 1995. The CCO report endorsed the 1994 ECOSOC resolution regarding the urgent need for a new joint program, emphasizing that "only a special United Nations system program is capable of orchestrating a global response to a fast-growing epidemic ... whose roots and ramifications extend into virtually all aspects of society."[4] ECOSOC acted immediately on the CCO report by proposing in a July 1995 resolution that a formal agreement should be signed by the participating agencies to become the co-sponsors of the new program.[5] This decision was made by ECOSOC without even first obtaining the clarifications it had requested from the CCO on the management and governance structures of the new program. ECOSOC was keen to get the joint program operational by its target date of 1 January 1996 and, to this end, acted immediately on the CCO report by proposing that the participating agencies should go ahead and sign a formal agreement among themselves to become the co-sponsors of the new program.

Furthermore, even before the CCO presented its report to ECOSOC, a candidate for the post of director of the joint program had been identified and recommended by the CCO for appointment by the UN secretary-general in December 1994. It was argued that lack of leadership was affecting the progress of the transition process, and that the new director should join the transition team immediately to fill this gap. The candidate selected for the post was Peter Piot, who at the time was the GPA's Director of Research and Intervention Development. As the head of the transition team, Peter Piot had the opportunity of influencing the structure and functions of the new program that was to be formally launched a year later in January 1996.

During 1995, the CCO, now effectively under the leadership of Piot, had to make important decisions on the governance, staffing and funding of the new program for approval by ECOSOC. As regards the governance structure of the new program, the CCO opted for the proposal in the 1994 ECOSOC resolution, which was that a "Programme Coordinating Board" (PCB), whose composition was to be determined later on the basis of wide-ranging discussions, should fulfill this important governance function. Piot interpreted this to imply that membership of the PCB should include not only government representatives but also non-state stakeholders. This did not go down well with some of the co-sponsoring agencies which resented the idea of the responsibility for governance of the new program vested in a body that included representatives of NGOs and civil society, as distinct from representatives of governments at the United Nations. Some agencies also wanted the CCO, rather than the PCB, to be the main decision-making body for the new program. Piot had a difficult time convincing the CCO that the PCB should be the governing body of the new program, as proposed in the 1994 ECOSOC resolution. Even more difficult was Piot's attempt to persuade the CCO that NGOs should be represented on the PCB, in line with his passionate conviction about the need for civil society to have a voice in the new joint program's decision-making body.[6] The CCO agreed to adopt the PCB model proposed in the 1994 ECOSOC resolution and, as a compromise, to include representatives of NGOs in the governing body of the new program but as non-voting members.

From the experience of dealing with the CCO on the functions and composition of the PCB, it was obvious to Piot that working with the co-sponsors in the transition team to secure consensus on a number of key issues was not going to be easy. Now firmly established as the leader of the transition process, Piot adopted a pattern of decision-making that increasingly relied on informal brainstorming sessions involving knowledgeable and influential "outsiders." These outsiders included diplomats, academics and technical specialists, representatives of the private sector and private foundations, and AIDS activists from both developed and developing countries. Piot was also able to secure financial support from non-UN sources for organizing these informal sessions.

The apparent success of this informal arrangement effectively assigned a lesser role to the representatives of the participating agencies on the CCO, and contributed eventually to the termination of the work of the CCO as a transition team by the spring of 1995. By then, Piot had put in place a preparatory team to work on the strategies and structures of the new joint program. The preparatory team was made up of representatives of the co-sponsors, some ex-GPA staff members and civil society actors. Piot also paid particular attention to consultation with stakeholders in the field and, with the active support of the preparatory team, organized a series of regional briefings in Dakar, Nairobi, New Delhi, Santiago, and Venice during 1995.

The launch of UNAIDS

Five of the six original co-sponsoring agencies signed a formal Memorandum of Understanding (MOU)[7] in October 1995 (the MOU is reproduced in Appendix 1). The exception was the World Bank, which signed the agreement later in 1996. The World Bank at the time was rather reluctant to assume responsibility and liability for the existence of UNAIDS, and initially wished to keep its involvement with the new program very limited. By then the Bank had in place its own HIV/AIDS program and was funding activities in several developing countries as part of its health sector and related programs.[8] Since then, four other UN agencies have signed memoranda of understanding with UNAIDS to become co-sponsors of the joint program: the United Nations Organization on Drugs and Crime (UNODC) in 2000; the ILO in 2001; the World Food Programme (WFP) in 2003; and the United Nations High Commissioner for Refugees (UNHCR) in 2004.

Although UNAIDS was officially launched on 1 January 1996 with the closure of the GPA at the end of 1995, the new joint program was already in operation by mid-1995 with Piot and key staff of the secretariat installed and functioning from office space and with administrative support by the WHO in Geneva. The program's governing body, the Programme Coordinating Board (PCB), was also constituted before the formal launch of UNAIDS and it met for the first time in Geneva in July 1995. The PCB focused its attention on the responsibilities of the co-sponsors, functions of the secretariat, and the budget of the program—issues which had not been addressed by the ECOSOC resolution which created UNAIDS. Discussions on the budget were protracted and divisive. Some donors wanted to fund only a small secretariat with only policy and program coordination functions, implying that the bulk of the new program's money should go directly to the co-sponsoring agencies to support their own HIV/AIDS activities as part of the global response. Others supported the view of Piot, who argued strongly for the funding of a bigger secretariat that could also carry out vital advocacy functions and disseminate strategic information, in addition to coordination.

Piot succeeded in convincing the PCB to agree to a larger secretariat and, hence, a much higher level of indicative biennial budget for the new program than had been initially proposed. The first UNAIDS budget was set within the range of US$120–140 million for the biennium 1996–97. Unlike the budgets of most UN agencies which are based on assessed contributions from member states, funding of the UNAIDS biennial budget was made contingent on payments derived from voluntary contributions and pledges from donor governments and other sources. Hence, the actual level of the joint program's budget would depend almost entirely on the amount of money raised during the biennium. In addition to funds raised by UNAIDS for activities by the joint program, the co-sponsors themselves are expected to allocate funds within their own regular budget resources to support agency-specific HIV/ AIDS activities carried out by them at country level.

The challenge of co-sponsorship

As the successor to the GPA which had been seriously affected by problems of inter-agency rivalry, there were expectations among the international donor community and recipient countries that the new joint program would overcome these problems and enable the UN system to provide a better and expanded global response. Joint ownership, as implied in a co-sponsored program, was intended to provide a firm foundation for improved collaboration on policy and cooperation in the planning and implementation arrangements among the co-sponsors. Even with this new arrangement based on the notion of co-sponsorship and joint ownership, the achievement of collaborative and harmonious working relationships among the co-sponsors and other UN agencies at country level could pose a major challenge.

According to the UNAIDS model, the effectiveness of collective action by the co-sponsors depended on cooperation among the agencies on the ground and the extent to which their respective interventions were integrated and aligned with national programs. In reality, cooperation among several UN agencies on a single agenda was not common in the UN system where different agencies tend to identify with their own mandates and technical competencies. Being a co-sponsor of the new joint program did not preclude an agency from having and operating its own HIV/AIDS program at country and regional levels; on the contrary, this was supposed to be the means through which co-sponsors as technical agencies were expected to contribute to the global response on the basis of their respective competencies and mandates. Given the necessity of attracting additional funds for their own HIV/AIDS activities in the field, individual co-sponsors would be inclined to emphasize their relevance and comparative advantage in order to attract resources from donors. Such a development could in fact result in competition among the co-sponsors for attention and resources and threaten the attainment of inter-agency cooperation which was required for the effective functioning of the new joint program.

The structure of UNAIDS

UNAIDS is the first and, so far, the only joint and co-sponsored program of the United Nations. It is an innovative formal partnership within the UN system that brings together the different technical competencies and resources of several agencies to act collectively as a single program on a specific agenda. This is unique in the history and experience of the United Nations. There are now ten UN co-sponsoring agencies within the UNAIDS partnership: ILO, UNDP, UNESCO, UNFPA, UNHCR, UNICEF, UNODC, WHO, WFP, and the World Bank.

The UNAIDS partnership benefits from the different competencies and technical resources of the co-sponsors which cover many disciplines and themes, as could be discerned from a useful summary put out by the UNAIDS secretariat.[9] The range of issues and sectors covered by the mandates of the 10 co-sponsors makes it possible for UNAIDS to engage a variety of partners, including governments, the private sector and civil society, to support an expanded response to the HIV/AIDS epidemic. For example, the tripartite membership structure of the ILO comprising of governments, employers, and workers gives UNAIDS direct access to the key actors and mechanisms in the world of work where the impact of the epidemic affects the health as well as the livelihoods and human rights of individuals, and which serves as a means of engaging the private sector. The global development network of the UNDP provides the UNAIDS partnership with the opportunity and means to integrate HIV/AIDS concerns into a development planning framework at country level and to address the governance challenge of AIDS response. UNICEF's focus on children and women has been particularly useful to UNAIDS for addressing the transmission of HIV from mother to child through pregnancy, and highlighting the plight of the millions of children orphaned by AIDS. The competence and resources of the WHO play a vital role in expanding access to antiretroviral treatment globally and in strengthening health sector infrastructures and personnel for effective HIV/AIDS response.

Although the roles of the co-sponsors are defined with respect to their respective agency mandates within the UN system, their responsibilities within the partnership and actual contributions to the implementation of the joint work program of UNAIDS are outlined in the biennial UBW. To avoid duplication of efforts among the co-sponsors and to ensure that countries receive the best technical support in specialized areas, a "division of labor" based roughly on the mandates and comparative advantages of co-sponsoring agencies was agreed upon by the CCO in 2005. A working group set up by the UNAIDS secretariat in consultation with the co-sponsors came up with 17 broad areas of UNAIDS technical support, and identified "lead organization" and "main partners" in each of these areas.[10] Each of the 10 co-sponsors and the secretariat leads in at least one technical area. For example, the lead agency responsible for addressing HIV/AIDS in the world of work is the ILO, while the UNHCR is responsible for dealing with the impact of the epidemic on refugees and displaced populations.

The 10 co-sponsors and the UNAIDS secretariat make up the Committee of Co-sponsoring Organizations (CCO) which meets at least once annually to review co-sponsors' activities and to agree on the level and allocation of UBW resources among the co-sponsors. The CCO reports to the governing body of UNAIDS, the Programme Coordination Board.

UNAIDS secretariat

The joint program is serviced by the UNAIDS secretariat, which is responsible for coordinating and streamlining the activities of the co-sponsors and for bringing consensus over policy and programming at global and country level. The secretariat has been the main advocate within the UN system for worldwide action against HIV/AIDS, and for promoting UNAIDS's global mission to "lead, strengthen and support" the global response to the epidemic.[11] Over time, the secretariat has expanded to become a recognized entity within the UN system and has taken on the character of a separate UN specialized agency in all but name.

The UNAIDS secretariat has its headquarters in Geneva and recently moved to its own purpose-built facilities in the vicinity of the WHO. The secretariat is headed by an executive director at the level of a UN under-secretary-general. The post was occupied by Peter Piot since the joint program was established until his retirement at the end of 2008, when he was succeeded by Michel Sidibe, a Malian national who served as Piot's deputy from 2004 to 2008. Under Piot's leadership, UNAIDS has been able to adapt to changes in the international development scene and hence ensure that HIV/AIDS remains a priority on the global agenda. Effective use has been made of advocacy and partnerships involving political, civic and religious leaders, international celebrities from all walks of life, and captains of industry, to raise awareness on HIV/AIDS issues and to promote initiatives, including campaigns at global, regional and national levels. Piot's high-profile style helped to regularly generate media coverage for UNAIDS and its activities; these included press releases on the linkage of HIV/AIDS with major global concerns such as poverty, human rights, food security, human trafficking and climate change. The program also issues major publications such as the biennial *Report on the Global HIV/AIDS Epidemic* and the annual *AIDS Epidemic Update*, which track and provide epidemiological data on HIV infection and AIDS trends at national, regional, and global levels. Though not a funding agency, the UNAIDS secretariat has used its advocacy role and partnership alliances to support resource mobilization efforts and new funding initiatives to finance the global HIV/AIDS response worldwide.

The field structure of the secretariat has grown over time, from a handful of Country Programme Advisers (CPAs) attached to UN offices in a few seriously affected countries in the early years of UNAIDS to the present complement of country representatives and offices in over 60 countries worldwide and full-time focal points in another 20 countries. In addition, the secretariat has liaison offices in Brussels, New York, and Washington, D.C., which serve as the primary links with major intergovernmental and multilateral institutions in those cities. More recently, as the secretariat increased its presence and capacity in the field and became more involved in technical programs at country level, it has established seven UNAIDS Regional Support Teams—two in Africa and one each in Asia and the Pacific, Middle East and North Africa, Europe, the Caribbean, and Latin America. Although the co-sponsors can contribute specialists to serve on UNAIDS country and regional technical structures, the pivotal role of the secretariat in the arrangement reflects its growing involvement, as distinct from that of the co-sponsoring agencies, in the provision of technical support for the implementation of national and regional HIV/AIDS strategies and programs.

The Programme Coordinating Board (PCB)

The PCB is the governing body of the UNAIDS program. Its main governance functions are to establish priorities and broad policies for the joint program, review and approve the program's biennial budget and work plan, and evaluate progress toward the achievement of its goals and objectives. On the basis of its review, the PCB can make recommendations to the co-sponsoring organizations and the secretariat regarding their activities. At present, the PCB is composed of 22 government representatives from the different regions of the world and the 10 co-sponsors, who are voting members, and 5 regional representatives of civil society including NGOs and People Living with HIV/AIDS (PLWHA) who do not vote (see Table 3.1).

In practice the oversight role of the PCB has been limited to the review of program activities related to coordinated action on jointly established priorities within the framework of the UBW, rather than the performance and impact of HIV/AIDS activities of the co-sponsoring agencies. This limitation is due partly to the fact that the PCB does not have any control over the regular budget activities of the 10 co-sponsoring organizations, each of which has its own governing body, and also because the co-sponsoring organizations have access to other sources of financing for HIV/AIDS activities outside the UBW. Furthermore, the full PCB meets only once a year and the long interval between meetings of this body makes it difficult to keep track of what has been going on even in the secretariat, let alone in all the co-sponsoring agencies spread out between Geneva, New York, Rome, Washington, and Vienna. In an attempt to foster a closer working relationship between the PCB and the UNAIDS secretariat, a Geneva-based "Bureau of the PCB," consisting of a chair, vice-chair and rapporteur from among the member states and one representative each of co-sponsors and civil society, was set up in 2006. Notwithstanding this development, the reporting link from the CCO to the PCB for governance and oversight purposes was found to be weak and ineffective, and the PCB was judged to have "no real authority beyond its moral stature over cosponsors' organizations or their boards."[12]

UNAIDS and the United Nations

UNAIDS has been fairly successful in keeping HIV/AIDS at the top of the global agenda over the past decade. This has been due largely to the leadership and advocacy role of the secretariat under Peter Piot and the efforts of the co-sponsors and external partners of the joint program, such as the Global Business Coalition on HIV/AIDS, to promote and intensify commitment at all levels. Former UN secretary-general, Kofi Annan—who is from Africa, the region most affected by the epidemic, and who is also familiar with humanitarian tragedies from his previous assignments in the UN—made HIV/AIDS one of his top personal priorities during his term of office from 1997 to 2007, which coincided with the first decade of UNAIDS. In June 2001, over 150 heads of state and governments met at the United Nations in New York for the first ever UN General Assembly Special Session on HIV/ AIDS (UNGASS) under the theme of "global action for a global crisis." The session resulted in the unanimous endorsement of a "Declaration of Commitment on HIV/AIDS"[13] by all the member states of the UN, and this document has since become a tool or point of reference for securing action and resources for the global response.

The UN Millennium Summit, which took place at the United Nations in New York in September 2000, was another occasion when HIV/AIDS was highlighted as a priority and a major development challenge at the world body. A specific target for halting and reversing the spread of the epidemic globally was set and included in the summit's Millennium Declaration as one of the eight Millennium Development Goals (MDGs) aimed at halving extreme poverty by 2015. Further-more, it was implied in the context of the Millennium Declaration that failure to control the spread of HIV/AIDS could be a major obstacle to the realization of the other MDGs in many developing countries.

On 10 January 2000, the UN Security Council at its first meeting of the new millennium discussed the impact of HIV/AIDS on peace and security. This was an historic occasion, being the first time the Security Council had discussed a health issue as a security concern. The dis-cussion at the Security Council was a significant development not just in terms of raising HIV/AIDS awareness at the highest level of the UN, but in construing and presenting HIV/AIDS as a national security problem which demanded international attention and action. The securitization of HIV/AIDS in the UN was subsequently reinforced by the adoption of a resolution on HIV/AIDS by the Security Council later in the year, which, inter alia, called for the development of a UN medical policy on AIDS for personnel associated with UN peacekeeping and other field missions.[14]

The 60th session of the UN General Assembly included a High Level Meeting on HIV/AIDS which took place in New York from 31 May to 2 June 2006. The main purpose of this meeting was to follow up on the outcome of UNGASS of June 2001 and in particular make progress on the implementation of the UNGASS Declaration of

Commitment The 2006 High-level Meeting adopted a political declaration which reaffirmed commitment to implement the UNGASS Declaration and the MDGs, and outlined new commitments by member states to deal with tough and emerging issues, such as the feminization of the epidemic, trade flexibilities in relation to access to

Table 3.1 Joint United Nations Programme on HIV/AIDS: composition of the Programme Coordinating Board (PCB) 1 January 2009

Member states

1. Brazil	12. Myanmar
2. Congo	13. Netherlands
3. Denmark	14. Russian Federation
4. El Salvador	15. Senegal
5. Ethiopia	16. Slovakia
6. France	17. Switzerland
7. Guatemala	18. Thailand
8. India	19. Turkey
9. Iran	20. United Kingdom
10. Japan	21. United States of America
11. Mauritania	22. Zambia

Co-sponsors
1. UNHCR
2. UNICEF
3. WFP
4. UNDP
5. UNFPA
6. UNODC
7. ILO
8. UNESCO
9. WHO
10. The World Bank

Representatives of NGOs/people living with HIV/AIDS
1. Africa: Southern African Network of AIDS Service Organizations (SANASO), Zimbabwe — The AIDS Support Organization (TASO), Uganda.
2. Asia/Pacific: The 7 Sisters, Thailand — AntiAIDS Association, Kyrgyz Republic.
3. Europe: Russian Harm Reduction Network — Action Against AIDS, Germany.
4. Latin America/Caribbean: Bolivian Network of people living with HIV/AIDS (REDBOL) — Caribbean Vulnerable Communities Coalition, Jamaica
5. North America: International Planned Parenthood Federation/Western Hemisphere Region, USA — Ontario HIV Treatment Network (OHTN), Canada Uniting the world against AIDS

AIDS drugs, and sexual and reproductive health and rights, which had been glossed over in 2001.[15] Another high-level meeting on HIV/AIDS took place at the UN in New York in June 2008, at which the present UN secretary-general, Ban Ki-moon, presented a comprehensive report to the General Assembly based on national situations and reaffirmed the commitment of the United Nations, spearheaded by UNAIDS, to the global response.

Conclusion

The assumption of the responsibility by UNAIDS in the late 1990s to coordinate the global response to HIV/AIDS was as significant as the formulation of a global AIDS strategy by the GPA which a decade earlier had defined the cause and impact of the epidemic beyond the domain of public health. The new joint and co-sponsored program had effectively taken on the responsibility to give operational significance to the broader conceptualization of the cause and impact of HIV/AIDS which was vital in later shaping the global response to the epidemic. This responsibility included calling attention to the multiple health and non-health characteristics of HIV/AIDS, which are discussed in detail later, and acknowledging the social, economic, political, and cultural dimensions of the epidemic, as well as the need to respond to the implications of these multiple characteristics of the epidemic.

UNAIDS was set up to serve as the mechanism for organizing the UN system and galvanizing the international community of nations to act promptly to combat a global epidemic of the exceptional nature of HIV/AIDS. This role has been undertaken against the background of the rapid globalization of the world economy, which has had the effect of producing other pressing global concerns that are vying for attention with the HIV/AIDS crisis on the international agenda. However, globalization has also resulted in increasing global interdependence which has, in turn, raised awareness among the international community of nations about the need for collective and coordinated action at the global level to control the spread of the disease. By the time UNAIDS was established, it was obvious at the international level that HIV/AIDS was a global epidemic and that no country was safe from the disease. The mixed results and lessons from earlier efforts to coordinate global responses to public health and humanitarian crises underlined the importance of the role of UNAIDS to foster improved collaboration among the UN agencies and to secure the cooperation of the international community of nations for an effective global response to the epidemic.

UNAIDS is still confronted with the challenges of coordinating the global response, which involves not only the activities of numerous UN agencies but also interacting with other actors in the public and private spheres who represent different perspectives of the global response to HIV/AIDS. These different dimensions of HIV/AIDS and its impact, such as human rights, security, socio-economic development, human resources, and the complexity of the financing and governance of the global response, are discussed and analyzed in the following chapters.

4 HIV/AIDS and human rights

Stigma and discrimination directed at people living with HIV and AIDS (PLWHA) have resulted in numerous cases of violation of human rights worldwide.[1] The need to protect the rights and freedoms of PLWHA ultimately gave rise to the incorporation of a "rights-based" approach by the United Nations system in its response to HIV/AIDS. The notion of a rights-based approach is based on the principles of non-discrimination and the universality of fundamental human rights, as enshrined in the Universal Declaration of Human Rights and other relevant international conventions.[2] In the specific context of HIV/AIDS, the essence of a rights-based approach is an essential requirement for ensuring that the biomedical needs, as well as other basic human needs that transcend healthcare, of PLWHA are satisfied as part of the overall process of human development. This implies that PLWHA should not be discriminated against with respect to the requirements for human development regardless of their HIV status. The concept of health as a universal human right thus becomes a channel for addressing broader questions of basic human needs and social justice.[3]

Several countries which have endorsed international conventions and resolutions for promoting universal human rights and social justice have, nevertheless, not made use of these instruments to legislate specifically to outlaw discrimination directed at PLWHA. On the contrary, some countries still have laws and policies that limit the effectiveness of basic interventions for HIV/AIDS prevention and care. Examples are laws criminalizing certain types of sexual behavior or preference, or those limiting sexual and reproductive rights. There are even instances where public authorities have evoked strict adherence to the traditional public health doctrine as a basis for imposing restrictive measures on HIV-infected persons, claiming that this is necessary for controlling the spread of the epidemics and promoting public health, and notwithstanding that such measures violate basic human rights and freedoms.

This chapter presents the human rights debate in the specific context of HIV/AIDS. This debate has been characterized by these two different but not mutually exclusive approaches, which differ in terms of the priority or emphasis given to (1) the protection of human rights, as against (2) the promotion of public health in HIV/AIDS response. The chapter starts with an overview of the two approaches, and makes a case for a balance aimed at the integration of the two objectives within the common framework of the global HIV/AIDS response. This is followed by restatement and justification of a rights-based approach, and examination of the existing institutional framework for adapting the approach to HIV/AIDS response. Next, the promotion of specific rights and freedoms, including the right to health, which underscore a rights-based to HIV/AIDS response, are reviewed with reference to the respective mandates of different UN agencies and global multilateral institutions that contribute to the global HIV/AIDS response. After exploring the contours of the human rights debate in the context of HIV/AIDS response, the chapter ends with the conclusion that the adoption of a rights-based approach is not only useful for protecting the human rights of PLWHA but can also be beneficial for promoting public health objectives and enhancing HIV/AIDS prevention and care.

Promoting public health versus protecting human rights: the need for a balance

The traditional public health approach to HIV/AIDS implies action by public authorities to protect society against the threat and spread of infectious diseases. To this end, action taken could cover a range of coercive or repressive measures, such as compulsory medical examination and screening, isolation and quarantine of infected persons, and maintaining records and disclosing information on infected persons as deemed necessary. These are measures which in effect could lead to human rights violations. Advocates of the traditional public health approach see these measures as justifiable, and have argued that individual human rights and freedoms should not override the urgent need for early detection of infectious diseases and the primary obligation of public authorities to control the spread among the general population. The primary objective of promoting public health is thus regarded as a good reason and a legitimate ground for imposing measures that might constitute discrimination directed at people living with HIV/AIDS (PLWHA) and the violation of the fundamental human rights.

Proponents of the rights-based approach to HIV/AIDS, on the contrary, have stressed that in addition to the inherent value of protecting fundamental rights of all as requirements for human development there are also advantages in this approach that could be of direct benefit to HIV/AIDS response in general. They argue that when human rights are protected through an enabling legal and policy environment, and PLWHA can live and have a voice in society without fear of being stigmatized and discriminated against, more people will present themselves voluntarily for confidential testing and seek treatment where available and, consequently, fewer people will become infected. This position has been endorsed by UNAIDS and its co-sponsors, emphasizing that the protection of human rights of PLWHA is not only right on legal and ethical grounds, but that this also produces positive public health results in terms of promoting HIV prevention and facilitating AIDS treatment.[4] The value of a rights-based approach to HIV/AIDS, as such, lies not only in the principles of international human rights law and the normative potential of the approach to eliminate discrimination, inequality and injustice against PLWHA, but also in its contribution to controlling the spread of the disease.

There is now widespread recognition within the United Nations and global system about the value of a rights-based approach to HIV/AIDS response at all levels. Adoption of this approach as an integral part of the global response imposes certain obligations on member states of the United Nations to respect and protect the rights of HIV-positive persons, as well as catering for their health and other basic human needs including access to treatment. The responsibility of governments in all regions to protect the rights of PLWHA is explicitly expressed or implied in the Declaration of Commitment on HIV/AIDS adopted by the UN General Assembly Special Session on HIV/AIDS (UNGASS) in New York in June 2001,[5] and other UN statements and declarations such as the "UN Millennium Declaration" of September 2000,[6] and the "Political Declaration on HIV/AIDS" adopted by the UN General Assembly High-Level Meeting on HIV/AIDS in June 2006.[7]

The promotion of a human rights framework as applied to HIV/AIDS, however, evokes a moralistic discourse that has surrounded the disease. The notion of a rights-based approach somehow implies the determination of rights and wrongs, which can even be more difficult to delineate in the complex economic, social, political and cultural context of the HIV/AIDS pandemic. The application of a rights-based approach could in fact clash with deep-rooted prejudice, ignorance and denial that still characterize HIV/AIDS, and gives rise to practical problems relating to situations in which the reality of PLWHA is far removed from the nuances of a rights-based approach. Nevertheless, this should not be an excuse for holding back on the application of a rights-based approach to HIV/AIDS. Furthermore, the application of a rights-based approach to HIV/AIDS may well go beyond the protection of individual rights to provide a framework for addressing wider development concerns like poverty, inequality, social exclusion, and gender imbalances.

Both the promotion of public health and the protection of human rights are essential requirements for increasing the effectiveness of HIV/AIDS prevention, treatment and care. However, it is important that specific measures are taken to safeguard the basic objectives of a rights-based approach in the general context of disease control and prevention. This would involve putting in place appropriate institutional arrangements and mechanisms, as well as enacting legislation or implementing law reform, to create a supportive environment for protecting basic rights and upholding human dignity, while at the same time pursuing the goal of controlling the spread of infectious diseases through, inter alia, the development and enhancement of public health systems.

The institutional framework for a rights-based approach to HIV/AIDS response

The problem of stigma and discrimination in the context of HIV/AIDS is often linked to the perception that the disease is deadly and incurable, and based on misconceptions about how it is transmitted. Being infected with HIV is perceived in some societies not only as being the carrier of a deadly infectious disease, but is even justified as punishment and retribution for immoral behavior and associated with shame. To the extent that HIV-related stigma and discrimination are based on deeply rooted social attitudes and traditions, protection against discrimination as a human right would require not only the reforming of laws and policies but also changes in perceptions and societal norms and practices, including those pertaining to gender roles. Ignorance and lack of knowledge about the disease and its impact may also have to be addressed in a rights-based approach, especially in cases where there is also little general understanding of underlying economic, social, and cultural factors that cause vulnerability to HIV. The main challenge therefore for the UN and the international system with respect to applying the principle of a rights-based approach to HIV/AIDS response is that of synchronizing the concept of the universality of fundamental human rights with the everyday realities of the epidemic in many societies.

One of the earliest initiatives taken at the international level to address HIV-related stigma and discrimination through the implementation of a rights-based approach was contained in the Paris Declaration that was adopted by an international AIDS summit meeting in 1994. This declaration assured the commitment and support of 42 countries for the "greater involvement of people living with AIDS" (GIPA) and established the so-called "GIPA principle."[8] Specifically, in addition to advocating the effective participation of PLWHA in decision-making and implementation of public policy affecting them, the GIPA principle also committed governments to protect and promote the individual rights of PLWHA through legal and social means.

UNAIDS has argued that publicly acknowledging and recognizing the rights of PLWHA, as called for under the GIPA principle, would increase awareness and understanding of the disease and, thereby, help to reduce stigma and discrimination related to HIV/AIDS.[9] To support this position, UNAIDS established a Reference Group on HIV/AIDS and Human Rights in 2002 to advise its secretariat and the co-sponsors on how they can work with governments, civil society, and the private sector to protect and promote human rights, including through the incorporation of the GIPA principle in HIV/AIDS policies and programs at country level.[10] At the same time, there were already developments within the United Nations human rights organ specifically aimed at addressing HIV-related violations of human rights.

The United Nations and the protection of human rights in HIV/AIDS response

The United Nations, through its Commission for Human Rights (later reconstituted as the Human Rights Council of the UN in 2006), had been active in promoting and strengthening the protection of human rights in the context of HIV/AIDS since the 1980s. The contribution of the Commission and its secretariat, the Office of the High Commissioner for Human Rights (OHCHR), had been mainly in the area of standard-setting through the development of international guidelines on HIV/AIDS and human rights. These guidelines, which are based on international human rights norms and the expertise of persons with several years of practical experience in responding to the epidemic, are especially useful for adopting and implementing a rights-based approach. The development of the guidelines was initially in response to rising concerns about HIV-related discrimination and possible violations of human rights.

The first set of guidelines emerged from collaboration between the UN Centre for Human Rights and the WHO's Global Programme on HIV/AIDS in July 1989, when they combined to organize an International Consultation on AIDS and Human Rights in Geneva. The participants included government officials, legal and medical experts, and AIDS activists from developed and developing countries, with representatives of the WHO and some other UN agencies participating as observers. They discussed and agreed on the idea of a set of guidelines for policy-makers and other stakeholders involved in HIV/AIDS response to ensure compliance with international human rights standards regarding law, policy, and practice.[11] Little action followed from this idea for a while, and it was not until several years later that the issue of international guidelines on HIV/AIDS and human rights came up again in the UN system.

This report of the UN secretary-general to the 51st session of the Commission on Human Rights in 1995 noted then that the guidelines could provide "an international framework for discussion ... in order to arrive at a more comprehensive understanding of the complex relationship between the public health rationale and the human rights rationale of HIV/AIDS."[12] The Human Rights Commission at its next session in April 1996 adopted a resolution requesting the UN High Commissioner for Human Rights to collaborate with UNAIDS "towards the elaboration of guidelines on promoting and protecting respect for human rights in the context of HIV/AIDS,"[13] and also requested the secretary-general to report to the Commission the following year specifically on the status of the guidelines.

A second International Consultation on HIV/AIDS and Human Rights was convened jointly by the UN Centre for Human Rights and UNAIDS in September 1996. The meeting, like the first consultation in 1989, took place in Geneva and brought together AIDS experts and activists from a variety of backgrounds, including representatives of national AIDS service organizations and organizations of PLWHA. It resulted in the drafting of a document entitled "International Guidelines on HIV/AIDS and Human Rights," which it submitted to the UN secretary-general for presentation to the Commission on Human Rights as requested.[14] The 1996 guidelines provided justifications for supporting both the protection of human rights and the promotion of public health in AIDS response, and emphasized the synergy between the two goals.

In July 2002, a third International Consultation on HIV/AIDS and Human Rights was jointly convened by the OHCHR and UNAIDS to update the 1996 guidelines in the light of advances made in AIDS-related treatment, including the availability of antiretroviral medication and the need to reduce global disparity in access to treatment between rich and poor societies. The original guidelines were therefore revised and eventually published in 2006.[15] Since the revision of the guidelines, the Human Rights Council at its annual sessions has adopted resolutions that stress the need to eliminate discrimination and address the vulnerability of specific groups (e.g. women, migrants, and children) in the context of responding to HIV/AIDS. Typically, these resolutions call on governments to take all necessary measures, including review of law and practice and enacting legislation, to achieve the various aims of a rights-based approach to the HIV/AIDS response. The resolutions have also called on the UN secretary-general to submit regular reports on international and domestic efforts to protect human rights in the context of HIV/AIDS. In addition, the Human Rights Council has retained the "Sub-Commission on Human Rights and HIV/AIDS" from its predecessor and now appoints a special rapporteur to undertake studies on the context and causes of HIV/AIDS-related discrimination. The OHCHR and UNAIDS secretariat have joint responsibility for engaging experts and various stakeholders to review the guidelines, in the light of new developments and changes in knowledge and understanding of the epidemic and its impact, as well as to allow for the provision of widespread law reforms.

The International Guidelines on HIV/AIDS and Human Rights constitute the core of the framework for the adoption and implementation of a rights-based approach in the context of HIV/AIDS response at country level. They articulate the obligations of member states with respect to protecting human rights in HIV/AIDS response through outlawing discrimination, including the crucial rights to health, information and education, employment, social welfare, and public participation for reducing vulnerability to the infection. The guidelines also provide a framework for dealing simultaneously with the protection of human rights and the promotion of public health. They are also intended to assist individual governments to fulfill their human rights obligations and responsibilities in the context of national HIV/AIDS responses, while at the same time emphasizing the universality and indivisibility of human rights as enshrined in the Universal Declaration of Human Rights of 1948.

Over the past decade, the United Nations has taken a robust stand against discrimination directed at PLWHA and others who are vulnerable to HIV infection. In 1999, the UN Commission on Human Rights condemned stigma and discrimination against PLWHA and reaffirmed that: "Discrimination on the basis of HIV or AIDS status, actual or presumed status, is prohibited by existing international human rights standards."[16] The 2001 UNGASS Declaration of Commitment on HIV/AIDS also identified stigma and discrimination as a major obstacle to prevention and treatment, and called on political leaders to take legal and practical steps to address the problem.[17] The Political Declaration on HIV/AIDS adopted by the General Assembly at the 2006 High-Level Meeting on HIV/AIDS in New York included a commitment by all member states toward "intensifying efforts to enact, strengthen or enforce, as appropriate, legislation, regulations and other measures to eliminate all forms of discrimination against and to ensure the full enjoyment of all human rights and fundamental freedoms by people living with HIV and members of vulnerable groups."[18]

The right to health and other related crucial rights in HIV/AIDS response

The right to health first appeared in the constitution of the WHO in 1946 when the agency was established, and this right was subsequently incorporated into the Universal Declaration of Human Rights of 1948. The WHO constitution committed the health agency to work with member states toward "the attainment by all peoples of the highest possible level of health."[19] States, on their part, are obliged under international law to respect, protect and fulfill the right to health, including the obligation to ensure accessibility, availability and quality of health facilities, infrastructures, and delivery services. They are also obliged to give sufficient recognition to the right to health in national political and legal systems and to adopt appropriate national health policies. Every country in the world is now party to at least one human rights instrument that addresses health-related rights, including the right to health and a number of rights related to conditions necessary for health. In the specific context of HIV/AIDS, the significance of the right to health is not just confined narrowly to ensuring access to HIV/AIDS prevention and treatment services, but interpreted by UNAIDS to extend to all things which promote the well-being of PLWHA, such as the right to education and information, food, shelter, social protection, and employment.

Although the notion of the right to health was first advocated six decades ago, it was only in the late 1980s that attention was given to the idea of linking the two domains of health and human rights in an explicit and practical manner.[20] Significantly, it was HIV/AIDS that acted as a catalyst in bringing together these two domains, through the explicit recognition of a rights-based approach to the prevention and treatment of the disease. As indicated in Chapter 2, it was in the context of its WHO/GPA's global AIDS strategy of 1987 that universal human rights were linked with the protection and needs of PLWHA. This was the first time that a public health strategy had been framed in human rights terms and anchored in international law and, by implication, made governments ultimately responsible for the health and well-being of their populations. This, in the context of HIV/AIDS, implied that the protection of basic human rights should not be in conflict with the promotion of good public health.

Initially, the WHO's role in promoting a rights-based approach in HIV/AIDS response was limited to providing normative and technical guidance, based on the need to promote public health while at the same time respecting human rights in key interventions such as testing and counseling services. Later, with the advent and availability of antiretroviral (ARV) drugs, the health agency turned its attention to the provision of ARV treatment as a key element of the right to health when it launched its "3×5" initiative in 2003.[21] By then, access to ARV therapy was widely regarded as a core component of a comprehensive health-sector response to HIV/AIDS, and AIDS activists in highly affected developing countries had already been demanding access to treatment as a right. The most notable case of this was in South Africa where a civil society pressure group, the Treatment Action Campaign (TAC), directed a long and harsh campaign at the government to provide treatment as a right to AIDS sufferers within the framework of the national response to the epidemic.

At the global level, the "3×5" initiative was a direct reaction by WHO to pressures from its constituents in developing countries about failure to deliver HIV/AIDS treatment in circumstances where the vast majority of those infected with the virus and suffering from AIDS-related illnesses cannot afford the cost of treatment. Furthermore, following the commitment by world leaders in 2006 to the goal of "universal access" to HIV/AIDS treatment, care, and support by 2010,[22] it was pointed out by both the WHO and the UNAIDS secretariat that this goal cannot be achieved without the provision of access to ARV drugs and HIV services as a right.

Access to treatment as a right

Access to HIV/AIDS treatment is now acknowledged by the international health community as a fundamental requirement in affected countries for the full realization of "the highest attainable standard of health," in accordance with the WHO constitution. The significance of access to

HIV/AIDS treatment is that it transforms the status of HIV infection from an inevitable fatal disease to a chronic but manageable condition, and allows those undergoing treatment to live longer and even to continue to lead a relatively normal life.

WHO and the UNAIDS secretariat have been at the forefront of international action to improve access to treatment in the broader context of the goal of universal access. WHO continuously monitors advances in the development of ARV and other drugs which are used for controlling HIV infection and treating AIDS, and together with UNAIDS advocate for change in pricing, production and marketing policies to support universal access to treatment. These actions have contributed to progressively substantial reductions in the cost of HIV/AIDS drugs in the last few years, which in turn have led to improved access to affordable drugs in the developing regions. However, the global situation is far from satisfactory, as millions of people in sub-Saharan Africa who need ARV therapy urgently are still unable to benefit from improved access to treatment. Even with the substantial reductions in the price of essential HIV/AIDS medicines, these are not affordable and available in sufficient quantities in resource-poor countries. In addition, access to effective treatment may be affected also by non-availability of the newer and more effective AIDS drugs and medical technologies in the developing regions for various reasons, as discussed later in Chapter 9.

The pricing policy of ARV drugs has been a major factor in restricting access to treatment. Until a few years ago, the average cost of ARV therapy was in the region of US$10–12,000 a year per patient, and many governments and health authorities in low-income developing countries could not afford to provide life-extending ARV therapy as a publicly provided service. Most ARV drugs are developed and manufactured by major pharmaceutical companies in the industrialized countries, which take out patents on them to protect their intellectual property rights and, hence, prevent the production of cheaper generic versions for a minimum number of years. The right to HIV/AIDS treatment is thus intertwined with states' obligations under relevant international agreements to protect and enforce intellectual property rights, and, as discussed in Chapter 9, there is a need for a satisfactory balance between the two in HIV/AIDS response.

The right to sexual and reproductive healthcare

The impact of HIV/AIDS on women and certain strategies and measures adopted to respond to the epidemic can create social and economic barriers to sexual and reproductive health. Discrimination and violence against women, and lack of access to appropriate healthcare facilities such as family planning and contraception, STI clinics, reproductive health services, and child and maternal healthcare, affects the sexual and reproductive health rights of women and girls. The United Nations Population Fund (UNFPA) has a mandate to promote universal access to sexual and reproductive health services. In the specific context of preventing HIV infection, UNFPA promotes reproductive health rights and safer sexual behaviors. This objective is pursued through actions to support gender equality and the empowerment of women and girls and to improve access to family planning and maternal health services, including programs to prevent mother-to-child transmission of HIV. The population agency supports voluntary testing and counseling to manage sexually transmitted infection, while insisting on rights to privacy and confidentiality. It also makes use of a rights-based approach to tackling socio-cultural barriers to effective HIV/AIDS response, such as problems of child marriage and wife inheritance.

In the context of HIV/AIDS response, access to family planning services as part of sexual and reproductive healthcare constitutes an essential element of the right to health. A recent report by Family Health International (FHI) stated that family planning currently prevents an estimated 190,000 unintended HIV-infected births each year in sub-Saharan Africa, and a similar number of unintended pregnancies can be avoided annually in the region with expanded access to family planning clinics.[23] The report concluded that preventing unintended pregnancies in women with HIV by contraceptive methods is one of the most cost-effective strategies to prevent new HIV infections.

Although access to sexual and reproductive health is based on rights recognized in international human rights law and international treaties,[24] there are certain harmful and criminal practices such as rape and violence against women, human trafficking and forced prostitution, child marriage, and sexual abuse of children, that pose a major challenge to the protection of these rights in general. In addition, efforts to promote sexual and reproductive rights in the specific context of HIV/AIDS have encountered opposition from traditional and conservative establishments which, for example, are opposed to the provision of condoms or access to sexual and reproductive health services on religious and moral grounds. The George W. Bush administration of the U.S.A., for example, was clearly opposed to the promotion of contraception and other aspects of family planning for reducing vulnerability to HIV infection, and withheld U.S. government resources from international agencies and NGOs advocating this approach.[25] This has proved costly to UNFPA and its constituencies in developing countries in terms of loss of potential donor funding or having to modify and scale down their HIV prevention programs with some loss of effectiveness.[26]

Gender equality and the situation of women affected by HIV/AIDS

For reasons linked to traditional discrimination against women and the existence of gender norms and societal attitudes that result in inequalities between women and men, particular attention should be paid to protecting the human rights of women in the context of HIV/AIDS. In many developing societies, women bear a disproportionate share of the burden of HIV/AIDS both in terms of the risk of being infected and the responsibility for taking care of family members who are infected and sick. Women now account for more than half of the total number of people infected with HIV worldwide, and they are more likely than men to be infected with HIV in the future. This is so especially in sub-Saharan Africa, where HIV infection rates among young women and girls are as high as four to six times those of young men and boys in the same age groups—an unacceptable situation that has been appropriately described as "the misogynistic arithmetic of male promiscuity and female powerlessness."[27]

The UN and a number of its agencies, such as UNICEF, UNFPA, UNDP, UNIFEM, ILO, and the UNAIDS secretariat, now routinely address systematic discrimination against women and girls and promote policies and strategies to reduce gender inequality as part of a comprehensive response to the global HIV/AIDS crisis. Technical assistance is provided by these and other agencies for programs at national and community level that seek to empower women, through ensuring access to education, sexual and reproductive health services, and employment, and providing them with social support. Such interventions are regarded as crucial in preventing the further spread of HIV among women as a vulnerable group. At the 2006 UN General Assembly High-level Meeting on HIV/AIDS, member states pledged in their Political Declaration to "eliminate gender inequalities, gender-based abuse and violence" and "to increase the capacity of women and adolescent girls to protect themselves from the risk of HIV infection."

The rights of children affected by HIV/AIDS

Because of HIV/AIDS, millions of children worldwide have become orphans due to the loss of one or both parents to the disease. In addition, infants become infected with HIV through transmission of the virus from mother to child, and the majority of these children die before they reach the age of five due to lack of access to treatment. UNAIDS reported in 2006 that every day about 2,000 babies were born HIV positive in developing countries or were becoming infected through breast feeding, and that an estimated 15 million children under the age of 18 had lost one or both parents to AIDS, including about 13 million in sub-Saharan Africa.[28] Despite proven and relatively simple treatment procedures for preventing the transmission of HIV from mother to child, the vast majority of HIV-positive pregnant women in sub-Saharan African countries do not have access to treatment which would allow them to give birth to babies not infected with the virus.

Guided by the UN Convention on the Rights of the Child, which establishes children's rights as enduring ethical principles and sets international standards for protecting children, UNICEF works with other UN system agencies and development partners to build and implement appropriate programs against HIV/AIDS for children, including prevention of mother-to-child transmission and providing care and support for children orphaned by the epidemic. The agency, in collaboration with UNAIDS and USAID, published a major report on the problem of children affected by HIV/AIDS in 2004,[29] and followed this up with a global advocacy and fund-raising campaign under the slogan "Unite for children, unite against AIDS." The campaign was boosted at the time of its launch with the personal support of then UN secretary-general, Kofi Annan.

The right to work for HIV-infected persons

As far back as 1988 the ILO had realized that HIV/AIDS was threatening fundamental rights in the world of work, mainly through HIV-related discrimination in the workplace.[30] Since then, the spread of the epidemic among workers and its negative impact on labor productivity, output and income led ILO to conclude at the start of the new millennium that HIV/AIDS is a major obstacle to the attainment of its decent work agenda and a threat to its fundamental principles, including the principle of non-discrimination in employment.[31] The right to employment in conditions of freedom, equity, security, and human dignity is enshrined in both the Constitution of the ILO, the ILO Declaration on Fundamental Principles and Rights at Work of 1998, and other core ILO instruments which are relevant for managing HIV/AIDS in the world of work.[32]

The ILO Code of Practice on HIV/AIDS and the World of Work,[33] which was adopted unanimously by the tripartite constituents from member states of the organization in May 2001, sets out key principles, including non-discrimination in employment, confidentiality and gender equality, as guidelines for policy and action to address HIV/AIDS in the workplace. The code is the basis of the labor agency's rights-based approach to combat HIV/AIDS in the world of work. According to the ILO, the fundamental rights of HIV-positive workers include the right to employment, training and promotion; the right to social protection and benefits; the right to confidentiality regarding health status; and the right to reasonable accommodation in terms of the provision of alternative work and working arrangements. On the highly contentious issue of HIV testing, the ILO code is clearly against compulsory testing and the use of testing to screen workers; the code clearly states that testing should be voluntary, supported by provision of adequate information and appropriate counseling and protected by confidentiality and privacy. The ILO code was implicitly recognized by the UN General Assembly as "established international guidelines on HIV/AIDS in the workplace,"[34] and now constitutes the basis of national HIV/AIDS legislation and policies and enterprise-level HIV/AIDS workplace programs in over 90 countries worldwide.

The situation of migrants and mobile populations

The special circumstances of migrants and mobile populations as a group make them particularly vulnerable to the risk of HIV infection. The majority of migrants are poor, and use migration to search for work away from home and as a survival strategy. They are often exploited and even abused; live in squalid conditions in slums, and usually not covered by legal protection. Being away from their partners and families, male migrant workers are exposed to the risk of HIV infection from patronizing the services of commercial sex workers. Similarly, women migrants are particularly vulnerable to sexual exploitation in the workplace, abuse, rape, and violence, which increases their risk to the infection. Trafficking of women and girls to work abroad as prostitutes, often on the basis of deception and the false promise of "good jobs," has become a major threat to the health of the victims through increased exposure to the risk of HIV and other sexually transmitted infections. Foreign migrant workers and their families are often discriminated against with respect to access to healthcare and social protection services. In a number of countries, the rights of migrants to move freely between countries and to pursue employment opportunities abroad are also breached by requirements that they should undergo an HIV test as a condition for residency and employment.

Foreign migrant workers who are found to be HIV-positive when already in employment are likely to be dismissed and sent home.

Recognizing and respecting the rights of migrants and mobile populations is regarded by the United Nations as essential for reducing their vulnerability and risk of HIV infection. This was given explicit recognition in the 2001 UNGASS Declaration of Commitment on HIV/AIDS, which specifically advocated national, regional, and international strategies to facilitate access to HIV/AIDS services for migrants and mobile workers, including information on health and social services.[35] The UNGASS Declaration also recognized their vulnerability and the higher than average risk faced by migrants and internally displaced populations to HIV infection, and called for measures to protect the health of these groups.[36] In June 2006 the UN General Assembly High-level Meeting on HIV/AIDS included the protection of the right to freedom of movement of PLWHA in the "Political Declaration on HIV/AIDS" which was annexed to a resolution adopted by the General Assembly.[37]

The OHCHR and UNAIDS International Guidelines on HIV/AIDS and Human Rights recognize the special circumstances of migrants and mobile populations and their vulnerability as a high-risk group. The guidelines therefore include measures to protect migrants against discriminatory practices and abuses that increase their risk of HIV infection. These measures are consistent with the provisions of the UN International Convention on the Protection of Rights of all Migrant Workers and Members of Their Family. To date, less than 40 member states, or one-fifth of the global body's membership, have ratified this convention, which is an indication of the obstacles still faced in convincing national authorities to recognize and ensure the rights of migrant workers.

Conclusion

This chapter has sought to highlight one of the most worrying aspects of the HIV/AIDS epidemic, that of stigma and discrimination directed at PLWHA, which often results in widespread violations of the basic human rights of those affected. It has explored the contours of the human rights debate in the specific context of HIV/AIDS, arguing that the promotion of public health does not conflict with the protection of human rights in responding to the epidemic, and that the adoption of a rights-based approach in managing the disease and its impact could in fact be beneficial for increasing the effectiveness of HIV/AIDS prevention and treatment and for the enhancement of public health delivery systems. Review of the institutional arrangements and the legislative framework for implementing a rights-based approach in HIV/AIDS response suggest that there are still obstacles that have to be overcome. It is also clear from the discourse that HIV-related violations of basic human rights contribute immensely to undermining conditions for creating and nurturing human security, as is discussed in detail in the next chapter.

5　HIV/AIDS as a security threat

Disease and insecurity co-exist in a vicious circle. Throughout human history epidemics have had destructive impacts on the capacities of individuals, families, and communities to secure and protect their livelihoods. Wars and armed conflicts have often resulted in humanitarian crises which increase the risk of exposure to infectious diseases and other health hazards. The emergence of HIV/AIDS and other potentially deadly infectious diseases in recent years, and the reality of how easily and quickly these can spread across borders, have given rise to heightened concern within the United Nations and the wider international community about the threat posed by global epidemics to national and international security.

This chapter looks at HIV/AIDS as a security threat in terms of the direct impact on human well-being and safety and, beyond that, the implications for state security and international peace and stability. The conceptual framework used for investigating HIV/AIDS as a security threat therefore depicts the connection between a global infectious disease and insecurity at both the personal and state level. Specifically, it addresses the impact of the epidemic both from the standpoint of a humanitarian crisis that impinges on personal safety and with reference to causal links between the epidemic and state-centric security concerns such as political instability, conflicts and civil wars, and regional and international insecurity. The basic hypothesis is that the extremely high rate of mortality identified with HIV/AIDS diminishes human capacity, with serious social and economic consequences which, in turn, could affect political stability and threaten national and international security.

HIV/AIDS and human security

Human security embraces more than the effects of the absence of conflict on human lives and livelihoods.[1] It encompasses the protection of rights and freedom from disease, poverty and deprivation, which was dealt with in the previous chapter, and includes the promotion of long-term and sustainable human development. In the specific context of HIV/AIDS, the most direct impact of the disease on human security is the unnecessary loss of life due to the absence of or inadequate treatment and care. This reflects a deficit in personal security requirements of those at risk to HIV infection, and a needs gap for those who require access to essential drugs for ARV therapy. The threat posed to human security by HIV/AIDS is greatest usually in the resource-poor developing countries which do not have the means and know-how to control the spread of the epidemic and to provide adequate treatment and care for those in need. This is in contrast to the rich industrialized countries which have the resources, infrastructure, and knowledge to guarantee HIV/AIDS prevention and provide life-prolonging treatment to those in need.

The human security implications of the HIV/AIDS epidemic are immense. According to UNAIDS, over 65 million people have been infected with HIV and about 25 million have died from AIDS-related illnesses so far.[2] The majority of these infections and deaths have occurred in sub-Saharan Africa (SSA), a region that has some of the poorest countries in the world and where AIDS is now a major cause of death. Millions of Africans are infected with HIV each year, millions have died from the AIDS-related illnesses, and millions more are likely to die in the absence of adequate treatment and care. The scale of the humanitarian tragedy associated with HIV/AIDS and the potential threat to personal safety and welfare prompted one specialist on global security issues to describe the HIV/AIDS pandemic as "a humanitarian and human security issue of almost unimaginable magnitude, representing one of the most pervasive challenges to human well-being and survival in many parts of the world."[3] With no known cure for AIDS, and no successful vaccine against HIV infection as yet, many believe that HIV/AIDS could turn out to be one of the worst humanitarian tragedies and gravest human security problems of our time, if the spread of this epidemic is not brought under control.[4]

The vicious cycle of poverty, HIV/AIDS, and human insecurity

Poverty is both a factor in HIV transmission as well as a manifestation of negative social and economic consequences of the disease for individuals, their families and communities. Conditions of human insecurity which are linked to poverty and deprivation, such as lack of access to income-earning opportunities, poor nutritional status and poor housing, and the absence of basic social services in a community, increase susceptibility and vulnerability to HIV infection and precipitate AIDS-related illnesses. Poverty due to the impact of HIV/AIDS on family incomes and productive assets means that more children from affected households have to forego schooling and, hence, miss out on opportunities and choices to develop their human capacity and fulfill their potential in the future. Worse still, many of these children end up losing one or both parents to AIDS and are left to cope with the insecurity of living as orphans. Gender inequalities and various forms of discrimination and abuse against women and girls within the household and in society have become part of the complex and vicious cycle of poverty, HIV/AIDS, and human insecurity.

The World Bank, in a series of studies entitled "Voices of the Poor," which were produced as background documents for the 2000/1 and 2001/2 issues of the Bank's *World Development Report*,[5] drew attention to the threat posed by diseases such as HIV/AIDS and poor health status in general to personal security, and elaborated the link between poverty and human insecurity. This threat was recognized by the UNDP as far back as the early 1990s when the development agency incorporated the notion of personal security into its conceptualization of "human development," and articulated an approach to measuring human well-being that took account of the link between health and human security and, conversely, disease and human insecurity. Subsequently, UNDP's 1994 *Human Development Report* extensively covered various dimensions of human security, including protection from the threat of disease, hunger, unemployment and environmental hazards.[6]

The Millennium Development Goals (MDGs), which were established by the United Nations in 2000 as time-bound targets for the elimination of extreme poverty worldwide, included a specific goal pertaining to controlling and reversing the spread of the global HIV/AIDS epidemic. This reflected the perception by the international community of nations of the epidemic being a major obstacle to the realization of poverty alleviation objectives globally, and convinced world leaders, and particularly those from the G7 group of rich industrialized countries, on the need for urgent and exceptional actions to combat the threat posed by HIV/AIDS to human development.[7]

Several of the specialized agencies of the United Nations regard the vicious cycle of HIV/AIDS, poverty, and human insecurity as an obstacle to the fulfillment of their mandates and primary objectives. For example, ILO is concerned about loss of employment due to the impact of HIV/AIDS and consequent income insecurity; FAO has warned that the impact of the HIV/AIDS epidemic on agricultural production could result in food insecurity; UNESCO has highlighted the problem of human insecurity due to lack of access to basic education and information on HIV prevention. Personal insecurity linked to poor health status, in terms of vulnerability to HIV infection and the lack of access to ARV therapy, is a major concern of the WHO; and UNICEF has taken on the responsibility within the UN system for addressing insecurity experienced by orphans and vulnerable children affected by the impact and consequences of HIV/AIDS.

HIV/AIDS and state security

While there is no irrefutable evidence of HIV/AIDS directly leading to the destabilization of states or state failures, there are well argued analyses of indirect links between the epidemic and threats to national security through catalytic factors such as poverty, population dislocation, and loss of vital human resource capacities.[8] The argument is that the spread of HIV within a population can have consequences that undermine the capacity of the state to govern; diminish military preparedness; and precipitate social and political unrest. AIDS-related deaths can also undermine productive capacity which, in turn, could affect the ability of the state to finance basic services and to function effectively. This can result in actions that challenge government legitimacy and exacerbate social and political tensions. Empirical evidence has been put forward to support the view that the HIV/AIDS epidemic stands to threaten political stability in Africa through erosion of democratic governance.[9] The abhorrent phenomenon of "child soldiers" in recent African armed conflicts and wars has, inter alia, been linked to the ease with which warlords are able to recruit children who have been orphaned by AIDS and who have no other means of sustenance. The impact of HIV/AIDS on the potential preparedness of the military and uniformed services is now well documented.[10] These analyses and studies constitute the basis for genuine concerns about the potential threat posed by the HIV/AIDS epidemic to the maintenance of peace and security at national and international levels.

Concerns about the security implications of the global HIV/AIDS epidemic at the international level resulted in the historic debate on HIV/AIDS at the United Nations Security Council on 10 January 2000, when for the first time a health issue was discussed in the Council.[11] At about the same time the U.S. National Intelligence Council (NIC) produced a study on the security dimensions of infectious diseases, which warned that the spread of HIV/AIDS and other infectious diseases globally could endanger U.S. citizens and interests at home and abroad and trigger or exacerbate political instability in strategic countries and regions.[12] This was probably the first time that a formal national security apparatus of the U.S. government had focused on the security threat posed by a global infectious disease.

At the historic first discussion of HIV/AIDS at the UN Security Council, then UN secretary-general, Kofi Annan, warned that HIV/AIDS threatens peace and security in Africa, and moved that the security implications of the epidemic should be addressed by the Council as a matter of priority.[13] At the same Security Council debate, the former U.S. vice-president Al Gore argued that:

> AIDS is not just a humanitarian crisis [but] it is also a security crisis ... because it threatens not just individual citizens, but the very institutions that define and defend the character of society ... It strikes at the military and subverts the forces of order and peacekeeping.[14]

Six months later in July 2000, the Security Council went on to adopt a U.S.–sponsored resolution which expressed concern about the potentially damaging impact of HIV/AIDS on the health of international peacekeeping personnel. The resolution recognized the threat that HIV/AIDS could pose to peace and security at national and international levels through impact on the armed forces and other uniformed services, and called for a range of actions as well as regular reporting by the UN secretary-general to the Security Council on this particular issue.[15]

HIV/AIDS was again discussed in the UN Security Council in January 2001 and in July 2005 when a presidential statement was made on progress achieved in addressing the impact of HIV/AIDS on UN peacekeepers globally.[16] Discussion of the epidemic at the Security Council on these occasions raised awareness about HIV/AIDS as a potential national security threat at the international level and, furthermore, legitimized the basis for intervention by the United Nations to combat this particular threat of the epidemic. In 2004, the United Nations High-level Panel on Threats, Challenges and Change, established by the secretary-general to examine present and potential threat to international security in a changing world, identified HIV/AIDS and other infectious diseases as a "bio-security threat." The panel saw the epidemic as a threat to international security which it had defined as "any event or process that leads to large-scale death or lessening of life chance and undermines States as the basic unit of the international system."[17]

In the aftermath of the 9/11 terrorist attacks on New York and Washington, D.C. in September 2001, some influential members of U.S. political circles began to establish links between states weakened by global infectious diseases such as HIV/AIDS and threats of international terrorism.[18] A second report by the U.S. National Intelligence Council in 2002, "The Next Wave of HIV/AIDS: Nigeria, Ethiopia, Russia, India, and China," presented evidence of rising trends in HIV infection in the five countries covered, each of which has a large population and was considered as strategic for different reasons by the U.S.A. This report noted that if these trends are not halted and reversed, the demographics of these "Next Wave" countries will be radically transformed both in terms of numbers and geographic distribution, with serious political and international relations implications.[19]

Perception of HIV/AIDS as a security threat at the United Nations and among influential politicians in the United States represented a shift from the traditional understanding of, and response to, the impact of infectious diseases on human well-being. It gave a wider interpretation to the concept of human security, which extended beyond the fundamental conditions for people to live in safe, secure, healthy and productive lives, and included the implications for state security.[20]

Relationship between HIV/AIDS, conflict and security

Conflict and the spread of diseases are intertwined. In the case of HIV/AIDS, the thinking has been that humanitarian emergencies caused by armed conflicts have served to facilitate the spread of the epidemic among affected populations. The presence of the military and peace-keepers in conflict zones has also been identified as a factor in the spread of HIV infection, as discussed in the next section of this chapter. The response of the United Nations and regional organizations to the higher risk of HIV infection during conflicts has therefore taken the form of interventions to incorporate prevention and treatment measures into humanitarian emergencies and similar programs, and aimed at both the general population and military personnel, especially international peacekeepers.

The security implications of HIV/AIDS in the context of humanitarian emergencies have attracted much attention within the UN and the wider multilateral system. Within the UN system, response to the risk of HIV infection in conflict-related emergencies has revolved around actions initiated by the humanitarian agencies, chiefly the United Nations High Commissioner for Refugees (UNHCR). Even before becoming a co-sponsor of UNAIDS in 2004, UNHCR had spearheaded the UN system's effort to protect refugees, internally displaced persons and other conflict-affected populations, including victims of gender-based violence, against the risk of HIV. UNHCR has been an active member of the inter-agency Task Force on HIV/AIDS in Emergency Settings, which was established in 2001 as a reference group within the framework of the United Nations Inter-Agency Standing Committee (IASC).[21] The work of the task force resulted in the issuing of the "Guidelines for HIV/AIDS Interventions in Emergency Settings" by the IASC in 2004, which deals with HIV/AIDS as a cross-cutting theme that should be integrated and reflected in all actions pertaining to the humanitarian reform process of the UN.[22] The coordinating mechanism of the IASC was intended to provide a comprehensive cover for addressing a broad range of HIV/AIDS response programs in emergency situations, ranging from prevention, treatment, and basic care to protection for conflict-affected populations and workplace programs for humanitarian workers.

The vulnerability of displaced persons and migrants and mobile populations to HIV infection prompted the Geneva-based International Organization for Migration (IOM), a non-UN system organization, to extend its activities into the HIV/AIDS sphere. IOM has been collaborating with the UNAIDS secretariat and co-sponsors such as UNHCR and ILO on advocacy, capacity-building and programming for dissemination of information on HIV awareness and prevention during the migration process. IOM has also contributed to the policy-formulation, standard-setting and program development activities of a number of UN agencies in the context of HIV/AIDS response, and provided technical support to national and regional institutions for the protection of migrants from the risk of HIV infection. Inputs from the migration agency have been beneficial to UN international peace-keeping operations, in terms of the provision of information and guidance to foreign peacekeepers and host countries on reducing the risk of HIV infection.

The challenge of effective response to the risk of HIV infection in emergency situations is complex and substantial, and there are gaps and weaknesses that should be addressed. The main problem with the multilateral response was the lack of comprehensive and coordinated action for HIV prevention and care needs of populations affected by humanitarian emergencies. Within the UN system, individual agencies at global and country levels had been inclined to design and implement separate programs which, in the absence of effective coordination, resulted in policy incoherence, disjointed activities and costly duplications of effort on the ground. Analysis of reports on the experience of humanitarian emergency operations in Sierra Leone, Côte d'Ivoire, and Liberia by the United Nations suggest that there is a need for better inter-agency coordination, as well as streamlining of HIV-prevention and care efforts in emergency and post-conflict situations.[23]

Lately, some progress seems to have been within the UN system to address the problem of coordination, with reference to the integration of HIV/AIDS into humanitarian and emergency programs as a cross-cutting theme. This is reflected in more use being made of a multi-sectoral approach involving the mandates of several UN agencies in the design of country-level programs, based on directives and guidelines coming from the secretary-general and heads of agencies. In addition, more attention is now given to the promotion of pragmatic measures to prevent HIV transmission, such as through the issuing of guidelines for dealing with gender-based violence, the development of early warning programming tools for prevention and protection in emergency situations, and the use of specific indicators to monitor the implementation of the IASC guidelines on HIV/AIDS in emergency situations.[24] Professional codes of conduct have also been developed for uniformed services and international peacekeepers involved in humanitarian assistance.

HIV/AIDS and the military

UNAIDS has provided evidence of higher rates of HIV among the military and other uniformed services than in the general population in a number of high-prevalence countries such as Ethiopia, Eritrea, Malawi, South Africa, and Zimbabwe.[25] One explanation for this is that military personnel are obliged to spend long periods away from home separated from their partners and, hence, more likely to engage in casual and commercial sexual relationships. Also, the military is usually made up of the age-group that is most at risk of infection, young unattached men who tend to have a more casual attitude toward sex.

As already stated, the initial interest of the United Nations in addressing the impact of HIV/AIDS as a security threat to the military was in response to concerns about the higher risk of HIV infection among international peacekeepers on UN missions. UN Security Council resolution 1308 of July 2000 referred to this problem, and it called on the global organization and its member states to take action to address the risk of contracting HIV faced by soldiers on international peacekeeping duties. The resolution required the UN Department of Peace Keeping Operations (DPKO) to report regularly to the

UN Security Council on efforts made toward its implementation worldwide, and instructed that action to address the risk of HIV infection should be specifically incorporated into UN Security Council resolutions establishing and extending peacekeeping operations in countries with a high prevalence of HIV. While the basis of resolution 1308 was apparently the concern of countries providing international peacekeepers to high HIV-prevalence countries, some of the host countries themselves regarded the presence of international peacekeepers as contributing to the spread of HIV among their own populations.[26]

The challenge to the United Nations then was to address the risk faced by peacekeepers of contracting HIV when on duty, on the one hand, and on the other, the concern of member states about the hazard posed through risky behavior of peacekeepers as a factor in the spread of HIV among the general population of host countries and those of their own countries when they return. The perceived link between international peacekeepers and the spread of HIV undermines the trust of the international community of nations in UN peacekeeping operations, and has in fact raised questions about the ability of some member states to contribute troops to UN missions. It has also led to calls for mandatory pre-deployment HIV-testing of peacekeepers, which itself is a highly controversial issue as it is not consistent with existing international guidelines for dealing with HIV/AIDS, such as ILO's "Code of Practice on HIV/AIDS and the World of Work," which is against mandatory testing in employment. The DPKO has therefore adopted a policy which encourages "Voluntary Confidential Counseling and Testing" (VCCT) as an element of its HIV/AIDS awareness program.

The UNAIDS secretariat has been collaborating with the DPKO in the development and implementation of policies and programs to support the implementation of Security Council resolution 1308. Under this arrangement, a UNAIDS policy adviser was deployed in Sierra Leone in 2001 to work with the UN peacekeeping mission in that country. Since January 2002, UNAIDS has also funded the post of an HIV/AIDS policy adviser attached to the DPKO at the United Nations in New York. A special "AIDS, Security and Humanitarian Response" unit has also been set up within the UNAIDS secretariat in Geneva to liaise with the DPKO, as well as to provide advice to regional organizations such as the African Union, the Caribbean Community (CARICOM), and the Commonwealth of Independent States (CIS) which covers the ex-Soviet Union countries. The UNAIDS secretariat also provided technical support to the Training and Evaluation Services of the DPKO toward the development of guidelines for integrating HIV prevention into pre-deployment training for all UN peacekeepers. At the country level, UN theme groups on HIV/AIDS are responsible for regularly providing advice and guidance to UN peacekeeping missions on HIV/AIDS awareness, prevention, and treatment.

Conclusion

This chapter has explored the links between the HIV/AIDS epidemic and the threat it poses to human and national security. The emergence and re-emergence of HIV/AIDS and other deadly infectious diseases in our time have led to growing concern at the United Nations, regional organizations and among national authorities about the effect on political stability at country level and international peace and stability. In the case of HIV/AIDS, situations of armed conflict and wars have increased vulnerability to the infection among affected populations through the consequences of displacement of people and destruction of livelihoods, and through the risky behavior of combatants and international peacekeepers. In order to effectively address the security threat posed by HIV/AIDS, the United Nations and other stakeholders at national and international levels should cooperate to develop strategies for incorporating broad security concerns and themes into HIV/AIDS responses and development programs and vice-versa. Greater efforts are needed to mitigate the impact of HIV/AIDS on human well-being and to address HIV/AIDS risk and impact in conflict situations and humanitarian emergencies. Such efforts could be enhanced through improvements in the provision of basic social services, including access to ARV therapy and socio-economic opportunities for those living with HIV and AIDS, and by the involvement of the armed forces themselves in HIV/AIDS awareness and prevention campaigns. Addressing HIV/AIDS as a humanitarian crisis that affects personal safety and well-being, and also with reference to implications for political and social stability, should also be seen in the context of the impact of the epidemic as a broader development challenge, which is discussed in the next chapter.

6 HIV/AIDS as a development challenge

This chapter is about the impact of the HIV/AIDS epidemic on national development goals and the living standards of individuals, households, and communities in the developing world. It is now known that in resource-poor countries, the impact of a high prevalence of HIV/AIDS among the population could be detrimental to economic growth and poverty reduction objectives, as well as pose obstacles to the satisfaction of essential human needs such as health, education, food, and social inclusion.[1] We have also seen in the previous two chapters that HIV-related discrimination leads to violations of fundamental human rights and freedoms, and that the threat posed by the epidemic to human and state security could undermine political institutions and democratic governance. The link between the HIV/AIDS impacts and a wide range of development problems and concerns in the economic, social, and political spheres has led to the conceptualization of HIV/AIDS as a development challenge. Furthermore, development problems which are linked to the impact of the epidemic on national development goals and on households and communities are themselves conditions that contribute to the spread of HIV and impede access to treatment of AIDS, thereby adding to the enormity and complexity of the challenge.

HIV/AIDS: a development issue

The relationship between HIV/AIDS and development can be analyzed through two sets of effects which are interlinked. The first set relates to the implications of HIV/AIDS for human development. AIDS is a fatal disease for which there is still no cure, nor is there a successful vaccine against HIV infection as yet. The impact of HIV/AIDS on mortality is therefore huge in countries where treatment is not readily available or affordable. The epidemic has already claimed over 25 lives worldwide. The implications of AIDS-related morbidity ~~rtality~~ are immense and far-reaching in terms of effects on ~~ods~~ and on the development of future generations. The second relat~~ to the impact of the epidemic on overall economic development and social progress. Loss of lives in exceptionally large numbers due to HIV/AIDS, as has occurred in some countries in sub-Saharan Africa (SSA),[2] can be harmful to development efforts. This is underlined by the fact that in the developing world, HIV/AIDS is concentrated in the working-age population, including those with critical economic and social roles in society.[3] Management of the disease at country level places a great financial burden on governments, which can be detrimental to long-term sustainable development.

The HIV/AIDS epidemic is therefore not only having a devastating impact on human life, but it is resulting in the loss of productive capacity in key economic sectors. The UN system and major stake-holders in the development business recognize the threat posed by the global HIV/AIDS epidemic to the achievement of national and inter-national development objectives, and have strived to keep HIV/AIDS as a priority issue on the international development agenda. The importance of HIV/AIDS as a global development issue was acknowl-edged by the UN General Assembly meeting at the level of heads of state in New York in September 2000 through the setting of a target for the control of HIV/AIDS as one of the eight UN Millennium Development Goals (MDGs). This is elaborated on later in this chapter. Since then, various UN agencies and international conferences have discussed the epidemic and adopted conclusions and declarations aimed at mitigating the impact of the epidemic on development goals and objectives. Concern about the impact of HIV/AIDS on develop-ment has led major development agencies in the multilateral system, including the World Bank and UNDP, and bilateral donors such as the U.K.'s DFID and SIDA of Sweden to advocate that development policies and programs should include as well as be part of the response to the epidemic at national and global levels.

HIV/AIDS and human development

The immediate impact of HIV/AIDS on human development is manifested in increases in mortality rates and reversals of gains in life expectancy. The well-being of individuals and households is affected by the epi-demic through loss of human productive capacity and livelihoods caused by AIDS-related deaths and illnesses. The global scale of the HIV/AIDS epidemic and the severity of its impact in developing countries in terms of loss of life and livelihoods make it probably the worst humanitarian tragedy in our time, and, hence, a major development challenge at global, national, and local levels. This is reflected in the preamble to the "Declaration of Commitment on HIV/AIDS" adopted by the UN General Assembly Special Session on HIV/AIDS (UNGASS) in New York in June 2001, which recognized HIV/AIDS as not just a health issue but a wider development problem, and noted that "the continuing spread of HIV/AIDS will constitute a serious obstacle to the realization of the. ... development goals. ... adopted at the Millennium Summit."[4]

In the specific context of sub-Saharan Africa, the UNGASS Declaration stated that "HIV/AIDS is considered a state of emergency which threatens [human] development, social cohesion, political stability, food security and life expectancy."[5] Crucially, the UNGASS Declaration recognized that obstacles to human development such as "poverty, underdevelopment and illiteracy are among the principal factors contributing to the spread of HIV/AIDS ... [which] is now reversing or impeding development in many countries."[6] Accordingly, the UNGASS Declaration's Program of Action included the need to evaluate the impact of the epidemic on human development, and recommended that the adoption of measures to reduce poverty and improve the standard of living should be an integral component of the global HIV/AIDS response. Recognition of the link between HIV/AIDS and human development in the UNGASS Declaration laid the foundation for action by the United Nations system and the international donor community to address the impact of the epidemic beyond the needs of the health sector.

Multilateral development institutions like UNDP and the World Bank and some major bilateral donors have advocated the linking of poverty reduction strategies with HIV/AIDS responses as an integrated approach to national development. The link with poverty constitutes one of the most critical relationships in the conceptualization of HIV/AIDS as a development challenge. Poverty plays a role as a determinant of the vulnerability and spread of HIV/AIDS in developing countries, and for many households in poor countries an important effect of HIV/AIDS is to deepen poverty. Studies by the World Bank, UNDP and UNAIDS secretariat, already cited, provide evidence which suggests that poverty and deficits in basic human needs at household level due to HIV/AIDS-related factors undermine efforts to cope with the disease. This is further compounded by the negative impact of the epidemic on the public provision of basic social services, such as health and education, which benefit the poor.

The WHO Commission on Macroeconomics and Health established by the then director-general, Gro Harlem Brundtland, stressed the need to assess the place of health and human well-being in economic development.[7] The Commission in its 2000 report presented health as both a central goal and an outcome of human development, and stressed that the MDGs cannot be achieved where there is a high prevalence of infectious diseases and debilitating illnesses. Specifically, the report identified HIV/AIDS as one of the main causes of avoidable deaths in low-income countries, and recommended that investment in the prevention and control of HIV and the treatment and care of AIDS patients should be given a high priority in development policies and programs.

HIV/AIDS and socio-economic development

It was not until the UN Millennium Development Summit in September 2000, that development impact of the global HIV/AIDS epidemic was directly addressed by the United Nations. Development programs and goals of the UN which were established as frameworks for global action in the 1990s did not focus on the development impact of HIV/AIDS, even though the epidemic was already seen as a threat to development. Following the inclusion of a specific target to control and reverse the spread of HIV among the Millennium Development Goals, the 2001 UNGASS Declaration recommended the adoption of "economic and social development policies to address the impact of HIV/AIDS on economic growth."[8]

Outside the UN, the impact of HIV/AIDS on development had been analyzed in various studies using economic models of the potential long-run effects of the epidemic on changes in GDP growth and per capita income.[9] Although these studies have not shown conclusively that there is a direct correlation between increase in HIV prevalence and decline in economic growth rates and incomes, there are indications from some of them that suggest an inverse relationship between HIV/AIDS prevalence and key economic indicators such as levels of output and household income and consumption in some of the highly affected countries in sub-Saharan Africa.[10]

Responding to HIV/AIDS as a development issue on the international agenda

The notion of HIV/AIDS being on the international agenda as a development issue is fairly recent. The first time that HIV/AIDS was addressed as a global development concern by world leaders was probably at the Okinawa G7/8 summit in June 2000 which adopted the "Okinawa Infectious Diseases Initiative." This initiative reaffirmed that infectious diseases such as HIV/AIDS and malaria are not only health problems, but also constitute a formidable challenge for global development in the new millennium. The G8 leaders committed their countries to support global efforts to control the spread of HIV/AIDS and other infectious and parasitic diseases. This was followed by developments at the global level spearheaded by the G7/8 which led to the agreement on a new global health financing mechanism, and ultimately the establishment of the Global Fund to Fight AIDS, Tuberculosis and Malaria (Global Fund) in 2002.[11] The shift in international development thinking, from viewing HIV/AIDS as a public health problem to the acknowledgment that the epidemic must be tackled as part of a broader global development agenda, was further evidenced by a number of initiatives taken from 2000 onward by the United Nations and the multilateral system, which are recounted below.

HIV/AIDS and the Millennium Development Goals (MDGs)

As part of the Millennium Declaration, world leaders agreed to a set of time-bound and measurable goals and targets for combating poverty, hunger, disease, illiteracy, environmental degradation, and discrimination against women.[12] The declaration represented a global agenda for achieving sustainable reductions in various dimensions of poverty by 2015, and these were packaged into eight Millennium Development Goals (MDGs). The sixth MDG is a commitment to halt and reverse the spread of HIV/AIDS, malaria and other major diseases found predominantly in the developing regions. Significantly, the Millennium Declaration also recognized the threat posed by the spread of HIV/AIDS to the achievement of the other MDGs. Crucially, the response to HIV/AIDS was seen as a key factor in determining whether or not highly-affected developing countries can attain their MDG targets for health, education, nutrition, gender equality, and child survival. This point was emphasized by the then secretary-general, Kofi Annan, in 2005 at the UN High-level Meeting which reviewed progress toward the MDGs: "Halting the spread is not only a Millennium Development Goal in itself; it is a prerequisite for reaching most of the others. Only if we meet this challenge can we succeed in our efforts to build a humane, healthy and equitable world."[13]

HIV/AIDS and the international financial institutions

At the 2001 spring meeting of the influential Development Committee of the World Bank and the International Monetary Fund (IMF), ministers from both developed and developing countries discussed HIV/AIDS as a development policy issue and agreed on the need for increased financial assistance to seriously affected developing countries. The World Bank had been financing HIV/AIDS awareness and pre-vention programs in a number of African countries since the late 1980s, and had later launched a special facility with an initial amount of US$500 million in flexible and rapidly funding grants and loans to assist African countries to scale up national HIV/AIDS efforts. The Heavily Indebted Poor Country Initiative (HIPC) which the World Bank launched in conjunction with the IMF in 1999 had also been used as a mechanism to release resources for HIV/AIDS programs through debt relief.

In the case of the IMF, the agreement reached on HIV/AIDS financing at the 2001 Development Committee meeting was important in that it highlighted the need for flexibility in the imposition of different types of "conditionality" on financial assistance provided by the institution. There were already concerns in African countries and regional organi-zations about the effects of IMF conditionalities on the capacity of high-prevalence countries to respond effectively to the threat of HIV/AIDS. Some of the African countries seriously affected by HIV/AIDS were constrained by public sector spending limits imposed under IMF-supervised macroeconomic country programs in using available resources at their disposal to scale-up their HIV/AIDS response, such as the hiring of additional health sector personnel and payment of cash incentives aimed at retaining doctors and nurses. It was therefore sig-nificant that the Development Committee of the World Bank and the IMF agreed to the idea of increased financing to support the HIV/AIDS response, without specifically linking this to macroeconomic performance.[14]

The decision of the 2001 spring meeting of the Development Com-mittee resulted in the provision of additional official development assistance (ODA) for the global HIV/AIDS response. It was consistent with the idea advocated by UNAIDS and the developing countries that spending on HIV/AIDS should come from additional ODA and not through a reduction in existing resources committed to other essential development programs. The decision also provided support for the view held by the developing countries that increases in ODA for financing HIV/AIDS response could be achieved under existing arrangements, if the major donor countries were meeting existing commitments to move toward the 0.7 per cent ODA/Gross National Income target they had pledged and if more aid was channeled through grants rather than credits.

HIV/AIDS in major international development conferences

Leaders from both developed and developing countries at the UN International Conference on Financing for Development, held in Monterrey, Mexico, in March 2002, recognized and included the cost of addressing HIV/AIDS as a development challenge in the context of matching MDG commitments with resources. The agenda of the conference addressed the fundamental question of how to put into practice the strategies needed to deliver on the MDGs and ultimately eradicate extreme poverty worldwide. Speaking at the conference, Marika Fahlen, then a director at the UNAIDS secretariat, reminded the delegates of "the profound impact of AIDS on growth, income and poverty" and welcomed the opportunity provided by the conference to give "international attention to the need for investment in global public goods, such as incentives for research on HIV/AIDS, including vaccine and microbicide development" and "the potential for using debt relief for public social expenditure, notably to combat HIV/AIDS."[15] In the context of the "Monterrey Consensus," which outlined policies and called for initiatives based on partnerships between the North and the South to achieve sustained economic growth and promote sustainable development in poor countries,[16] the Global Fund to Fight AIDS, Tuberculosis and Malaria (Global Fund) which then had just been established underlined the resolve of the international development community to mobilize the necessary finance to achieve the internationally agreed MDG target for controlling and reversing the spread of HIV.

The World Summit on Sustainable Development (WSSD), which took place in Johannesburg, South Africa, in August 2002, brought together over 100 heads of states and governments, leaders from the private sector and civil society, and over 20,000 delegates. The WSSD reaffirmed the commitments made by the international community at the Monterrey conference to finance development activities in support of meeting the MDGs, and highlighted the threat posed by HIV/AIDS to sustainable development in highly affected countries such as the host, South Africa. The summit, which discussed the importance of health as a resource for sustainable development, among other things, provided an opportunity for the international community to reflect on the fact that the concentration and impact of the HIV/AIDS epidemic in Africa had transformed a health problem into a major development challenge for some of the poorest countries in the world. The "Political Declaration" issued at the end of the summit identified the fight against HIV/AIDS as one of the key global development issues to be addressed by the international community, and the "Johannesburg Plan of Implementation," which was adopted by the world leaders, included a separate chapter on health in which the threat posed by HIV/AIDS and other infectious diseases to sustainable development was recognized, and proposals were made to strengthen the capacity of healthcare systems and to improve access to essential ARV drugs.[17]

HIV/AIDS, globalization, and international cooperation

Recognition of HIV/AIDS as a development issue by the international community of nations has more or less coincided with the current rapid globalization of the world economy. Globalization and growing interdependence among countries has generated an enormous increase in global economic activity, including the movement of people and the pathogens they carry across borders. A high level of population mobility creates conditions ideal for the spread of epidemics such as HIV/AIDS, SARS and the avian flu. In the case of HIV/AIDS, which is now perceived as a long-wave event with devastating human and economic consequences, key member states of the international community, including the U.S.A. see a real danger in the spread of the epidemic globally particularly in certain large and strategically important countries in Asia and the transition economies of the former Soviet Union, in terms of effects on the growth of the world economy and the threat posed to international peace and security.

Globalization has therefore increased the interest of the rich nations in addressing HIV/AIDS as a global crisis, and prompted them to cooperate with the developing countries on joint action to control the spread of a major global epidemic because it is in everyone's interest to do so. Lack of action can have consequences for all in a globalizing and increasingly interdependent world. The application of the doctrine of international cooperation to the global HIV/AIDS response can be illustrated by the decision of the G8 leaders at their Gleneagles summit in July 2005 to finance HIV/AIDS prevention and treatment in Africa. The Gleneagles summit endorsed a comprehensive plan for Africa's recovery and development proposed by the U.K. government as host, which identified HIV/AIDS as "the greatest development challenge of the time."[18] The Africa plan endorsed the need identified at the 2001 UNGASS to mobilize billions of dollars annually to fight AIDS, and accordingly proposed a timetable for meeting the target of 0.7 percent of gross national income for aid from rich to poor countries which could boost HIV/AIDS response. In addition, the plan specifically called for an additional US$25 billion per year in aid for Africa by

2010, some of which will go toward HIV/AIDS response in seriously affected countries in the region. In their final communiqué, the G8 leaders at Gleneagles emphasized the need "to take action to combat HIV/AIDS, Malaria, TB and other killer diseases," focusing on investment in health and education.[19] In this connection, the communiqué included an agreement on new initiatives to cancel debts owed by eligible heavily-indebted poor countries (HIPC) to the international financial institutions and G8 countries.

Responding to the development challenge of HIV/AIDS: examples from the World Bank, UNDP and the UN Economic Commission for Africa

World Bank

The World Bank views HIV/AIDS as disruptive to major development objectives and poverty reduction, and became involved in providing financial resources to support national responses to the epidemic in low- and middle-income countries more than two decades ago. From the early 1990s, the Bank had been inputting estimates for the effects of HIV/AIDS into its population projection for all countries, and had also developed simulation models for assessing the impact of HIV/AIDS on economic growth.[20] In a 1997 report entitled *Confronting AIDS: Public Priorities in a Global Epidemic*,[21] the World Bank highlighted the bi-directional links between HIV/AIDS and development: the epidemic could be harmful to economic development, while gains in development could improve HIV/AIDS responses. The report therefore argued strongly that governments must be directly involved through economic policy and planning in confronting HIV/AIDS as a development challenge. By 1999, the World Bank had come to recognize the enormous threat posed by the HIV/AIDS epidemic to development prospects in sub-Saharan Africa, and published a regional HIV/AIDS strategy paper aimed at addressing this threat.[22]

Within the overall framework of its global HIV/AIDS program, the World Bank had funding for HIV/AIDS programs in sub-Saharan Africa and other developing regions since the late 1980s.[23] In 2000, the Bank launched the Multi-Country HIV/AIDS Program (MAP) for Africa as an emergency response to the impact of the global epidemic in the region. The MAP provided the institutional framework for the World Bank to substantially scale-up its financial support to affected countries and to relax eligibility requirements, in order to address shortfalls in resources for national AIDS responses in poorer countries.

The MAP now covers other developing regions although SSA remains the major beneficiary. More than $1.5 billion has now been committed by the World Bank through the MAP to support about 170 health sector and multi-sectoral HIV/AIDS projects in over 40 low– and middle-income countries, including sub-regional (inter-country) projects. The program also extends its activities to non-state actors by providing financial support for the mobilization of civil society and the involvement of the community-based organizations in national HIV/AIDS response.[24] The significance of the MAP in the context of the World Bank's relationship with poor countries as a development partner is that the program has added a strategic but flexible and predominantly client-driven dimension to financial support provided by the institution.

Total World Bank financing and technical support for HIV/AIDS responses globally since 1988 is estimated to be in excess of $3.5 billion.[25] Most of this amount has gone into interventions for scaling-up national responses and strengthening HIV/AIDS program implementation, including capacity-building, and for mainstreaming HIV/AIDS into the Bank's operational programs in health and other key development sectors. The World Bank's contribution to responding to HIV/AIDS as a development challenge has also included the incorporation of HIV/AIDS concerns into national Poverty Reduction Strategy Papers (PRSPs) that the institution has developed in collaboration with governments in several developing countries, including some that are highly affected by the epidemic. This integrated approach is clearly intended to link HIV/AIDS responses with poverty reduction goals within the overall framework of national development planning. As part of the integration of HIV/AIDS into PRSPs, the World Bank has collaborated with the IMF and UNDP in assisting countries to ensure that macroeconomic and public expenditure frameworks for poverty reduction also support the implementation of effective national AIDS response programs.[26]

The World Bank has recently revised the orientation of its AIDS Campaign Team for Africa program (ACT Africa), which was originally set up in the late 1980s to support the implementation of project funding for HIV/AIDS prevention. A new five-year "Agenda for Action" was launched by ACT Africa in late 2007, which seeks to reinforce support within the Bank's policy and operational structures for the MAP and to strengthen the Bank's relationships with UNAIDS and its co-sponsors and with other partners at the country level, including bilateral donors, the private sector, labor unions and civil society. In addition, the World Bank's Global Programme on HIV/AIDS now operates at a sufficiently high level within the management structure of the institution to give it the authority to coordinate HIV/AIDS and development policy issues throughout the Bank, as well as to serve as the focal point for partnerships with UNAIDS, WHO, the Global Fund and the U.S. government HIV/AIDS initiative, PEPFAR.[27]

UNDP

As the UN's global development agency, UNDP was given responsibility in 2001 by then secretary-general, Kofi Annan, to coordinate the UN system's development efforts at the country level for attaining national MDG targets. Halting and reversing the spread of HIV/AIDS, as called for by MDG 6, is perceived by the UNDP as requiring an operational framework that links the causes and consequences of the epidemic to action against poverty and a range of development concerns such as gender inequality, unemployment and poor governance.[28] UNDP's approach to addressing HIV/AIDS as a development challenge is built around the integration of the national HIV/AIDS response with broader country-wide development efforts in key sectors and at both central and local levels. The development agency therefore strongly advocates that policy and programming responses to HIV/AIDS should be multi-sectoral and decentralized, and has developed an operational framework and implementation guidelines for mainstreaming HIV/AIDS in development planning.[29]

As the coordinator of the UN development efforts for achieving the MDGs at the country level, UNDP is thus responsible for coordinating the HIV/AIDS activities of different UN agencies to ensure a coherent UN system response toward the attainment of MDG 6. In collaboration with the UNAIDS secretariat, UNDP has been instrumental in the setting up of inter-agency UN "Country Teams on HIV/AIDS" and "HIV/AIDS Theme Groups" at country level to assist and work with national HIV/AIDS commissions, development planning ministries and external development partners of the government. This enables the structure of the UNDP resident coordinator at country level to play an important role in promoting and facilitating the incorporation of HIV/AIDS concerns into the overall development process, specifically linking progress in meeting the target for MDG 6 with progress in other development goals such as poverty reduction and gender equality. The UNDP's focus on national development planning as the framework for HIV/AIDS response reflects the thinking that the development impact of HIV/AIDS is best analyzed and addressed in the specific context of the economic, social, cultural, and political characteristics of individual countries, rather than in terms of global strategies.[30]

Development policy-makers and practitioners at international and national levels therefore need to start from a common base of understanding the causes and consequences of the epidemic in particular socio-economic settings, as a way of generating more effective outcomes. In terms of causes, they need to know what the main factors are that make individuals, families, and entire populations more susceptible to HIV infection, and how these are related to key indicators of human well-being which are included in the UNDP's Human Development Index (HDI).[31] With regards to consequences, policy-makers should understand the effects of HIV/AIDS on households and communities in terms of vulnerability to the impact of the epidemic and implications for national development, as the basis for mainstreaming HIV/AIDS into national development planning.

United Nations Economic Commission for Africa

Operating in the region most affected by the HIV/AIDS epidemic, the Addis Ababa-based UN Economic Commission for Africa (ECA) gave prominence to "the development challenge of HIV/AIDS for African development" at the start of the new millennium when it adopted this concern as the theme of the ECA's first African Development Forum (ADF 1) in December 2000. Particular attention was given at ADF 1 to the economic and social impact of HIV/AIDS in Africa and the costs for future generations in the region, and to obstacles that the epidemic could pose to the achievement of the MDGs to which African (and other world) leaders had committed themselves at the UN in New York in September 2000. The main document prepared by the ECA for the ADF 1 recognized the threat posed by HIV/AIDS to long-term sustainable development in Africa, in addition to being a humanitarian tragedy, and called for special initiatives to deal with the problems of HIV/AIDS as a broader development challenge.[32]

As a follow-up to ADF 1, then secretary-general Kofi Annan established a Commission on HIV/AIDS and Governance in Africa (CHGA) in 2003, and made the ECA the secretariat for CHGA which was made up mainly of eminent persons and specialists from the region. CHGA was mandated to examine the multiple ways in which HIV/AIDS impacts upon development and governance in Africa, and to make recommendations for assisting governments to formulate and implement policies and programs for effective response to the epidemic.[33] ECA organized a number of interactive sessions for CHGA on different themes pertaining to the development challenge of HIV/AIDS, such as impact on agriculture, education, public administration, labor, and the role of the private sector. After a long interval, the final report of the Commission was released and presented to Secretary-General Ban Ki Moon in June 2008.[34]

Conclusion

There is ample evidence that the HIV/AIDS epidemic is having a disastrous impact on social and economic development in highly affected countries, and this has been identified as a major obstacle to the attainment of the UN Millennium Development Goals in many developing countries. This leads to the conclusion that HIV/AIDS is a formidable development challenge, and that combating the epidemic and promoting development are complementary strategies. The link between HIV/AIDS and poverty illustrates the need for an integrated approach to deal with the challenge of reducing poverty in the midst of an HIV/AIDS crisis. Another conclusion is that HIV/AIDS is a longwave event, both in terms of its unending spread globally and its impact on long-term sustainable development, which is justification for keeping the epidemic on the international agenda as a development issue. However, for HIV/AIDS to remain high on the international agenda as a development issue, the evolutionary nature of the epidemic and the complexity of its impact on development in a globalizing and changing world must not be lost on decision-makers in the governance structures of key global multilateral institutions. This is all the more crucial in the light of other competing priorities, such as climate change, the global food crisis, and water shortages, on the international development agenda. It is also important to stress the centrality of human resources for sustainable development, in the context of the development challenge of HIV/AIDS, as a strong argument for keeping HIV/AIDS as a priority on the international development agenda. This critical dimension of the development challenge of HIV/AIDS is addressed in the next chapter.

7 HIV/AIDS and human resource capacity

In the previous chapter, it was noted that the impact of the HIV/AIDS epidemic, which is concentrated on the working-age population in many developing countries, constitutes a drawback to development efforts. In this chapter, we explore further the adverse demographic impact of the epidemic on development in terms of losses in human resource capacity in key economic and social sectors. It is not realistic to assume that losses in human resource capacity due to HIV/AIDS can be replaced without costs. In developing countries, this might involve training and retraining programs, including in the health sector, which may not be feasible in many cases because of shortages of training facilities and personnel, or lack of money.

This chapter addresses two key challenges stemming from the impact of HIV/AIDS on human resource capacity. The first concerns the impact of the epidemic on labor and employment, in terms of the effects on the size and quality of the workforce and the implications for labor cost and demand. The second challenge relates to the loss of qualified and experienced professionals in key sectors, including health, due to AIDS-related mortality and morbidity and to labor migration. Millions of lives have been lost to HIV/AIDS in the developing world, resulting in significant quantitative and qualitative losses in labor supply which are generalized across all sectors of the economy. The concentration of the epidemic among the working age population and its economy-wide impact underline the immensity of the challenge faced by the high HIV-prevalence countries to sustain the requisite human resource capacity for present and future development needs.

Impact of HIV/AIDS on labor and employment

ILO reported in 2005 that an estimated 28 million workers had been lost to the global labor force due to AIDS-related mortality and morbidity, and this number was projected to reach 48 million by 2010 and 74 million by 2015 if the spread of the epidemic is not contained.[1] HIV/AIDS is therefore having a huge impact on human resource capacity through its effects on population growth and life expectancy, and the implications for labor and employment. The demographic impact of HIV/AIDS is particularly severe in sub-Saharan Africa, which is the region that has been most severely affected by the spread of the epidemic. According to UNAIDS, some countries in the region have up to a third of their adult population infected with HIV,[2] and the majority of those infected could die due to lack of adequate treatment and care. Life expectancy in some countries in the region has dropped substantially from over 55 years in the early 1980s to below 40 now, and there have also been marked increases in infant and child mortality rates due to HIV/AIDS. An increase in the spread of the epidemic among women in the developing regions is likely to affect the rate of population growth in the future, as HIV-positive women are having fewer babies and dying in their reproductive prime.[3] Furthermore, orphans and other vulnerable children affected by HIV/AIDS are missing out on schooling and education, which in turn is affecting the development of the next generation of human capital.

The impact of HIV/AIDS on human resources is of particular concern to the ILO, which sees the epidemic as an obstacle to the attainment of employment and labor market objectives and a threat to fundamental rights at work.[4] This impact is particularly serious in resource-poor developing countries, many of which were already experiencing significant shortfalls of critical skills in their human resource endowment even before the advent of HIV/AIDS. In many of those countries economic activities are predominantly labor-intensive, and a decline in labor supply and productivity in sectors such as agriculture and mining could have serious implications for development and welfare. Global estimates of the impact of HIV/AIDS on labor made by the ILO indicate that over two-thirds of the losses in human resource capacity worldwide have occurred in sub-Saharan Africa.[5] The ILO estimates show significant losses across sectors in several economies in the region, including evidence of labor shortages in agriculture and the loss of qualified and experienced professionals, technicians, and administrators who are hard to replace in the short term.[6]

The public sector

The public sector in many developing countries is a major employer, and the sector fulfills a key developmental role in terms of the planning, coordination, and delivery of essential public services. Because of the dominance of the public sector in the economy in developing countries, the majority of those in the labor force with technical skills, professional qualifications, and management expertise are likely to be employed in the sector. The effects of human resource losses in the public sector are therefore wider and systemic and the consequences may be particularly costly overall, especially as public sector human resource requirements involve high levels of public investment in education and training. Public sector institutions in some African countries are already experiencing difficulty in filling key vacancies caused by AIDS-related morbidity and mortality.[7] In addition, HIV/AIDS not only threatens the effective functioning of the public sector through loss of personnel, but also generates more demand for publicly provided health services which can be costly for developing countries.

HIV/AIDS has exerted a heavy toll on human resources in the education sector in Africa. The impact on teachers, administrators, and support staff in the education sector is of immense importance for the delivery of educational outputs, both currently and in the medium to long term. There are reports from high-prevalence countries of very high overall teacher attrition, which not only creates critical shortfalls in the supply of teachers but also raises the demand for newly qualified teachers, thus prolonging the dependence of the system on unqualified teachers.[8] The United Nations Educational, Scientific and Cultural Organization (UNESCO), which is a co-sponsor of UNAIDS, has been working with national authorities in several highly affected countries, specifically to increase the capacity of education and training institutions to replace teachers lost to the system due to AIDS. UNESCO has also collaborated with ILO at country level to better prepare new entrants to the labor market in order to alleviate human resource losses under the impact of HIV/AIDS.

There impact of HIV/AIDS on human resource capacity can also affect the capacity of the state to govern, as the impact extends to those who are directly involved in government and to parliamentarians and members of the judiciary. There is already evidence from a number of African countries linking HIV/AIDS-related mortality and morbidity with the erosion of democratic governance and threats to political stability.[9] Furthermore, the impact on the military and uniformed services within the public sector, as discussed in Chapter 5, could threaten national security and the maintenance of law and order.

The private sector

Within the private sector, the impact of HIV/AIDS on human resource capacity affects labor productivity and costs of production. The issue, however, is not simply one of costs to the enterprise that are directly identifiable, such as those caused by HIV/AIDS-related sickness and absenteeism, medical and related costs including funeral expenses, and payments to relatives of deceased workers. While these are important for many entrepreneurs, they are in no sense the sum total of all the labor costs associated with the impact of HIV/AIDS on enterprises. In both the present and the medium to long term, the critical factor is how to sustain human resources capacity with respect to specialized skills and managerial experience, given the key role that these play in enterprise profitability and survival. These skills are usually scarce in many developing countries and are often derived from years of experience. Loss of key personnel with job-specific skills and experience in particular enterprises can cause disruption to production, a decline in product and service quality and an increase in production costs. Addressing this problem implies additional costs linked to the recruitment and training of replacement staff and retraining of existing workers.

Both subsistence production and commercial agriculture engage a large proportion of the labor force in the developing regions, and in several African countries agriculture is the main source of livelihood for the majority of the population. Not only do livelihoods depend on sustaining agriculture, but so does food security. The loss of workers in agriculture to HIV/AIDS is affecting food production and distribution in Africa. The UN Food and Agricultural Organization (FAO) estimated that about 7 million workers had been lost to agriculture due to AIDS between 1985 and 2000, and that an additional 16 million deaths could occur in the sector in the next two decades if the trend continues.[10] Ensuring that agriculture remains productive in the face of the impact of HIV/AIDS on agrarian systems is thus one of the main development challenges of the epidemic.

The informal economy

The informal economy is a dynamic source of employment and income in many developing countries, and the impact of HIV/AIDS on labor in this sector threatens the livelihoods of a large percentage of the population in those countries. Because of the precarious nature of employment in the informal sector, the impact of HIV/AIDS is pervasive and complex. Morbidity and mortality place a great strain on the sustainability of informal sector enterprises. Illness or death not only results in loss of income but possibly in the collapse of the business, because such informal sector enterprises are highly dependent on labor and internal generation of flows of revenues and savings for their survival. Savings are also threatened by the demands on revenues for higher levels of health expenditure when owners or key workers fall ill. Of particular concern in informal sector production is the loss of experience and specific skills that are essential for survival in small, labor-intensive businesses. Vulnerable groups such as women and migrants are prominent in the informal sector labor force, and the greater risk that they face to HIV infection makes their situation as workers and breadwinners even more precarious. Premature deaths of artisans and craftsmen due to HIV/AIDS could cause disruption in the inter-generational transfer of traditional skills, and consequently the demise of economic activities vital to rural livelihoods.

The UN system's response to the impact of HIV/AIDS on human resource capacity

In line with its responsibility within the UN system for labor and employment matters, ILO has been a major player in addressing the impact of the HIV/AIDS epidemic on human resources. The labor agency's response focuses on the world of work and revolves around the mobilization of the constituents of its unique tripartite membership structure (governments, employers, and workers) at country level. Activities carried out by the ILO include raising awareness about the disease and its mpact on labor and related social objectives in the workplace; promoting relevant international labor standards to combat HIV-related discrimination in employment; applying occupational health and safety regulations to HIV/AIDS management in the workplace; and providing guidelines for the development and implementation of specific workplace HIV/AIDS policies and programs. ILO's main instrument in its response to the impact of HIV/AIDS on human resources is its "Code of Practice on HIV/AIDS and the World of Work," which was adopted in May 2001 on the basis of consensus among the tripartite constituents. The ILO Code provides specific guidelines derived from ILO standards for protecting workers from HIV infection, prohibiting discrimination, and mitigating the impact of the disease on workers and their families through access to social protection.

FAO, in collaboration with ILO, has been providing policy advice and training for replacing skilled and semi-skilled agricultural workers lost to HIV/AIDS, and implementing country-level programs for sustaining output and income in agriculture under the impact of the epidemic. The UN World Food Programme (WFP), which is a co-sponsor of UNAIDS, assists affected countries to minimize the impact of HIV/AIDS on food security. WFP provides food directly to HIV-infected persons who require adequate nutrition to support ARV therapies; to support prevention of mother-to-child transmission programs (PMTCT); and for school-feeding schemes catering for orphans and other vulnerable children affected by HIV/AIDS.

A number of UN agencies have initiated actions to address the growing concern about gender inequality linked to HIV/AIDS prevention, treatment, and care, which impacts upon the roles of women in the labor market and access to opportunities for gainful employment. It has been observed that women and girls are at much greater risk of HIV infection than their male counterparts, and that they bear a disproportionate burden in the provision of care and support to family members who are sick. The need to empower women by aiming to reduce gender-based inequality is now prominent in HIV/AIDS response programs of the ILO, UNDP, UNICEF, UNFPA, and World Bank.

Responding to human resource losses in the health sector

In addition to loss of health sector personnel through HIV/AIDS-related death and illness, some of the developing countries worst affected by the epidemic are also losing skilled and experienced health sector professionals through labor migration that has been influenced by the impact of the epidemic, among other things. The exodus of qualified and expensively trained doctors and nurses from developing to mainly developed countries represents what has been described as a "brain drain" at high economic and social cost to the sending countries. While the brain drain is nothing new, the problem has hit Africa particularly hard at a time when the region needs all of the skilled health sector workers it can mobilize to combat HIV/AIDS. Sub-Saharan Africa is losing thousands of doctors and nurses every year to Europe, North America, and Australia. Not surprisingly, this flight of health workers from the region has triggered a health crisis, according to the WHO.[11] The World Bank reported that the exodus of skilled labor in health and allied services is as high as 50 percent of the total in the Gambia, Cape Verde, Malawi, Sierra Leone, and Zimbabwe, which is affecting the response to HIV/AIDS and hindering overall development in the continent.[12]

The problem of brain drain in the health sector

A study on the migration of doctors and nurses from Africa to developed countries, undertaken on behalf of the Washington, D.C.-based Center for Global Development (CGD), reported that approximately 65,000

African-born doctors and 70,000 African-born nurses were working in a developed country in 2000, representing respectively about one-fifth and one-tenth of the global total of African doctors and nurses at the time.[13] The loss of qualified and experienced health professionals is already affecting the capacity of African countries to respond effectively to HIV/AIDS. The shortage of health workers in many African countries was a major constraint on the implementation of the "3×5" initiative that the WHO launched in 2003 with the objective of providing ARV therapy to 3 million HIV/AIDS patients in low- and middle-income countries by the end of 2005. The UN health agency had to put in place crash training programs, and adopted special measures to shift and share tasks among available staff to alleviate personnel shortages affecting the implementation of the 3×5 in several developing countries.[14]

The migration of health professionals from developing to developed countries has sparked highly charged and emotive debates at international and regional levels. African countries and their international development partners have accused the developed countries of poaching expensively trained doctors and nurses without compensation of any kind.[15] Writing in the *Lancet* recently, one impassioned commentator went as far as to suggest that the recruitment of health personnel from Africa "should be viewed as an international crime."[16] There are indications of concern about the brain drain from the receiving countries themselves, as evidenced from a plea from by the chair of the British Medical Association Council in 2005 to bring an end to "the rape of the poorest countries."[17]

The problem of the brain drain in medical fields is complex and, as such, a solution would involve several considerations. Given the huge differentials in salaries, benefits, and opportunities between developed and developing countries, some argue that the migration of health professionals from the South to the North is a response to the "pull factor" of market forces in the context of the globalization of the world economy. Lack of facilities and opportunities for post-qualification training in many developing countries has been identified as a pull factor in the decision of newly qualified doctors to leave home. The developing countries themselves realize that one of the best ways for them to retain their health professionals is to pay them higher salaries and provide better facilities for them to work in, which unfortunately health systems in many African countries cannot afford. Then there is the case of those countries in the region which can afford to provide incentives to retain skilled workers, but may be otherwise constrained by externally imposed conditions.[18]

Incentive schemes to combat the brain drain

There is consensus emerging globally on the need for incentives to retain health professionals and to encourage those who are already abroad to return home. Incentive schemes are bound to be costly, and substantial external financial assistance will be needed by most countries affected by the brain drain to make such schemes operational, let alone successful. The case has been made for rich countries which need and benefit from foreign health workers from developing countries to pay compensation to the sending countries, including contributing to the costs of training doctors and nurses in those countries. The idea of encouraging qualified and experienced health professionals who are working abroad to return home has been seriously considered by specialized international agencies such as the IOM, WHO, and World Bank, and a number of proposals and initiatives have emerged.

The IOM supports incentive schemes to encourage foreign doctors abroad to return home. Realizing that part of the reason for qualified health professionals going abroad is lack of facilities and opportunities at home, IOM sees some merit in the idea of skilled health workers from developing countries going abroad and investing in furthering their knowledge to avoid a "brain waste," and then encouraging them to return home eventually or even temporarily to share their skills.[19] This approach recognizes that there is an advantage for everyone concerned, developed and developing countries and the health professionals themselves. The U.K. National Health Service (NHS), which ended "active recruitment" of healthcare personnel from sub-Saharan Africa in 2001, has since taken steps to provide financial assistance to some countries in the region to improve conditions locally for medical staff and thus help mitigate the brain drain. In 2005, the U.K. government provided £100 million in aid to Malawi to train and improve conditions for health sector workers under a six-year program which aims to double the number of nurses and triple the number of doctors in the country.

WHO's Treat, Train, and Retain (TTR) initiative

At the June 2006 UN General Assembly High-Level Meeting on HIV/AIDS, member states agreed to work toward the goal of "Universal Access" to comprehensive prevention programs, treatment, care and support by 2010. One of the main constraints to universal access is the serious shortage of health workers in low- and middle-income countries needed to treat HIV/AIDS patients. According to the WHO, providing ARV therapies for 1,000 HIV-infected persons in resource-constrained settings will require one or two doctors, up to seven nurses, three pharmacy staff and a large number of community workers.[20] The reality falls far short: in some highly affected countries in southern Africa, there are districts that have no doctors or pharmacy staff at all.

In response to this chronic shortage of trained health workers for HIV/AIDS response, the WHO launched the "Treat, Train, and Retain" (TTR) initiative in August 2006. TTR is an important component of WHO's overall effort to strengthen human resources for health and to promote comprehensive national strategies for human resource development across different disease programs. Focusing on HIV/AIDS, the TTR initiative aims to build and expand human resource capacity in the health sector by addressing both the causes and effects of HIV/AIDS on health workers. The three key elements of the program are: (1) HIV treatment including prevention for health workers who may be infected or affected by the disease; (2) training for health workers to enable them to deliver universal access to HIV/AIDS services; and (3) strategies for retaining heath sector workers and other measures to improve working conditions in the sector and initiatives to control the migration of workers from the sector. TTR fits in with the global mandate of the WHO to coordinate efforts for establishing and sustaining strong and effective healthcare systems worldwide. As the lead agency, WHO works with other international agencies, such as the ILO, IOM and World Bank, and with local health authorities to help countries implement national plans based on the TTR initiative. WHO also monitors and evaluates progress of TTR around the world, and gathers experience and examples of best practice that can be shared with others. It is estimated that it will cost between US$7.2 and 14 billion over the next five years to implement the TTR initiative in the 60 countries with the highest HIV burden in the world.[21]

In the context of implementing the TTR, the WHO Africa Regional Office has estimated that the region has a shortfall of over 800,000 qualified health personnel—doctors, nurses and midwives.[22] This means that there is a need to more than double the existing workforce of these categories of health professionals in the region to support effective HIV/AIDS responses at country level. Given that it takes about six years to train a doctor and three to four years for a nurse and a midwife, and that current training facilities in the region are insufficient, WHO recently launched the "Task Shifting" project, in collaboration with the Office of the U.S. Global AIDS Coordinator and other bilateral donors, to support the implementation of the TTR.

The idea behind task shifting is to delegate certain tasks, where appropriate, to less specialized health personnel to compensate for the shortage of higher-level personnel. For example, when doctors are in short supply a qualified nurse can prescribe and dispense ARV therapy, or trained community health workers can deliver a range of HIV/AIDS services to free the time of qualified nurses for other higher-level duties. WHO claims that task shifting is cost-effective and can expand human resource capacity in the health sector rapidly since, for instance, the training of a community health worker takes substantially less time and costs only a small fraction of the time and resources required to train a fully qualified nurse. WHO also emphasizes that task shifting has the added advantage of building bridges between the health system and the local community, and that the use of community workers creates employment locally. An international conference of health ministers was organized by the WHO in Addis Ababa in January 2008 to unveil guidelines for implementing the initiative, as part of the global effort to facilitate universal access to HIV/AIDS services.

WHO was instrumental in the establishment of the "Global Health Workforce Alliance" (GHWA) in 2006, which it hosts at its Geneva headquarters. The purpose of GHWA is to mobilize global support and coordinated action for overcoming the crisis in human resources for health in developing countries. GHWA brings together a variety of stakeholders from both the public and private sectors, including international and local NGOs. It has formulated a 10-year plan of action (2006–15) and developed a global platform to strengthen health sector human resource development programs and activities around the world for the accelerated achievement of health-related MDGs.[23]

The World Bank's "Human Resources for Health" program (HRH)

In addition to the challenge of retaining skilled health workers, many developing countries are also faced with the problem of getting available health professionals to work in rural and remote areas. According to the World Bank, the situation is particularly severe in several African countries where more than 90 percent of doctors work in urban areas which also have most of the available health facilities.[24] This imbalance in the distribution of health professionals and facilities effectively means that the poor, who live in the rural areas and far away from the capital cities, including those infected with and vulnerable to HIV, cannot benefit from health services that are available in urban areas.

To address this particular human resource problem, the World Bank, with funding from the Gates Foundation and the Norwegian aid agency NORAD, launched a specific "Human Resources for Health" (HRH) program in 2006 to provide technical and financial assistance to sub-Saharan countries. The program operates closely with and coordinates the efforts of other multilateral and bilateral agencies and NGOs at the country level. Assistance is provided to governments to obtain and make use of evidence-based information and data for targeted policy and program interventions, and to provide incentives that motivate health personnel to work in rural and poorer areas. The aim is not only to redress the rural/urban imbalance in the distribution of health workers in a country, but also to ensure health service coverage for the poor through access to doctors and other health workers who are responsive to their needs.

Conclusion

This chapter has illustrated that the impact of HIV/AIDS on human resource capacity is a major development challenge, particularly in Africa. Many levels and types of human resource capacity which are needed for sustainable development are affected by the impact of HIV/AIDS on labor. It was noted that losses of human capital due to HIV/AIDS are not only confined to skilled workers; some African countries are already experiencing shortages of labor in subsistence agriculture, which is vital to the livelihood of the majority of the population. An important policy conclusion is the need for action to sustain different types and levels of skill as required for an effective response to the epidemic, to ensure that labor supplies are maintained in key sectors like health and education as the epidemic takes its toll on the workforce.

The adverse impact of HIV/AIDS on human resource capacity in health sector personnel is of particular concern to policy-makers at international and national levels. As shown, in addition to loss of human resource capacity due to AIDS-related mortality and morbidity, there is also an exodus of qualified and experienced health professionals from developing to developed countries. This is seriously affecting national capacity to respond effectively to the threat posed by HIV/AIDS to development. Innovative policies and programs focusing on the restructuring of education and training systems, as well as the introduction of new methods of work organization and incentives, have been proposed and implemented by relevant global institutions in cooperation with governments in affected countries. It is obvious that developing countries still need to be assisted financially to implement policies and programs for sustaining human resource capacity and maintaining the necessary facilities for responding effectively to HIV/AIDS. The next chapter looks at the financing of the global HIV/AIDS response, which can be decisive to the outcome for developing countries in meeting the human resource and broader development challenges of the epidemic.

8 Financing the global HIV/AIDS response

Donor governments provide the bulk of the money that funds HIV/ AIDS prevention, treatment, and care programs in low- and middle-income countries today. The main donor governments are the members of the OECD's Development Assistance Committee (DAC), which includes the G7 group of rich industrialized countries. Financing of the global HIV/AIDS response is mainly through donor contributions to relevant multilateral institutions such as UNAIDS, the Global Fund, and WHO, as well as by direct bilateral transfers to recipient governments and national or regional institutions. In the early years of the epidemic, none of the wealthy nations funded HIV/AIDS programs in developing countries directly through bilateral aid programs. In the absence of a clear funding strategy and guidelines from the UN at the time, donor governments were uncertain about how to proceed and chose instead to direct funds for HIV/AIDS through the multilateral channels.[1]

Financing of the global HIV/AIDS response has skyrocketed over the past two decades. It increased from just US$200,000 in 1986 to an estimated $53 million the following year, when the Global Programme on AIDS was established by the WHO and provided a multilateral mechanism through which donor governments can fund HIV/AIDS prevention and care. Annual donor financing had exceeded $225 million by 1990, and this upward trend continued throughout the 1990s and exceeded the $1 billion mark by the end of that decade. Since 2000, the increase in HIV/AIDS financing has been much faster with the appearance on the scene of major resource mobilization initiatives, chiefly the Global Fund, the World Bank's Multi-Country HIV/AIDS Program (MAP) and the U.S.A.'s President's Emergency Plan for AIDS Relief (PEPFAR). Funding of HIV/AIDS programs in low- and middle-come countries from all sources increased from an estimated $1.6 billion per annum at the end of 2000 to US$6.1 billion in 2004, then to US$8.9 billion in 2006, and was projected to reach US$10 billion by the end of 2008.[2] The huge upsurge in HIV/AIDS financing, and the outpouring of new resources from a variety of sources, has recently precipitated key debates about whether or not the global HIV/AIDS response is over-financed relative to its share of the burden of global diseases and in relation to other development needs.

This chapter presents and analyzes the main sources of HIV/AIDS financing globally. The analysis is also undertaken in the light of the debates and queries raised about the amount of money being spent on the epidemic and the impact of this spending. It brings into focus the problems and challenges of financing the global response, and explores policy options and practical proposals for improving the efficiency and effectiveness of the different financing arrangements and mechanisms. The chapter also addresses the paradoxical situation in global HIV/AIDS financing of unspent commitments and allocations co-existing with resource and need gaps, which raises questions about the competence and governance of resource mobilization strategies and funding mechanisms.

Bilateral financing

Following the demise of the WHO's Global Programme on AIDS, and throughout the 1990s, bilateral assistance was the major source of financing for the global response until the emergence of the Global Fund in 2002. Prior to the establishment of the Global Fund, seven major OECD donor governments, namely the U.S.A., U.K., France, Sweden, Denmark, Germany, and the Netherlands, and the European Commission accounted for as much as two-thirds of the total amount spent on the global HIV/AIDS response during this period. In line with the general pattern for bilateral aid, donor governments often targeted specific countries which were considered to be of special interest to them and, accordingly, the number of countries benefiting from this source of HIV/AIDS financing tended to be rather limited in relation to the total number of countries affected by the epidemic.

Although HIV/AIDS is no longer a growing public health problem in the United States and other rich countries, growing awareness of the impacts of the epidemic at the global level and on international development objectives such as the Millennium Development Goals has contributed to continued and increasing financial support for the global response from the rich countries. The most important example of this was the decision by the U.S. president, George W. Bush, to propose an initiative to combat HIV/AIDS in poor countries in his

2003 State of the Union address. In response to President Bush's proposal, Congress passed the "U.S. Leadership Against AIDS, Tuberculosis and Malaria Act" on 27 May 2003, which authorized the administration to spend up to US$15 billion over five years.[3] The legislation also created the Office of the Global AIDS Coordinator (OGAC) within the Department of State to manage the initiative, rather than the U.S. Agency for International Development (USAID), which had managed previous U.S. bilateral HIV/AIDS assistance. OGAC was mandated by the legislation to develop a "comprehensive, integrated. ... strategy to combat AIDS. ... [and] to strengthen the capacity of the United States to be an effective leader in the international campaign against AIDS."[4] In February 2004 the Global Coordinator, Ambassador Randall Tobias, duly prepared and presented to Congress a five-year global AIDS strategy, titled "The President's Emergency Plan for AIDS Relief" (PEPFAR). As a result of PEPFAR, the United States became the largest single contributor to the global HIV/AIDS response. In 2006, the United States committed over $2.5 billion for the global response, which was nearly half of the total contributed by all donors.

PEPFAR: the U.S. global HIV/AIDS initiative

PEPFAR, which described itself as the "largest global health initiative directed at a single disease that any nation has ever undertaken,"[5] established three objectives: to encourage bold U.S. leadership at every level to fight HIV/AIDS; to apply best practices within U.S. bilateral HIV/AIDS prevention, treatment, and care programs; and to encourage partners to coordinate efforts to ensure the most effective use of resources. About two-thirds of the initial PEPFAR authorization was earmarked as grants for HIV/AIDS prevention and treatment in 15 "focus countries" selected by the administration (twelve in Africa, two in the Caribbean and one in Asia).[6] PEPFAR's overall targets for all of the focus countries were as follows: provision of ARV treatment to 2 million people by 2008; prevention of 7 million new infections; and provision of care and support for 10 million HIV-infected persons and AIDS orphans over the five-year period. The remaining one-third of the initial PEPFAR money was intended to go toward the U.S. contribution to the Global Fund over the five-year period. Although the PEPFAR legislation refers as well to action against malaria and tuberculosis, in line with the wider mandate of the Global Fund for the same three diseases, about three-quarters of the total authorization was for HIV/AIDS.

PEPFAR was established on the implicit belief that HIV/AIDS prevention, treatment, and care could be addressed by allocating a very large amount of aid which would make a big dent on the epidemic and change the landscape of the global response significantly. The argument advanced in favor of this approach was that the rate of HIV infection was rising faster than the rate at which ARVs are being supplied worldwide, so financial resources needed to be mobilized and disbursed quickly to bring the problem under control. However, it should be noted that mobilizing and providing massive doses of capital to solve a major problem can downplay obstacles to the efficacy of donor assistance, posed by weaknesses and drawbacks of aid and constraints and limitations of internal capacity.

The PEPFAR legislation outlined priorities for spending the money, irrespective of the evolution of the epidemic and changing impact and response patterns over time and in different circumstances. It was decreed that 55 percent of total spending on HIV/AIDS should go to treatment; 20 percent for prevention activities, of which 33 percent should be spent on abstinence-until-marriage programs; 15 percent for palliative care of people with AIDS; and 10 percent for support of orphans and vulnerable children.[7] The imposition of a common formula in terms of priorities and spending patterns for all the focus countries essentially does not allow for flexibility in the use of PEPFAR grants by individual countries, which could be counterproductive to effective HIV/AIDS response. For example, the requirement that one-third of PEPFAR money to be spent on prevention should go to abstinence programs denotes an implicit bias against the use of condoms and could even undermine efforts to control the spread of HIV.

The selection of a very small number of countries as beneficiaries, in relation to the much larger number of developing countries affected by the epidemic, leaves the program open to the criticism that it ignores some of the poorest and neediest countries. The selection of countries, it would appear, was based on political and other considerations that benefit allies and constituencies of the United States rather than the worst-affected countries and those most in need of assistance. In addition, the U.S. administration had decided against giving PEPFAR money directly to UN specialized agencies operating in the focus countries, preferring to rely on the expertise available within the local U.S. embassies on the ground. This deprived the initiative at country level of the opportunity to benefit from available specialized technical skills and knowledge of local conditions that come with many years of experience of UN agencies' involvement in program planning and implementation in some of those countries.

Initially, PEPFAR was not in favor of buying and using cheaper generic ARV drugs in its country operations, including those which had been approved by the WHO. Whether this decision was influenced by the preference of the Global Coordinator of PEPFAR, who was previously the chief executive officer of a major U.S. pharmaceutical company, is unknown, but it nevertheless gives the impression of a donor that was more interested in protecting the commercial interests of U.S. pharmaceutical companies that were already the leading global producers of patented AIDS medicines than in providing treatment for as many people as possible in the developing countries. Countries benefiting from PEPFAR assistance were thus obliged to buy more expensive patented drugs even when cheaper and safe generic versions were available in the market.

Despite these criticisms, the added value that the PEPFAR money gave to the global HIV/AIDS response was widely regarded as significant and crucial. Peter Piot, then executive head of UNAIDS, believed that the PEPFAR initiative was a great boost to HIV/AIDS funding and one of the important developments in the history of the fight against the epidemic.[8] When PEPFAR was launched in 2003, there were only about 50,000 AIDS patients on ARV therapies in sub-Saharan Africa; this number had increased to an estimated 1.5 million people receiving ARV drugs in 2008, due largely to PEPFAR-funded projects in the 12 focus countries in the region.

Action was taken by the U.S. administration in 2006 to make use of local organizations in the implementation of country projects with the launch of the "New Partner Initiative" (NPI), as part of a broader effort within PEPFAR to work with new partners, including community- and faith-based organizations. NPI grants are provided directly to local implementing partners to provide HIV prevention, treatment, and care in the focus countries. This is in line with one of the main objectives of PEPFAR, which is to enhance technical and organizational capacity at local level and support community ownership to ensure continuity and long-term sustainability of HIV/AIDS programs.

Following a visit by President Bush to a number of the focus countries in Africa in late 2007, where he saw at first hand the devastating effects of HIV/AIDS and the impact of PEPFAR in the fight against the disease, his administration submitted a new request to the U.S. Congress to authorize an extension of PEPFAR over another five-year period, 2009–13, and at a much higher level of funding. In July 2008 the U.S. Congress eventually approved an extension of PEPFAR, authorizing $48 billion for HIV/AIDS, tuberculosis and malaria for another five years.

Multilateral financing

As already indicated, multilateral financing of the global HIV/AIDS response got a big boost with the establishment of the Global Fund to Fight AIDS, Tuberculosis and Malaria (Global Fund) in 2002. Before that, World Bank funding of HIV/AIDS projects at country level, which goes as far back as the late 1980s, was the main source of multilateral financing of HIV/AIDS activities. The World Bank's effort was intensified in September 2000 with the launching of its innovative Multi-Country HIV/AIDS Program (MAP), which is now central to its multi-sectoral and development-oriented HIV/AIDS strategy.

UN agencies, particularly WHO and later UNAIDS, and the World Bank had been at the forefront of efforts within the multilateral system to combat the global HIV/AIDS epidemic until the Global Fund appeared on the scene in 2002. The Global Fund represented a new approach to international health financing within the multilateral format.

The Global Fund

The Global Fund was established as a financing mechanism with the support of the G7. Its main purpose is to attract and disburse financial resources to developing countries for preventing and treating HIV/AIDS, tuberculosis, and malaria. In many ways, the Global Fund is an innovative financing mechanism in the area of global health. First, it is structured as public–private partnership between governments of developed and developing countries, the private sector, civil society, and affected communities. Second, it operates outside the UN system as an independent non-intergovernmental organization, but works in close collaboration with other bilateral and multilateral organizations, such as WHO and UNAIDS, and the World Bank. Since 1 January 2009, the Global Fund has become an administratively autonomous organization, terminating its original administrative services agreement with the WHO. Third, funding for country-level HIV/AIDS activities is provided to developing countries in the form of grants awarded on the basis of project proposals prepared and submitted to the Fund and reviewed by an independent technical panel. Fourth, the governing body of the Global Fund is a 24-member international board of directors that consists of an equal number of representatives of donor and recipient governments, two representatives of NGOs from the North and South respectively, and two private sector members representing businesses and philanthropic foundations. The WHO, UNAIDS, and the World Bank (which is the Global Fund's trustee) have non-voting seats on the board. In addition the Global Fund convenes a biennial Partnership Forum, which brings together a broader group of stakeholders with diverse perspectives and intimate knowledge about the impacts of the epidemic.

The Global Fund is served by a secretariat based in Geneva and headed by an executive director. Compared to UN agencies, the secretariat of the Global Fund plays mainly a facilitating and coordinating role, and is characterized by a lean management and administration structure with less than 300 regular staff in Geneva and no institutional representation or direct presence in the countries where it operates. Instead, it relies on a wide range of partners to carry out key activities, including contracting an independent Local Fund Agent in each country where it operates to oversee the administration of funds provided and to verify progress in project implementation. Until the beginning of 2009, the Global Fund secretariat also relied on the WHO to provide it with a range of administrative and financial services, which enabled it to become operational almost immediately after it was established.

A high priority is attached by the Global Fund to local involvement in and ownership of the projects that it funds, and it specifically encourages broad-based participation in its program activities at country level. This point is best illustrated by the unique arrangement that the Global Fund has adopted for project development and execution, which requires all countries dealing with the Fund to constitute a broad representative body known as the Country Coordinating Mechanism (CCM) for the preparation and submission of grant proposals and for monitoring the implementation of projects which have been approved for funding. Typically, a CCM will include representatives of government agencies, private sector institutions, civil society (including community- and faith-based) organizations, and those living with and affected by HIV/AIDS.

Proposals submitted by countries to the Global Fund must meet the approval of the CCM, and are then reviewed by an independent Technical Review Panel (TRP), appointed by the Fund's board of directors and made up of experts drawn from all regions of the world. The TRP makes recommendations to the Fund on the basis of the technical merit of proposals, and may recommend that proposals be funded without condition, approved conditionally, revised and resubmitted, or not approved.

While the methods used by the Global Fund for the approval of proposals and award of grants to countries are designed to ensure local ownership and transparency, concerns have been expressed that grants can be awarded on the basis of well written proposals which have probably been put together by outside specialists hired specifically for this purpose, rather than on the basis of a consultative process involving various stakeholders within the CCM, as was intended. Furthermore, with little or no prior feasibility studies carried out regarding particularly absorptive and technical capacities of countries before the proposals are approved, there is the danger of bottlenecks and efficiency-related problems arising in the implementation phase. It is only after a grant has been awarded that a Local Fund Agent (LFA) is hired by the Global Fund to assess the capacity and systems of a country to implement and manage the project. This has resulted in long delays between commitment and disbursement whenever the LFA is unconvinced about the efficacy of local implementation capacity and structure.

Proposals approved by the Global Fund are usually negotiated into an initial two-year grant agreement between the Geneva-based secretariat and a Principal Recipient (PR) nominated by the CCM and confirmed by the Global Fund. The PR may be an agency of the recipient government such as the finance or health ministry. Following clearance by the LFA and the signing of the agreement, the first disbursement is made by the Global Fund to the PR; the PR in turn makes money available to local implementing organizations. Subsequent disbursements are made by the Global Fund on the basis of evidence of progress achieved and verified by the LFA. The flow of funds over the initial two-year program period is linked to continued progress. At the end of the two-year period, performance is evaluated by the Fund to determine whether to renew the grant for another two-year period or more up to the full term of the project. This rather cumbersome procedure may be justified in terms of necessary financial and program monitoring and the provision of safeguards against mismanagement, but it is leading to long delays in implementation of projects which are meant to deal with a problem that is regarded as an emergency. For example, a recent report in a Ugandan newspaper stated that the country has been able to access only about a third of Global Fund money awarded as grants over the past five years, and it cited an analysis by Aidspan, an independent watchdog that monitors Global Fund disbursements, which revealed that Uganda grants are on average 28.3 months behind schedule.[9] As far as safeguards are concerned, there is no guarantee that the procedure is effective. The same newspaper report stated that part of the reason for the delay in disbursement is that "Uganda was in August 2005 suspended from the

Global Fund after an audit indicated that the Ministry of Health had misused $1.6 million."[10]

As of July 2008, the Global Fund had gone through eight funding rounds of grant approvals,[11] and committed over US$10 billion to more than 550 programs and projects run by governments and other recipients including NGOs, community- and faith-based organizations and the private sector, in about 140 countries. This makes the Global Fund the primary multilateral mechanism for funding HIV/AIDS programs in low- and middle-income countries. Governments account for the largest share, at over 60 percent of the Fund's disbursements to date. Distribution of all Global Fund commitments indicates that about 60 percent of the Fund's money goes to HIV/AIDS, 24 percent to malaria, 14 percent to tuberculosis and 2 percent to health system strengthening.[12] Over two-thirds of the total Global Fund grants so far have gone to low-income countries, the majority of which are in sub-Saharan Africa. About half of the Global Fund's total commitments to date have been used for procurement and delivery of drugs and commodities linked to treatment; 20 percent to human resources and capacity-building; 12 percent to physical infrastructure; 8 percent to administration; and the rest to monitoring and evaluation and other services.[13]

The Global Fund depends entirely on voluntary contributions, and these come from mainly donor governments, philanthropic foundations, and the private sector. Most of the Fund's money is raised from the public sector, and the major donor governments are the U.S.A., Germany, U.K., Japan, France, Italy, and Canada. Since its inception, the Global Fund has received an estimated US$9 billion in contributions and pledges, mainly from the G8 countries.[14] Businesses and private foundations play an important role in the Fund's operations, although more as partners than donors. So far, efforts to raise private sector contributions to the Global Fund have not been particularly successful. In addition, some recipient countries make cash contributions and contributions in kind toward local costs of Global Fund-financed projects.

In order to make its resources more predictable and sustainable, the Global Fund in 2004 established the Voluntary Replenishment Mechanism, which at the time was chaired by the UN secretary-general. This arrangement provides for the holding of regular replenishment meetings to which major donors and other stakeholders are invited. Quite recently, the Global Fund has begun to give serious consideration to the idea of lending money in the form of an interest-free loan to upper-middle-income developing and transition countries, such as those in the Eastern Europe and Central Asian regions, which may no longer qualify for Global Fund grants (which are for low- and middle-income countries).[15] This move, according to the head of the Global Fund, would help to ensure that civil society groups are not deprived of resources for fighting HIV/AIDS as countries become richer and move away from being eligible for grants.

Guided by the "additionality principle,"[16] which implies that grants awarded by the Global Fund should not in any way subtract from commitments made by other development partners or agencies to recipient countries to address the three diseases, the Global Fund grants are intended to fill gaps and add value to existing national programs. The fact that the Global Fund was originally conceived as a financing instrument and not an implementing agency has meant that from the start the institution has by and large confined its operations to mobilization and disbursement of funds. It was left to experts and operating agencies acting on its behalf and the recipient country to decide on what to spend the money on and how. This, however, again raises questions about the Fund's responsibility for the use of its grants. While the practice of relying on the CCM and LFA to oversee implementation has worked well in some countries, in others it has given rise to concerns about government domination and the quality of oversight. The Global Fund has actually had to cut off funding to a small number of countries because of alleged mismanagement of resources and outright corruption. The situation imagined by the G7 and other stakeholders—that the international organizations would step up and provide recipient countries with technical and other types of support needed for implementation—has not always come to pass, and country capacity to absorb funds and implement programs has remained a major challenge. It may no longer be out of context to think that the Global Fund, in addition to providing money, also needs a functioning system on the ground to ensure that its money is well spent.

The World Bank

The World Bank began funding HIV/AIDS projects in 1986 when it included the sum of US$150,000 for blood screening in a much larger health sector loan to Niger.[17] By 1989, the Bank was already financing various elements of HIV/AIDS response including prevention strategies, epidemiological research, and blood screening within the framework of health sector projects in over a dozen countries. During the 1990s, the World Bank's funding for HIV/AIDS response in developing countries was extended to include activities within non-health sector projects such as education and transport, in recognition of the wider development implications of the epidemic. The launching of the MAP initially for African countries in 2000 enabled the Bank to provide affordable financial resources to low-income countries that would dramatically increase access of their populations to HIV/AIDS prevention, care, and treatment programs, and in the process build local capacity to address HIV/ADS as a development challenge.

The funding of MAP projects was significantly different from the typical World Bank lending or even the institution's existing mechanism for funding HIV/AIDS response activities. The exceptionality of HIV/ AIDS and the urgency of its response led to the adoption of flexible approval arrangements and less stringent eligibility criteria for MAP funding. This marked the beginning of the period when the Bank increased its support for HIV/AIDS sharply to meet the development challenges of the epidemic in poor countries.

A number of innovations in World Bank funding operations were introduced under the MAP, including simplified procedures for the approval and disbursement of funds; funding of operating and recurrent costs of projects; and the financing of civil-society-led projects within national HIV/AIDS programs. Following the appraisal and negotiation of a MAP country program, it is submitted to and fast-tracked through the Bank's board for approval as part of the flexibility accorded to the MAP to speed up commitment and disbursement arrangements. The MAP had been specifically designed to encourage and provide support for the mobilization of civil society through the Bank's transactions with governments. So far, nearly 49,000 NGO, faith- and community-based projects have been funded within the framework of the MAP. In addition, MAP resources have also been used to finance cross-border HIV/AIDS projects and interventions that cannot be supported through individual country programs.

It is significant to note that the World Bank has made use of the MAP to facilitate the incorporation of HIV/AIDS programming into poverty reduction programs as part of national development planning. In this regard, the Bank has collaborated with the UNDP to develop methodologies and guidelines for integrating HIV/AIDS concerns into Poverty Reduction Strategy Papers (PRSP) in a number of African countries, including Tanzania, Burkina Faso, Ghana, Ethiopia, Malawi, Rwanda, and Zambia. The MAP is regarded by the World Bank as a vital component of its strategy to fight poverty. In principle, all International Development Association (IDA) member countries of the World Bank[18] affected by the epidemic can request and have MAP projects approved. However, there are eligibility criteria that can prevent an IDA country that is in need of assistance to support national

HIV/AIDS efforts from getting access to MAP resources. Priority is usually given by the Bank to IDA countries of "good standing," rather than to the neediest irrespective of standing in their relationship with the Bank. As a controversial provider of development assistance that has long been the object of criticisms about the conditions and effects of its assistance to developing countries, the World Bank should avoid the criticisms that could arise from the imposition of conditions that would exclude some of the poorest countries in the world from benefiting from IDA grants and low-interest credits for fighting HIV/AIDS.

The MAP was also designed to address the need for strong political commitment to the delegation of authority and resources to local levels to tackle HIV/AIDS: money has been included in MAP loans to help governments put in place institutional arrangements for promoting decentralization of HIV/AIDS implementation structures to provincial and district levels and to increase local-level participation in the process. Unlike other HIV/AIDS funding mechanisms which are directed at programs built around types of activities or objectives such as prevention education, treatment, or poverty reduction, most MAP projects are organized around the funding of an implementing entity such as the National AIDS Council (NAC), line ministries, local program administration and community-based organizations.

Total HIV/AIDS commitments and disbursements by the World Bank from 1990 to the end of 2007 were estimated at US$9.2 billion and $5.9 billion respectively for 174 approved projects.[19] A sizeable proportion of this total has been channeled through the MAP, which now includes a regional component for Latin America and the Caribbean, in addition to Africa. By the end of 2007 the MAP had committed about US$1.4 billion to HIV/AIDS projects in 33 countries in the two regions it covers, and over US$120 million to regional and sub-regional (i.e. cross-border) projects such as the Abidjan to Lagos transport corridor and the Great Lakes region projects. MAP programs were originally meant to last between four and five years, which may not fully address the Bank's commitment to long-term efforts to combat HIV/AIDS and the sustainability of interventions. Since 2005, the Bank has made provision for the renewal of MAP funding to address this need.

The first phase of the MAP (2000–6) helped to stimulate an unprecedented global response to HIV/AIDS in African and low-income countries, and the approach has shown that it is possible to respond relatively quickly to a global epidemic and development emergency situation by an innovative, flexible, large-scale funding program. The support provided to recipient countries by the MAP for institutional strengthening and capacity-building effectively laid the foundation for developing countries to be able to use the billions of dollars of HIV/AIDS financing which became available after 2002 with the establishment of the Global Fund and the PEPFAR initiative. Additional funding is critical for the rapid expansion of treatment and the achievement of the commitment to universal access. At the same time, the growth of the MAP (and other international) funding initiatives has resulted in significant challenges, not least of all the severe burdens placed on under-resourced and fragile health and development planning systems to use additional resources efficiently to sustain an effective response to the HIV/AIDS epidemic.

Some of these challenges were outlined in a report on the first phase of the Africa MAP program which was published in June 2007.[20] While noting that the investment made through MAP and other sources of international funding is beginning to have an impact in terms of slowing the pace of the epidemic in the region, the report acknowledged that there are still weaknesses in service delivery at country level and lack of coordination of donor efforts that impede more efficient use of donor funds. The report, prompted by internal Bank-led criticisms, also emphasized the need to fully integrate HIV/AIDS with the broad development agenda and to channel more money to local communities for grassroots actions that are crucial for reducing stigma and changing beliefs, perceptions, and social and individual behaviors. The lessons from the first phase of the MAP revealed a need for effective impact evaluation in order to better assess results and contribution to wider development objectives including poverty reduction. It has therefore been proposed within the Bank that ex-ante impact evaluations should be explicitly built into and funded in the next phase of the MAP.

The World Bank has launched a new strategy for the implementation of the second phase (2007–11) of the MAP,[21] which advocates a flexible and multiple approach to HIV/AIDS response that balances treatment and prevention efforts tailored to the conditions of individual countries. Assistance to the hardest hit countries in the region in terms of prevalence rate will be expanded on the basis of partnership with local organizations as part of the new strategy. The Bank would also make use of innovative financial instruments to expand engagement in middle-income countries in the African region, such as Botswana and South Africa, in order to ensure sustainability of key interventions which tackle the drivers of the epidemic. Through the second phase of the MAP, the World Bank hopes to contribute toward filling financing gaps not adequately met by other donors by providing support for programs aimed at vulnerable groups, such as sex workers and those exposed to greater risk of HIV infection in conflict-affected countries and zones.

The UNAIDS Unified Budget and Workplan

Numerous organizations of the United Nations system carry out HIV/AIDS activities within the framework of their respective mandates. Some of these are co-sponsors of UNAIDS, and as such plan and implement their activities within the framework of the UNAIDS biennial Unified Budget and Workplan (UBW). Following the approval of the UBW by the UNAIDS governing body, the Programme Coordination Board (PCB), the budget is financed through contributions and pledges from donors over the biennium. The principal contributors to the UBW are the rich industrialized countries; in recent years the leading donor governments have been the Netherlands, United Kingdom, United States, Sweden, Norway, Finland, Denmark, Ireland, Canada, and Spain.[22]

The UBW is the mechanism through which funds raised by UNAIDS are allocated to the secretariat and each of the co-sponsoring agencies for specific activities, based on a division of labor agreed upon by the secretariat and the co-sponsors. In addition, individual co-sponsors are encouraged to use their own regular budget funds as well as mobilize additional donor resources to support HIV/AIDS activities which they undertake outside the context of the UBW. These activities should be consistent with the respective mandates of the co-sponsoring agencies within the UNAIDS partnership. For example, the WFP provides direct food assistance to those affected by the epidemic such as AIDS patients on ARV treatment; the World Bank provides technical assistance for project planning and management; WHO implements programs to expand access to ARV drugs; ILO promotes the development and implementation of workplace HIV/AIDS policies and programs; and UNICEF helps governments and NGOs at country level to procure medicines to prevent transmission of HIV from mother to child. The UNAIDS secretariat and co-sponsors and other UN agencies have committed themselves to implement an HIV/AIDS policy in their own workplace, and are obliged as such to provide HIV-related services for their own employees and their families.

The approved UBW for the 2008–9 biennium amounted to US$470 million, in addition to an estimated US$1.9 million allocated by the ten co-sponsors from their own regular budgets for HIV/AIDS activities to be implemented by them at country level. The distribution of the UBW resources for the biennium is as follows: US$135 million to be shared among the 10 co-sponsors; US$182 million for the UNAIDS secretariat; US$147 million for inter-agency activities; and US$5 million for a contingency fund for unexpected expenditures linked to the UBW.

Private and business-linked foundations and international NGOs

Philanthropic foundations and charitable arms of private sector businesses represent an important funding stream for HIV/AIDS programs worldwide, often contributing to the development of innovative strategies and practices. UNAIDS estimated that contributions from foundations and business-supported charities were about US$400 million per annum for 2006 and 2007.[23] About two-thirds of contributions from charitable and business-linked foundations to the global HIV/AIDS response have come from the Bill and Melinda Gates Foundation; other contributors in this category include Bristol-Myers Squibb Foundation, Rockefeller Foundation, Kaiser Family Foundation, Merck Company Foundation, Ford Foundation, Elizabeth Glaser Pediatric AIDS Foundation, and Pfizer Foundation.[24] Most of these foundations are based in the United States, where tradition and law support a higher level of private philanthropic activity than exists in other developed countries. Foundations have tended to concentrate their contributions in critical areas that are vital for the global response, but may not be attractive to ODA donors because the results are less predictable and long-term in nature. Hence, foundations have been prominent in the funding of scientific research for the development of a successful HIV/AIDS vaccine and more effective prevention and treatment regimes. For example, the Bill and Melinda Gates Foundation has provided large amounts of money to scientific institutions and to international alliances and regional programs for microbicide development which could lower the risk of the transmission of HIV through sexual intercourse.

Private sector businesses have made use of "business coalitions" on HIV/AIDS at global, regional, and country levels to provide financial support for prevention and treatment programs in low- and middle-income countries, and have also developed partnerships with the public sector in some of those countries. The Global Business Coalition against HIV/AIDS (GBC), which was established in 1997, works with business-linked foundations to contribute to the global response, not only in terms of funding but also through non-cash mechanisms and in-kind contributions such as price reductions and donation of HIV/

AIDS medicines, and by encouraging their membership at country level to promote and support HIV/AIDS workplace programs in their own enterprises.

International NGOs such as Oxfam, ActionAid, Médecins Sans Frontières, Save the Children, and World Vision provide critical support for the global HIV/AIDS response, even if not so much in terms of direct financial contributions. Some of them act as local implementing partners at country level for bilateral and multilateral donor agencies and foundations, making use of their specialized experience in selected fields and their relationship with local civil society organizations. International NGOs also raise funds to finance their own HIV/AIDS operations in developing countries, and have been particularly successful in getting money from donor governments who prefer to channel funds for HIV/AIDS programs through civil society rather than governments. Significantly, international NGOs have been instrumental in drawing attention and responding to the non-health impact and the broader development challenges of the epidemic, such as the linking of HIV/AIDS with poverty, the promotion of prevention through gender equality and the education of girls, and the incorporation of nutritional requirements in ARV therapy.

Domestic sources of HIV/AIDS funding

Total spending on HIV/AIDS prevention, treatment, and care from domestic sources, which includes both spending by governments of affected countries and expenditure by households and individuals within those countries, now represents a substantial contribution to the global HIV/AIDS response. UNAIDS estimated that funding of the HIV/AIDS response from domestic sources within low- and middle-income countries was about US$2.6 billion in 2005 and projected to increase to US$2.8 billion in 2006 and US$3 billion in 2007.[25] The extent to which affected governments provide resources for HIV/AIDS will depend on a number of factors, ranging from a country's wealth or income to the level of political commitment and influence of pressure from local activists and civil society organizations. The ratio of domestic spending on HIV/AIDS to external contributions shows distinct differences between the developing regions, reflecting both the severity of the HIV/AIDS problem and the income differentials between countries. For example, in Latin America, domestic spending by governments accounts for about three-quarters of the region's overall HIV/AIDS expenditures, whereas in sub-Saharan Africa, which receives the bulk of international HIV/AIDS financing, the corresponding ratio is less than one-quarter.[26] At the same time, households in highly affected countries in Africa contribute a higher proportion to overall HIV/AIDS expenditure at country level than in Latin America.

Apart from a few countries such as Brazil, Thailand, and more recently South Africa which announced a new program for increased domestic funding of its HIV/AIDS program in 2008, most of the highly affected countries in the developing regions do not provide any sizeable contribution to HIV/AIDS services within their national budget. The situation is of particular concern in Africa, where government spending on HIV/AIDS is negligible, despite commitments made by African heads of state at the special Abuja summit on HIV/AIDS in 2001 "to allocate at least 15 percent of our annual budget to the improvement of the health sector ... and that an appropriate and adequate proportion of this amount is put at the disposal of the National Commissions/Councils for the fight against HIV/AIDS, tuberculosis and other related infectious diseases."[27] A similar pledge was made by African leaders five years later, when they met again in Abuja in May 2006 at a special African Union (AU) summit on HIV/AIDS; that summit adopted the "Abuja Call for Accelerated Action towards Universal Access" which set bold targets for achieving universal access to prevention, treatment and care by 2010, and established a mechanism for reviewing progress. Not much seems to have been done in terms of acting on this declaration since then.

HIV/AIDS financing and spending: cost-effectiveness and efficiency issues and key debates

Despite the dramatic increase in financial commitments for the global HIV/AIDS response over the past decade, there is little evidence that the spread of the epidemic is being controlled and reversed globally, according to conclusions of the 2006 and 2008 UN General Assembly High-level Meetings on HIV/AIDS. Analysis of HIV/AIDS financing and impact at global and national levels reveals significant gaps and time lags in the disbursement and implementation processes, which result in sizeable proportions of committed funds remaining unused over time. These gaps have resulted in cumulative resources amounting to hundreds of millions of dollars which are not being put to use on the ground, and the trend affects the effectiveness of money committed as measured by the impact on prevention and treatment. There is evidence that large amounts of funds committed for HIV/AIDS programs globally are not being utilized in time or effectively, while at the same time the UN, international development agencies, governments of affected countries, and AIDS activists worldwide are claiming that there is not enough money for an effective global response to HIV/ AIDS, and are backing these claims with estimations of huge funding gaps that exist between what is already committed and what is needed overall. What we have, then, is a paradoxical situation in which large amounts of committed and disbursed resources co-exist with substantial funding gaps. This paradox, and other concerns about the dangers of aid money going mainly to support HIV/AIDS response to the exclusion or neglect of other international development needs, have opened up key debates in HIV/AIDS financing, which are summarized below.

Gaps in disbursement and implementation are not unique to HIV/ AIDS financing and programs in the wider context of the world of development assistance. For a variety of reasons, commitments tend to lag behind disbursements, and disbursements often take place at a slower pace than planned or expected. In the case of the global HIV/ AIDS response, financial flows are measured in terms of commitments rather than disbursements. This means that reported levels of "available" money do not accurately reflect actual funding efforts or funds already provided. The gap between commitments and disbursements globally was estimated by UNAIDS at US$2.3 billion in 2004 and projected to reach US$3 billion in 2007, with the cumulative disbursement gap estimated to be US$14 billion by 2007.[28] Even the Global Fund, which was established specifically to mobilize and disburse additional money quickly to low- and middle-income countries, is experiencing significant gaps between commitments and disbursements. Constraints linked to limited absorptive and technical capacities at the country level, plus the rather complex procedures adopted by the Global Fund itself for disbursement, may have contributed to this situation.

Experience in the provision of development assistance has also shown that there are gaps between pledges and actual commitments. For example, several of the pledges made by G8 donor governments at the Gleneagles summit to support the doubling of aid to Africa from US$25 billion a year to US$50 billion by 2010 have not been matched by commitments. The lack of credibility of the Gleneagles pledges came to light just a couple of months later when the replenishment of the Global Fund fell short of its target by several billions of dollars. A similar experience is reflected in the failure of the majority of the OECD/DAC member governments to meet the 0.7 percent of GDP target for ODA transfers.

Claims regarding the existence of a funding gap in the global response

Gaps in disbursement and implementations, resulting in the under-utilization of committed and available funds for the global HIV/AIDS response, co-exist with a "funding" gap in terms of estimated total resources needs for HIV/AIDS globally, if we go on the basis of claims made by relevant global institutions. According to data compiled for UNAIDS, the gap between resource needs for HIV/AIDS globally and total commitments made by donors was estimated at about US$700 million in 2003.[29] This gap in funding requirements has widened significantly after 2005, with the setting of new targets linked to the goal of Universal Access by 2010, which increased resource requirements for the full package of prevention, treatment, care, and support interventions. Estimates for 2007 indicated a funding gap globally of US $8.1 billion, this being the difference between the UNAIDS estimate of US$18.1 billion that was needed to address the epidemic in low- and middle-income countries and the US$10 billion that was available from all sources.[30]

In October 2007, UNAIDS published a new report on the estimated financial resources required for the global HIV/AIDS response covering 132 low- and middle-income countries.[31] The report presented three different approaches to financing the global response for achieving Universal Access targets:[32] (1) scaling-up at current rates of annual increase in countries which estimated that resource requirements would be between US$14 and 18 billion in 2015 and would provide ARV treatment for 8 million people globally, which would fall far short of the Universal Access target levels for prevention, treatment, care and support; (2) significant increases in available resources and a dramatic scale-up of coverage in all countries for achieving Universal Access by 2010, which would require an increase in annual resource inputs of between US$32 and 51 billion in 2010 and between US$45 and 63 billion by 2015 and would provide ARV treatment for 14 million people by the target date; and (3) phased scale-up to Universal Access by 2015 which assumes different rates of scale-up for each country based on current coverage and the achievement of Universal Access by all countries by 2015, and would require between US$41 and 58 billion in 2015. Estimations of global resource needs of these orders of magnitude represent an upward trend in the exponential increase in HIV/AIDS financing. UNAIDS has consistently maintained that because HIV/AIDS is an exceptional disease and both an evolving and long-wave condition, it requires additional resources in order to bring the epidemic under control and reverse its spread globally. Only about a third of those in need of treatment in low- and middle-income countries are getting treatment, according to UNAIDS which believes that predictable and assured additional resources are critical to an effective global AIDS response and argues that lack of investment 10–20 years ago in the global response has resulted in a more serious global epidemic and the higher level of funding needed today.[33]

The Global Fund estimated that it would need approximately US$89 billion for the global HIV/AIDS response and TB and malaria for the period 2008–10.[34] This amount is linked to the achievement of both the global targets for Universal Access by 2010 and the Millennium Development Goals in 2015. Pledges made to the Global Fund at its September 2007 replenishment meeting in Berlin amounted to nearly US$10 billion over three years, and the fund plans to disburse between US$6 and 8 billion annually between 2008 and 2010. Hence, at the High-Level Meeting on HIV/AIDS in New York in June 2008, the executive secretary of the Global Fund, Michel Kazatshkine, announced an estimated funding gap for 2008 of around US$8 billion, which was expected to increase to US$10–12 billion per annum in the next two to three years, to meet projected demand. This amounts to a tripling of the institution's existing funding level, and will require significant additional contributions from existing and new sources, as well as innovative financing mechanisms.

Arguments against increased HIV/AIDS spending

Without any doubt, HIV/AIDS has attracted more resources than any other medical condition in human history. UNAIDS and other stakeholders have consistently maintained that the disease is exceptional and different from every other health problem and, therefore, requires an unprecedented response in terms of money and strategy to combat it. Notwithstanding the exceptionality of HIV/AIDS, there are those who oppose increased spending on the disease. They argue that the disease has received a larger share of total health spending than its role in the global burden of disease would justify; that the large increase in HIV/AIDS finance is having negative effects on the rest of the health system; that big spending on HIV/AIDS is distorting development planning priorities and diverting funds from other pressing development needs and programs, such as education, social welfare, and healthcare in general; and that current levels and patterns of spending could actually undermine HIV/AIDS efforts in the long term.[35]

One of the leading proponents of the view that too much money is going into HIV/AIDS at the expense of other killer diseases and other health system and development needs, is Roger England, chairman of the Health Systems Workshop, a health policy charity based in Grenada, West Indies. England has argued in articles and opinions written over the past 2–3 years that HIV/AIDS is receiving a larger share of total health spending than its contribution to the burden of disease would justify, and that this large increase in AIDS financing could in fact have negative effects on the rest of the healthcare system in recipient countries.[36] He challenged the claim that HIV/AIDS is exceptional, and maintained that there is little evidence that the massive investments in HIV/AIDS are having an impact on the spread of the disease. England has gone as far as to suggest that UNAIDS is serving no useful purpose and should be abolished.[37]

Another opponent of increased spending on HIV/AIDS, Laurie Garrett, a senior fellow for Global Health at the Council on Foreign Relations in the United States, has similarly argued persuasively that large amounts of money going to global health problems such as HIV/AIDS may not only fail to improve health conditions in developing countries, but may well make things worse.[38] Garrett goes on to recommend that support should be provided for integrating disease-specific programs, like HIV/AIDS, into general public health systems.

James Chin, formerly an epidemiologist at the WHO/GPA and currently a clinical professor of epidemiology at the University of California–Berkeley, has made use of scientific evidence from his analysis of epidemiological data to claim that a good deal of spending on HIV/AIDS is misdirected and wasted and, hence, supports the case for much-reduced spending on the epidemic. Chin argues that UNAIDS has ignored this evidence to focus on and persuade donors to put billions of dollars into the wrong interventions, thus promoting "a range of myths that have more to do with political correctness than science."[39] He saw a parallel in HIV/AIDS spending with, in his opinion, the billions that have been wasted on the prevention of general epidemics such as SARS and avian flu in Asia that were never going to happen.

Elizabeth Pisani, an epidemiologist and journalist who worked for UNAIDS in the area of epidemiological surveillance, recently published a book, *The Wisdom of Whores: Bureaucrats, Brothels and the Business of AIDS*, in which she argued that a substantial portion of the funding devoted to HIV/AIDS is wasted on ineffective programming; this, in her opinion, being the result of politics, ideology, and morality triumphing over the results of science and good public health policy. She also suggested that data on HIV incidence, including the annual rate of new infections, were exaggerated, even if not deliberately, to attract the attention and resources of the international community.[40]

Response by UNAIDS and other key stakeholders

UNAIDS and key stakeholders, as to be expected, have reacted with anger to these calls for a shift of focus and funds away from HIV/AIDS. Responding to a personal view by Roger England in the *British Medical Journal* of 10 May 2008, Paul De Lay, director of the UNAIDS Evidence, Monitoring and Policy Department, and his colleagues argued that current spending is not enough and pointed to the "fact that only about 3 percent of African adults living with HIV are receiving ARV treatment at present," and without treatment AIDS patients will die.[41] This, according to UNAIDS, is clear indication that current spending is not enough, when looked at in relation to unmet needs and taking into account the exceptional nature of the disease in terms of its impact and magnitude as both public health and humanitarian crises.[42]

The leadership of the Geneva-based International AIDS Society (IAS), which is the largest HIV/AIDS scientific and advocacy organization with over 10,000 members worldwide and organizer of the biennial International AIDS Conference, has also come to the defense of UNAIDS in the face of questions raised by Roger England and others about the present cost-effectiveness of UNAIDS. In a comment posted online in the *British Medical Journal* in response to one of Roger England's articles, the president and the executive director of the IAS stressed that HIV/AIDS is an exceptional disease with unforeseen and constantly changing challenges, and that UNAIDS is best structured to lead the institutional response to these challenges. According to the IAS, more money and physical and human resources should be mobilized to deal with the threat of HIV/AIDS worldwide. IAS also saw no conflict between directing additional resources at HIV/AIDS and strengthening of health systems, and even argues that general healthcare systems and infrastructure have improved in poor countries as a result of HIV/AIDS financing in those countries.

Conclusion

This chapter has reviewed the existing sources of funds for financing the global HIV/AIDS response, and drawn attention to the problem of not enough money being available for HIV/AIDS programs while the money that is available is not being spent as fast as it is being committed. This paradox has given rise to key debates relating to questions about the effectiveness of the extraordinarily large amounts of donor money that have been directed at this single disease alongside claims about the need for more money. The paradox also underlines specific challenges that are highlighted in the chapter to bring to the attention of policy-makers aimed and action aimed at increasing the effectiveness of HIV/AIDS financing.

The big surge in HIV/AIDS financing over the past decade has further compounded the main challenge of cost-effectiveness or how to use the money that is available effectively in terms of positive impact on prevention and treatment. Peter Piot, former head of UNAIDS, has on numerous occasions stated that the major challenge in HIV/AIDS financing is that of "making the money work."[43] There may be plenty of HIV/AIDS money around, but what is of particular importance in the global response is that available money should be made to work hard to support effective responses and value-added impacts. This requires efforts toward increased efficiency from both donor and recipient governments, including better coordination of donor inputs, and also improvements in the governance structures of relevant global institutions, an issue which is discussed in detail in the next chapter.

9 Global governance and HIV/AIDS response

This chapter makes the point that the governance of global institutions matters for an effective response to HIV/AIDS. The linkage between existing governance structures and mechanisms of global institutions and effectiveness of the global response is explored in three specific areas: (1) governance of intellectual property rights (IPRs) as applied to pharmaceutical products, which affects access to essential medicines for treating AIDS; (2) governance of global financial institutions with respect to the regulation of international capital flows and macro-economic management, which affects the ability of resource-poor countries to meet the immediate public health threat and longer-term development challenges of HIV/AIDS; and (3) global economic governance which concerns the relationship between the rich countries of the Global North and the poor countries of the Global South, and more specifically how the imbalance of power between the North and the South in terms of voice and influence in key global institutions affects the capacities of developing countries to respond effectively to the threat posed by the epidemic to their populations and to their economies.

In addition to examining the global governance of HIV/AIDS response within the framework of institutions in the traditional multi-lateral system, the chapter also looks at the emergence of the G8 – the group of rich developed countries, Canada, France, Germany, Italy, Japan, Russia, the United Kingdom, and the United States of America, with the participation of the European Commission – as part of a new generation of global institutions that has broadened its agenda to address the rapid spread of HIV/AIDS globally and major illnesses afflicting the world as a whole. The wealth, power, and influence of the G8 in the context of the global economy and politics make it a potentially powerful catalyst for innovation in global health governance, as already illustrated by its role in the creation of the Global Fund in 2002.

The main argument in the chapter is the current system of global health governance is not addressing the needs of the developing countries with respect to facilitating access to essential life-prolonging HIV/AIDS medicines and enhancing the mobilization of additional financial and human resources for responding effectively to the epidemic. Weaknesses in the current system of global governance in relation to HIV/AIDS response are evidenced by the contrasting situations of the North and the South. Historically, the governance structures of major global institutions have been characterized by imbalances in power relationships and influence over decision-making between the North and the South. Decision-making authority within key global institutions has been dominated by the rich countries of the North, which also have the resources required to address the global HIV/AIDS crisis but are less affected by the epidemic. On the other hand, the developing countries of the South where the epidemic is concentrated do not have the resources to combat HIV/AIDS, nor the power and authority in key global institutions to influence decisions concerning access to ARV drugs and resource flows in their favor.

Different definitions and conceptualizations of global governance have emphasized the exercise of power and authority in the management of decision-making processes and economic and social resources.[1] Democratic deficits between the North and the South in the context of the global governance of HIV/AIDS response relate to differences in power relationship and authority, which are derived partly from institutional structures and relationships that are no longer relevant to present day realities of global geopolitics and economic relations. Furthermore, the existing multilateral system allows for global institutions which have non-health mandates, such as the IMF, the World Bank and the WTO, to exert powerful influence on important global and national health policies through decisions taken by them in areas such as trade liberalization, financial regulation, and macroeconomic management. Growing concern about the relevance and efficacy of the current system of global governance for HIV/AIDS response has prompted demands from developing countries and their supporters, including international NGOs, for a re-examination of global governance structures and mechanisms. The case is made in the chapter for changes in the role and governance structures of concerned global institutions, and particularly the need to adapt existing rules, policies, and practices to meet the wider development challenges of HIV/AIDS. In concluding, the chapter draws attention to the necessity of a new architecture of global governance for HIV/AIDS response, and highlights key requirements including policy changes and practical suggestions for redressing the balance between North and South.

Intellectual property rights and access to HIV/AIDS drugs

The high cost of antiretroviral (ARV) drugs for treating HIV/AIDS has kept treatment out of the reach of most of those affected by the disease in developing countries. Until recently, major pharmaceutical companies in the United States, Europe, and Japan which develop and produce essential HIV/AIDS medicines had insisted on the full life of their patents on those drugs in accordance with the protection provided by the international system of intellectual property rights (IPRs). In the case of pharmaceutical products, the responsibility for the protection of IPRs has been accorded to the World Trade Organization (WTO), rather than the World Intellectual Property Organization (WIPO) which has the mandate to promote and protect IPRs overall.[2] The protection of IPRs through patents had enabled Western pharmaceutical companies initially to set and maintain high prices for ARV drugs, especially as WTO rules originally prohibited the production of lower-priced generic copies during the life of those patents. Consequently, ARV drugs which could slow the progress of AIDS and prolong life were too expensive and unaffordable in low- and middle-income countries. The urgent need for treatment of millions of HIV/AIDS patients in Africa and other developing regions therefore remained unmet due to the lack of access to medicines.[3] Recent modifications in WTO agreements governing patents on essential medicines needed to treat AIDS and other serious infectious diseases have improved access in developing countries, but the majority of those needing HIV/AIDS treatment in sub-Saharan Africa, for example, are still not getting any, for reasons that are linked to availability and affordability.

The linked issue of availability and affordability with respect to AIDS medicines involves two distinct interests. First, there is the obligation of governments to fulfill the right to health for their populations, including ensuring the availability of and access to essential medicines and treatment therapies. Second, there is the business imperative of the pharmaceutical companies which depend on the protection of their IPRs under the international patent system. It is worth pointing out at the onset that the objectives of these two different interests are not regarded by the UN and the stakeholders in the international community as conflicting or irreconcilable.

A strong case has been made by the developing countries, and their supporters, that access to life-prolonging AIDS medicines should be provided as a "right" by making those drugs available and affordable for their populations. This amounts to keeping prices low in line with income levels in the majority of developing countries. Pharmaceutical companies, on the other hand, argue that they invest huge amounts of money and time on research and development (R&D) for new medicines, and rely on the patent system to be able to recover the costs of this investment over a reasonable period of time. Furthermore, they make the point that it is only through the application of the patent system that they could go on to develop new and more effective drugs for treatment of infectious and other diseases. This argument has not gone down well with the developing countries and their supporters, and some have even accused Western pharmaceutical companies of benefiting from the misfortune of HIV/AIDS sufferers in poor countries by putting profit ahead of saving life.

The "patients rights versus patent rights" confrontation represents one of the most contentious issues in the global HIV/AIDS response, especially as both positions are equally valid from the perspective of the international system: recognition and commitment to the right to health, on the one hand, and adherence to the rules of international trade, on the other. The UN and its specialized agencies have played a sort of "middleman's role" in the confrontation. The UN system has been instrumental in bringing the two sides together to find feasible means for ensuring that developing countries have access to affordable drugs for treating AIDS and other diseases, without at the same time jeopardizing the business interests of the big pharmaceutical companies and the incentives for them to develop new and more effective drugs.[4]

The TRIPS agreement

The availability of lower-priced generic medicines which would enable AIDS patients in poor countries to have access to treatment is central to affordability. This is vital since, in the absence of a vaccine and cure, treatment represents the next best option for those suffering with AIDS. However, WTO agreements on protection of patents had until recently been a major obstacle to the production and marketing of cheaper generic copies of ARV drugs. The most important agreement in this regard is the one on "Trade-Related Aspects of Intellectual Property Rights" (TRIPS) which was concluded under the Uruguay Round of international trade negotiations in 1994.[5] TRIPS, which took effect on 1 January 1995, originally provided patent protection for both products and processes for at least 20 years. Developed countries were given one year to ensure that their laws and practices conform to the agreement; developing countries were given five years; and the UN-designated least developed countries (LDCs) until 2006. While the agreement allowed countries to issue compulsory licenses for medicines that could be manufactured in their own countries, this was of little use to most developing countries, which lacked the knowledge and high-tech manufacturing capacity to do so.[6]

The limits placed by the original TRIPS agreement to the production of generic medicines before patent protection runs out was not only a barrier to free trade, but by restricting access to treatment it was also in conflict with the universal recognition of health as a basic human right. In the light of the heavy toll of the impact of HIV/AIDS on human development in poor countries, and considering a patent life of 20 years under TRIPS, governments of developing countries and AIDS activists felt that it was morally unjust to wait until patents run out before producing cheaper generic drugs while millions were dying and getting infected annually. They argued for modification to TRIPS, to make it more responsive to the interest of public health and to overcome barriers to affordable access to treatment in low-income and poor countries.

Hence, at the WTO's Doha ministerial conference in November 2001 it was agreed to renegotiate and introduce flexibility to the TRIPS agreement, so that it could be implemented in a way that supported public health objectives. While recognizing the need for flexibility to address national emergencies in the form of grave public health threats, the negotiations at the same time also highlighted the importance of the protection of intellectual property rights for development of new and more effective medicines. The Doha Declaration on the TRIPS Agreement and Public Health as adopted was intended to remove impediments to the availability of generic drugs under certain conditions and, thereby, make it possible to use TRIPS to address HIV/AIDS and emerging health crises in those developing countries with no manufacturing capabilities. The Doha Declaration also gave rights to member states to grant compulsory licenses and freedom to determine grounds on which licenses are granted, such as public health crises and national emergencies. It was only in 2003, and under a pilot scheme, that manufacturers were allowed to obtain compulsory licenses to export their products to other developing countries as a form of emergency relief for treating serious epidemics such as HIV/AIDS, but while at the same time respecting intellectual property rights. The 2005 WTO Hong Kong ministerial meeting agreed to make the 2003 pilot scheme a permanent part of the TRIPS agreement, and also to extend the exemption on pharmaceutical patent protection for the least developed countries for another 10 years to 2016.[7]

However, to date only a handful of WTO member states have ratified the Doha extension to the TRIPS agreement within their national legislation. Again, the main reason for this is the problem of manufacturing capability and resources. Apart from a few developing countries, such as India, Brazil, and South Africa, the majority of the WTO developing-country members lack sufficient capacities in the pharmaceutical sector to make effective use of compulsory licensing under the amended TRIPS. Furthermore, while progress has been made in driving down prices of certain ARV drugs, the availability of new and more effective next-generation medicines for the treatment of AIDS and other opportunistic diseases is still a challenge for developing countries which lack the resources and technology to carry out the necessary R&D. At the same time, there are concerns that Western pharmaceutical companies may be less inclined to undertake R&D on new drugs for the treatment of global diseases that are found mainly in developing countries, if they cannot be protected by and derive benefits from patent rights.[8]

Despite a progressive fall in the price of patented ARV drugs over the past five years, the cost of HIV/AIDS medicines in relation to financial capacity of poor countries still remains a major obstacle to access to treatment. The production and marketing of low-priced generic drugs is about the only feasible solution to the problem. Although the Doha Declaration established the right of countries to take action to secure essential drugs at affordable prices as a means of protecting public health and addressing a national emergency, there are still provisions in the TRIPS agreement that support stringent patent protection which can artificially raise prices of vital life-extending AIDS medicines. Thus, there may still be a need to further reduce the patent protection currently afforded by TRIPS in the interest of public health—a sort of "TRIPS minus" position as advocated by the ILO in its Social Dimension of Globalization Commission report.[9] But this may not be easy to achieve.

WTO's role is still strongly influenced by the rich industrialized countries of the North which are determined to protect their own national and international pharmaceutical industries. Developing countries from the South are often under pressure to make concessions and compromise on their interests and stated positions within the WTO, where their influence is still minimal despite their larger total membership as a group in the organization. There are still disagreements between the North and the South with regard to the implementation of Doha, for example, over what constitutes public health crises and national emergencies in developing countries. It is significant to point out that the WTO has not been keen to involve the WHO in its negotiating processes on the TRIPS, even though the health agency could offer valuable advice on essential pharmaceutical products and their effectiveness.[10]

Governance of international financial institutions and HIV/AIDS response

Some of the countries worst affected by the global HIV/AIDS epidemic are also incurring heavy and unsustainable external debt burden, which represents a huge barrier to progress in the fight against HIIV/AIDS. Repayment of debts by these countries amounts to diverting scarce financial resources needed for responding to HIV/AIDS and other development needs, and represents a transfer from poor developing countries to international financial institutions (IFIs) and governments of rich countries which are the major lenders. There is ample evidence of debt repayment taking precedence over spending on health and other vital human needs in developing countries. A study by Oxfam reported that Zambia was spending 30 percent more on debt servicing than on health; Malawi's health budget was equivalent to its debt servicing; Cameroon's debt repayment amounted to three-and-a-half times the country's spending on health; and for every dollar that Mali spent on health, $1.60 was paid to creditors.[11]

In such a situation, debt repayment impedes effective HIV/AIDS response, which cannot take place without efficient service delivery capacity within the health system. There is growing consensus within the international community that debt relief could help release resources needed to boost development efforts, including for addressing HIV/AIDS and poverty. In this regard, it is useful to review current debt relief initiatives and mechanisms, and to see if they are relevant and adequate for mobilizing additional resources needed to protect current and future generations from the impact of the HIV/AIDS epidemic.

The Heavily Indebted Poor Countries Initiative (HIPC)

The Heavily Indebted Poor Countries (HIPC) initiative, which was launched by the World Bank and the IMF in 1996 to provide debt relief to poor countries, represents a scheme that in principle could convert debt repayments into public investment in health, education, and other human development areas. Initially, HIPC had two primary goals: (1) to reduce the debt burden of poor countries to levels that would allow them to achieve sustainable growth; and (2) to enable poor countries to use the dividend from debt relief to promote poverty alleviation and human development. The scheme was based on the assumption that an adequate amount of predictable debt relief was an efficient way of transferring resources to poor countries. Benefits from such transfers, however, were made conditional on reasonable economic management by the recipient government. Hence, the HIPC scheme was extended only to countries that committed themselves to sustaining an improved debt situation over the medium term in compliance with an IMF program. It was realized that this criterion for eligibility could not be met by some of the poorest and neediest countries in the world, and the HIPC program had to be modified in 1999 and renamed the "Enhanced HIPC" (HIPC2) initiative to establish a closer link between debt relief and poverty reduction.

Even after the introduction of the HIPC2, there were reports by international NGOs that certain poor countries which are seriously affected by HIV/AIDS still could not qualify for debt relief under HIPC while others who qualified were spending a sizeable part of government revenue to finance debt servicing.[12] Oxfam reported that 13 of the 26 HIPC countries in 2002 were spending more on debt than on public health. Another study indicated that half of the HIPC countries were spending at least 15 percent of their total revenues on paying off debts at a time when public investment in health and education for fighting HIV/AIDS was badly needed.[13] It became increasingly clear that the HIPC initiative was not providing countries with a sufficient level of debt relief to allow them to benefit from sustained growth in order to reduce poverty and combat HIV/AIDS.

For HIPC to have a positive impact on poverty and enhance the budgetary capacity of poor countries to respond effectively to HIV/AIDS, practical ways have to be found to make debt relief more predictable and sustainable at the country level, and to effectively integrate debt relief with improvements in health services and poverty reduction strategies. This could involve, for example, the setting of a ceiling of approximately 5–10 percent on debt-servicing as a ratio of government revenue, and the linking of debt servicing to actual export earnings of countries. In the specific context of HIV/AIDS, the international community would need to consolidate the efforts of various stakeholders into a commitment to broaden and deepen debt relief as a mechanism for mobilizing additional resources for HIV/AIDS response. In addition, there is also a need on the part of developing countries for their governments to make a stronger commitment and willingness to use HIPC debt relief dividends for improving the efficiency of health services and effectiveness of AIDS response. Data from the World Bank for 10 low-income African countries benefiting from debt relief under HIPC indicated that together only about 5 percent of their total HIPC debt relief dividend was budgeted for HIV/AIDS activities in 2001.[14]

Integrating HIV/AIDS needs with the Poverty Reduction Strategy Paper (PRSP) initiative

Discussion on how the HIPC initiative could operationalize the link between debt relief and poverty reduction led to the launch of the PRSP initiative by the World Bank and IMF as a complementary scheme to the HIPC.[15] Given the critical link between poverty and HIV/AIDS, the World Bank seized the opportunity to use the PRSP as a planning tool for enhancing the effectiveness of HIV/AIDS response at the country level. The Bank teamed up with the UNDP to promote an integrated approach for responding to HIV/AIDS and poverty simultaneously within the development planning framework of the PRSP. The two institutions jointly undertook pilot projects in a number of highly affected countries in sub-Saharan Africa that were in the process of preparing PRSPs in 2005 and 2006, and used the experience from these projects to develop and refine the methodology for a wider application of the approach. The World Bank reached the conclusion that in addition to channeling benefits from debt relief into HIV/AIDS response, the PRSP could also serve as an instrument for mobilizing additional resources from both multilateral and bilateral sources for financing integrated poverty reduction and HIV/AIDS programs. All eligible HIPC countries were required to prepare PRSPs to ensure that savings on debt relief go toward poverty reduction.

However, it would appear that so far the PRSP has not been particularly useful as a tool for helping poor countries to mobilize additional resources for HIV/AIDS response. It has been observed that only few PRSP documents have operationally linked HIV/AIDS and poverty in a planning context or connected PRSP expenditures with goals and targets of national HIV/AIDS strategies and plans.[16] An examination of PRSP documents in sub-Saharan African countries would reveal that while most countries included HIV/AIDS concerns in their documents, there were hardly any estimates of resource requirement for responding to the epidemic in a planning context.

Part of the reason for this lack of country specificity may have been due to the influence of World Bank staff in the preparation of country PRSP documents. Contrary to the stated intention that the preparation of the PRSP should be a country-driven process, some countries involved in the preparation of PRSPs had to rely on substantial technical assistance from the World Bank. The involvement of advisers who lacked knowledge about local conditions concerning the nature and impact of the HIV/AIDS could have contributed to the failure of country PRSP documents in some cases to include credible analyses of costs and of how resources should be allocated for breaking the vicious circle of HIV/AIDS and poverty in a comprehensive and systemic manner. The effectiveness of the PRSP as a mechanism for linking debt relief with HIV/AIDS response would therefore depend on more being done in policy and operational terms toward ensuring "national ownership" of the process to reflect needs and priorities of the government, backed by the willingness of donors to use the mechanism to boost public expenditure on HIV/AIDS response at national level.

The IMF and health spending in poor countries

Controversy surrounds IMF-supported macroeconomic programs in developing countries and their effects on the health sector. Critics of the IMF approach to macroeconomic management argue that the financial institution's programs could constrain health and other social expenditures in developing countries, even when donor support for such expenditures is potentially available.[17] While developing countries can set priorities and targets for improvements in the health sector, the IMF can through its country programs impose policies that unintentionally undermine efforts to improve health conditions in countries that are heavily burdened by disease. The issue could become more serious for HIV/AIDS response, as governments of developing countries with ongoing IMF programs find that they are unable to utilize available funds from donors, such as Global Fund grants, to recruit additional health professionals or to increase salaries and provide other incentives for experienced doctors and nurses who would otherwise go abroad or move to the private sector. This could happen where an IMF country program, in the interest of financial stability, imposes a ceiling on government wage bills or a freeze on public sector recruitment, which in effect conflicts with the need to strengthen the public health workforce as required for responding effectively to HIV/AIDS and other health problems.

The IMF has responded to allegations of obstructing effective HIV/AIDS response through the imposition of wage ceilings and recruitment freezes by pointing out that its circumscribed role does not include sector-level decisions, such as specifying cuts in the health sector. It then went on to elaborate that IMF programs merely set targets for overall spending, and it is up to countries themselves to decide what part to allocate to health as well as to ensure that health priorities are protected in overall budget cuts.[18] In addition, the IMF has also argued that its macroeconomic programs are designed to ensure fiscal stability, as required for promoting economic growth and reducing poverty, which could eventually have a positive impact on public health standing.

This may be so, but the report of a working group of experts on IMF programs and health spending, established in 2007 by the Washington-based think tank, the Center for Global Development, found that IMF fiscal policies and programs on the whole have been too conservative and risk-averse and, as such, have tended to constrain health spending in poor countries.[19] The report noted that while the IMF has no mandate for health sector issues, its recommendations and activities often have important indirect effects on health sector spending in countries following an IMF program. The report concludes that this situation needs to be redressed through flexibility in IMF's policies and, crucially, through changes in the role and governance structure of the institution. Specifically, this implies an explicit recognition of the need to link IMF macroeconomic management with health policy-making at country level. Overall, more attention should be paid by the IMF to the social consequences of its macroeconomic policies and public expenditure targets, and the institution should explore alternative scenarios and a broader range of feasible and less draconian options.

It is equally important to recognize that any change in IMF policy to protect health spending should be supported by action on the part of governments of developing countries and their development partners. These governments must take the lead in making an effective case for health spending and present clear priorities, objectives, and targets for the health sector in the context of the overall budgetary process. Donor, governments as external partners, should improve the predictability of their aid by making a longer-term commitment for overall budget support and, furthermore, they should better coordinate their diverse actions at country level.

Global economic governance and HIV/AIDS response

Rapid globalization of the world economy, and the consequent growing interdependence among countries, have increased the need for collaborative global action to address a broader range of international and cross-border issues. This in turn has generated an interest in global economic governance in terms of the impact of globalization on both developed and developing countries, as well as with respect to the important role of multilateral institutions in managing globalization. Focusing on multilateralism as the organizing principle of global economic governance, the rules and institutions of the multilateral system then become important to the nature of the impact of globalization, including the distribution of benefits from the process.

Marginalized countries on the fringe of the world economy, such as those in sub-Saharan Africa (SSA), are structurally underdeveloped and have weak links with the global economy and, hence, are more vulnerable to the negative impact of globalization. The wider implications of the impact of globalization for overall development in those countries have on balance acted as a constraint on their capacity to respond effectively to the range of development challenges confronting them, including the ability to cope with the threat posed by HIV/AIDS to their development. Only a few developing countries have so far been able to benefit significantly from the opportunities created by globalization for increased economic growth and social development.[20] In the absence of action at the international level to improve global economic governance in favor of poor countries and, thereby, facilitate their integration into the global economy, these countries are likely to remain poor and disadvantaged.

Current global economic governance has not helped the situation in most of the countries in SSA in an era of globalization, including some of those worst hit by HIV/AIDS. For many countries in the region, the process of globalization has resulted in anxieties rather than challenges and in global risks rather than global opportunities. HIV/AIDS has increased these anxieties and risks and, in turn, made it difficult for marginalized and disadvantaged countries to become fully and beneficially integrated into the global economy.[21] Being thus marginalized, the negative impact of globalization on economic growth has de facto reduced national capacity to respond effectively to HIV/AIDS and other health problems.[22] At the same time, poor economic performance by marginalized countries, due in part to the impact of globalization, has nurtured conditions for international financial institutions to continue to exercise enormous influence over macroeconomic policy-making in those countries, often to the detriment of social expenditures. The current pattern of global economic governance is thus affecting global health governance in two ways: first, through its direct impact on national capacity to respond to health and other development problems, and second, through the creation of conditions that encourage interventions by international financial institutions in the economies of marginalized countries on the basis of global governance structures and rules that were established for a different purpose, time, and context.[23]

Globalization may have created opportunities for accelerated development of life-extending drugs and technologies to treat HIV/AIDS, but weaknesses of global economic governance arrangements against the interests of resource-poor and marginalized countries have left them with less chance to benefit significantly from these breakthroughs. While it is widely accepted that the process of globalization is irreversible, changes in the governance structures of relevant global institutions could lead to fairer outcomes of globalization and improve the chances of poor countries benefiting from the opportunities created by the process.[24]

Innovation in global economic governance to redress the balance can play a crucial role in creating conditions that would enable developing countries to respond more effectively to the threat of HIV/AIDS in their economies and populations. A key issue in global economic governance concerns the nature of the partnership between the countries of the Global North and the Global South and, linked to that, their relative strength and influence on decision-making in global institutions. The power structure within international institutions is usually determined or influenced by the relationship between the member states and by relationships between the institutions and other key stakeholders such as external donors, international NGOs, and civil society organizations. Bold initiatives need to be undertaken in a number of key areas pertaining to the governance of economic globalization, including the enhanced participation of developing countries in multilateral governance. This should be supported by the development of open and innovative partnerships, between rich and poor countries, between donor and recipient governments, between the public and the private sectors, among governments of the developing countries themselves, and among governments and their social partners and civil society.

The G8 and governance of the global HIV/AIDS response

Though strictly speaking not a global institution, the G8, which is made up of the world's economically most powerful countries, can, and does, play an important role in addressing issues of global concern including global governance. For over a decade now the G8 has been interested and involved in global public health issues and, as can be deduced from the examples listed below, has emerged as a promoter of global health governance in a globalizing world.[25] The actual and potential influence of the G8 in the global system therefore has to be taken into account in the context of the global governance of HIV/AIDS response. Since 1999 when the leaders of the G8 began focusing on international development issues at their annual summit, the deliberations and conclusions of the group's annual meetings have led to important multilateral initiatives of relevance to global governance and the global HIV/AIDS response.

The 1999 Cologne summit led to the launch of the HIPC initiative by the World Bank and IMF as a way of linking debt relief to poverty reduction and social development; the 2000 meeting in Okinawa recognized infectious diseases as a threat to development and laid the foundation for the establishment of the Global Fund; the 2003 Evian summit produced a health action plan that included measures to tackle a range of diseases afflicting mainly the developing world; in 2004, the Sea Island meeting of the G8 leaders explored the prospects of developing an HIV/AIDS vaccine; the Africa action plan for debt relief for some of the poorest countries in the world, including several of those worst affected by HIV/AIDS, was based on the report of the U.K.-led Africa Commission which was unveiled at the 2005 Gleneagles summit; the 2007 Heiligendamm meeting in Germany recognized the need to strengthen healthcare systems in developing countries to fight HIV/AIDS and other health problems; and the 2008 Hokkaido meeting similarly dealt with health problems in developing countries. These examples clearly suggest that in many ways the G8 is fulfilling important global health governance functions and even filling gaps that have been left or avoided by the organizations of the traditional multilateral system.

However, from the standpoint of impact, there is a need for the G8 to work more closely with key global multilateral institutions, such as the WTO, WHO, IMF, and World Bank, which deal with specific issues on the international development agenda and where developing countries themselves are represented. More recently, the G8 summits have included a session of informal discussions with selected leaders from developing countries as a way of developing a better understanding of each other's perception of development issues and promoting fruitful partnership between the North and the South. This process should perhaps be institutionalized, as already suggested in a number of proposals such as the one calling for the creation of a "G-N" group (where N is for neutral) that would allow for the participation of a more representative group of world leaders on substantive discussions of global and international development issues.[26] The current focus of international attention on the G20 and the growing importance of this more representative group as the forum for debating and reaching agreement on global economic and financial issues, with the participation of the World Bank and the IMF, seems to be a step in that direction.[27]

Toward a new architecture of global governance for HIV/AIDS response

We have argued that under the current system of global governance, imbalances in the governance structures of key global institutions tend to impede progress in responding effectively to the threat of HIV/AIDS at national and international levels. The existing governance structures of global institutions represent obstacles to effective response by developing countries to global health problems that affect their overall development prospects.[28] Changes and adaptations to the governance structures of global institutions, ranging from greater flexibility in application of rules to assist weaker member states, to the giving of more voice to developing countries with the aim of a more balanced representation in multilateral decision-making and processes, are therefore required. Reforms to global governance structures should not only recognize common interests of members, but also diversities and differentiated responsibilities among nations of the global community in general, and particularly countries of the North and the South.

To avoid the drawbacks of the current system of global governance, the ideal is that the governance structures of global institutions should be both fair in terms of democratic representation and efficient with respect to decision-making. In the specific context of HIV/AIDS response, the need for improvement in global governance should focus on the decision-making processes and mechanisms of global institutions which at present put developing countries as a group at a disadvantage and limit their capacities to respond effectively and in timely fashion to the epidemic and its impact. The link between global governance and effective HIV/AIDS response should be analyzed as an endogenous and bidirectional relationship, implying that improved governance would not only lead to more effective HIV/AIDS response, but that good governance would also be enhanced by lower prevalence of HIV/AIDS at a national level. However, the most appropriate correction of deeply entrenched imbalances in institutional governance structures at the global level might require a radical and comprehensive approach to international system reform, which may not be not feasible and practical within an acceptable period for both geopolitical and economic reasons.

What, therefore, is being proposed by way of a new architecture of global governance for HIV/AIDS response is the application of certain conditions and modifications that could make the organization and management of global governance more responsive to the needs of developing countries, rather than proposing the replacement of the current system by completely new institutional frameworks and operational arrangements. There are a number of key requirements that should be met in order to ensure that the new architecture of global governance is appropriate to the demands of an effective global response to HIV/AIDS.

First, the new architecture should pay more attention to the effects of the outcomes of globalization on the capacities of poor countries to respond to the threat of the epidemic. Second, it should include elements that are responsive to the economic needs of poor countries, as well as reflect the scale of the global HIV/AIDS epidemic as an international development issue. Third, it is important to link elements of the new architecture with the ability of developing countries to implement strategies and policies that address HIV/AIDS and poverty simultaneously and in an integrated manner. Fourth, the new architecture should address the relationship between poor countries and their development partners in HIV/AIDS response processes, and this should cover key development policy and planning issues such as ownership, convergence between partners, consensus on short-term needs and long-term goals, and policy guidelines and coherence. Fifth, the main operational mechanism of the new architecture should be a comprehensive international development agenda that covers aid, debt relief, trade, and macroeconomic management, and one that recognizes the need to provide developing countries with much needed technical assistance within a fairer global system, to enable them to participate competitively in the world economy and to build effective institutions to improve governance at national level. In this regard, the proposed reform of the UN system could serve as the overarching framework of a new architecture for global governance based on global consensus.

With reference to the global HIV/AIDS response, the proposed reform of the UN system—as outlined in the report of the High-level Panel that was appointed by the former secretary-general, Kofi Annan, in 2006[29]—called for changes in the governance, funding, and management of UN system-wide agencies, which were aimed at strengthening global development efforts. The proposed UN reform recommended measures to improve the governance of the world body, such as the establishment of a more representative Global Leaders Forum within the United Nations through which the developing countries would have some influence on global economic and social policy issues. It is likely that, if fully implemented, the proposed reforms could facilitate the integration of HIV/AIDS into international development policy by means of the reforms implied for the UN system as a whole, the achievement of a coordinated and more coherent approach, improved cooperation with the international financial institutions, and constructive engagement with civil society and the private sector.

The proposed UN reform recognized the need to give a voice and influence to developing countries in the multilateral system, and multilateralism should include arrangements for solving problems collectively and in the common interest of everyone. Effective participation of the developing countries in the decision-making process of key global institutions could go some way toward addressing current governance imbalances between the North and South. At the same time, global institutions in the framing of governance policy should recognize the principle of "constructive pluralism" which underlies the reality of different developing countries having different approaches and paths to development and, hence, allowing for countries to make their own choices rather than imposing a global model on them.

Reflection on a new architecture of global governance for HIV/AIDS response will undoubtedly bring into focus the distinction between the "hard" issues (i.e. global economic governance based on the models of the Bretton Woods institutions and WTO) and the "soft" issues (i.e. guidelines and standards based on UN declarations and commitments such as the MDGs, UNGASS targets, WHO's 3×5 initiative, and ILO's Code of Practice on HIV/AIDS) of the global HIV/AIDS response.[30] Hence, the new architecture should have a clear and appropriate "division of labor" between the "hard law" and the "soft law" institutions, which could be useful for providing a benchmark and serving as a framework for the interpretation and implementation of international agreements like the TRIPS.

Conclusion

In conclusion, this chapter has argued that imbalances and drawbacks in the present system of global governance stand in the way of effective response to HIV/AIDS at national and global levels. The need for improved governance of global institutions has become more obvious, with the growing recognition by the international community and other stakeholders that the global HIV/AIDS epidemic threatens everyone, and that the consequences are beyond the realm of public health alone. We have explored alternatives to existing rules, norms, and policies of global governance, and proposed more flexible arrangements and "exit clauses" to allow poor and marginalized countries to reassert their priorities as a national concern when these priorities clash with obligations to international institutions and unnecessary market discipline. These alternatives should be seen as an integral part of sustainable international economic and financial arrangements, characterized by stable and egalitarian global growth and based on policies built around the achievement of the MDGs.

We have also faced the realization that in a world of unequal partners, globalization does not seem to be benefiting poor countries with marginalized economies—many of which are also seriously affected by HIV/AIDS. Attention therefore has to be focused on the conditions and requirements for better managing globalization and arriving at fairer outcomes of the process in terms of greater economic well-being and social justice for all. The market-driven process of globalization should be made conducive to a more egalitarian style of economic development and a more broad-based pattern of social development. This would also require improved global governance of multilateral institutions which, in turn, should improve the prospects of developing countries for responding effectively and on a sustainable basis to the challenges of the HIV/AIDS epidemic and other development problems.

10 Critical and emerging issues in HIV/AIDS response

Although the HIV/AIDS epidemic has been around for more than a quarter of a century, it is still evolving differently across regions and countries. During this period, tens of millions of people worldwide have been infected with HIV and over 25 million have died from AIDS-related illnesses, but at the same time there have been significant developments and changes in the surveillance and response to the epidemic. Most significant is the emergence of antiretroviral (ARV) therapy, which transformed the response to the epidemic by introducing the possibility of life extension for AIDS sufferers. Until then, being infected with HIV was considered to be a "death sentence" sooner rather than later, in contrast with the situation today wherein the latest generation of ARV drugs can offer an almost normal lifespan. Initially, treatment was not affordable in resource-poor developing countries because of prohibitively high costs of ARV drugs, but progressive and substantial reductions in cost over time and increased donor funding have made treatment accessible to some of the millions of AIDS sufferers in the developing regions, and particularly in sub-Saharan Africa, which has some of the poorest countries with the highest HIV prevalence rates in the world. Despite advancement in tracking and treating HIV/AIDS worldwide, indications today are that the spread of the epidemic is far from being brought under control. Access to treatment and the implementation of effective prevention programs remain limited in the regions and countries most affected by the disease, for various reasons ranging from resource constraints to social, cultural, and political factors which undermine efforts to respond effectively.

The rapid spread and deadly impact of HIV/AIDS worldwide, and the realization that the epidemic is a long-wave event with longer-term development implications, have led to an extraordinary mobilization of human and financial resources and the establishment of exceptional global partnerships and programs in response, such as UNAIDS; the

Global Fund to Fight AIDS, Tuberculosis and Malaria; the Global Business Coalition on HIV/AIDS; and the International AIDS Society. Billions of dollars have been raised from various sources to support the fight against HIV/AIDS at global, national, and community levels.

The diversity of the global HIV/AIDS epidemic and its transitional and multidimensional characteristics have produced different approaches and mixed experiences in the context of the global response. At the same time, the variety of experiences and lessons from the global response have also brought into focus critical and unresolved issues, as well as new and emerging challenges. HIV/AIDS has continued to spread globally and, more worryingly, to large and populous countries in Asia such as China, India, and the former Soviet Central Asian countries, with potential strategic economic and political implications. In sub-Saharan Africa, where AIDS is now the leading cause of death, some progress has been made in slowing down the spread of the epidemic in the region, but the epidemic appears to be outpacing both physical and human resources in the worst affected countries. Inadequate healthcare facilities and ignorance have meant that only about a third of infected pregnant women in Africa receive ARV drugs for prevention of mother-to-child transmission, something which has been entirely avoidable for years. HIV/AIDS has maintained strong causative links with poverty in low- and middle-income countries, and stigma and discrimination and other social problems, including gender inequality, remain powerful barriers to prevention and treatment programs in those and many other countries worldwide. Two decades of efforts by the scientific community involving hundreds of millions of dollars in research and experimental trials have so far failed to produce a successful vaccine against HIV infection, let alone a cure for the disease. The emerging threat of TB-HIV and other HIV-linked co-infections does not seem to be getting sufficient attention in the response to HIV/AIDS at global and national levels.

This chapter summarizes these critical and unresolved issues, as well as emerging challenges which must be addressed in the context of further efforts to control and reverse the spread of HIV infection worldwide and to mitigate its impact on the millions who are already infected, their families, and communities. The summary takes into account that HIV/AIDS is now facing stiff competition from new and emerging global concerns, such as climate change, energy security, food shortages, water access, terrorism, and the financial crisis, to remain a priority issue on the international agenda. It notes that while some of these competing global concerns are significant to the current state of the world, they also have important links with and implications for HIV/AIDS.[1]

Effective use of HIV/AIDS funds

Despite the massive upsurge in the funding of the global HIV/AIDS response over the past decade, there are claims from many quarters, including UNAIDS and the Global Fund, that more money is needed for an effective global response. While this may be so, more effective use of available money could increase the coverage and impact of HIV/AIDS spending on prevention and treatment programs. This in fact has been recognized by UNAIDS and donor governments as a critical issue that needs to be addressed. Peter Piot, while head of UNAIDS, had consistently emphasized the importance of "making the money work" as a strategy for increasing the effectiveness of HIV/AIDS financing, a theme which was embraced by the wider UN system and external development partners at country level.[2]

The agreement reached in April 2004 between major multilateral institutions, donor governments, the World Bank, the Global Fund, and UNAIDS on the "Three Ones" principles[3] as the basis for harmonizing and coordinating donor efforts at the country level, was a significant step toward improving the effectiveness of HIV/AIDS funding. Support for the Three Ones principles among the developing countries was immediate, as indicated by the adoption of a resolution endorsing the Three Ones by African leaders at their summit in January 2005.[4] Many of the affected countries in the region were no longer able to monitor, let alone manage, the increased inflow and variety of donor funding that was being directed at their national HIV/AIDS response.

Endorsement and application of the Three Ones principles implied a recognition that while an increase in aid to fight HIV/AIDS may be necessary, this by itself is not sufficient to ensure an effective response. The spending of money should be matched by policy and institutional changes on the part of both donor and recipient governments to ensure effective functional coordination of efforts, better understanding of global roles and responsibilities, and improved national capacity to develop and implement an effective country-driven action program. For example, given large inflows of HIV/AIDS funds from sources such as the Global Fund and PEPFAR into developing countries with rather limited absorptive capacity, the provision of assistance should include technical support to improve absorptive and implementation capacities at country level, and countries should be allowed the flexibility to spread HIV/AIDS spending over a longer period, if necessary, to avoid overloading existing capacities. At the same time, improved monitoring and tracking of HIV/AIDS spending is required to address governance-related problems at country level. Poor governance and weak regulatory systems have resulted in HIV/AIDS money not being used effectively, as implied from concerns about mismanagement and fraud linked to Global Fund grants in some countries, which led to suspension of disbursement by the Fund.

The longer-term effectiveness of HIV/AIDS financing could be enhanced through external donors providing more predictable and sustainable funding for HIV/AIDS to minimize uncertainties and support longer-term responses. In this connection, longer-term financing of HIV/AIDS programs should be executed in tandem with measures for building effective health infrastructure and personnel in resource-poor countries. The response to HIV/AIDS should, therefore, be linked to adoption of sector-wide approaches to health development and implementation of cross-sectoral activities for improving health. The need to invest in health systems in general may be affected by the current massive spending on fighting HIV/AIDS, if the two needs are not dealt with in an integrated and complementary manner. It is therefore important to ensure that HIV/AIDS response initiatives support, rather than supplant, health system development and service delivery.

Access to cheaper but effective generic drugs could contribute to more effective spending of HIV/AIDS money in terms of the achievement and sustainability of treatment targets and programs in developing countries. There are still regulatory barriers at country level which impede timely access to licensed ARV drugs, and lack of knowledge and manufacturing capacity prevent many developing countries from taking advantage of the flexibilities introduced under the TRIPS to produce generics. Continued pressures are needed at the international level to reaffirm public health flexibilities in WTO intellectual property rules, and to draw attention to and demand action against bilateral free trade agreements which could undermine TRIPS provisions.

Prevention or treatment?

At the June 2006 UN General Assembly High-level Meeting on HIV/AIDS, countries made a commitment to achieve as close as possible the goal of universal access to required HIV/AIDS services by 2010. Universal access implies a comprehensive response to the epidemic, incorporating prevention and treatment interventions. However, for a variety of reasons associated with resources and, more importantly, policy preferences and actions of both donor and recipient governments, the HIV/AIDS response has sometimes involved a choice between prevention and treatment or a preference for one over the other. Given the different implications of treatment and prevention interventions separately in the context of HIV/AIDS response, the issue of a choice or trade-off between prevention and treatment has to be addressed and resolved, ideally through the integration of these two vital interventions as complementary components of a comprehensive package.

Insofar as new HIV infections annually add to existing financial and social costs of managing HIV/AIDS programs and prolongs the epidemic, it seems reasonable to make prevention the key component of a comprehensive HIV/AIDS response, particularly in high-prevalence, resource-poor countries. Yet, the tremendous attention given to treatment, especially with the advent of antiretrovirals, has meant that prevention efforts have been lagging behind treatment initiatives even in low- and middle-income developing countries. While it is true that the level of treatment in a region like sub-Saharan Africa is still low relative to the large number of AIDS cases, and the majority of those in need of treatment in the region are not covered due mainly to cost, it is also a fact that the incidence of new infections has not been brought under control, which sooner than later adds to the burden of treatment. Furthermore, there is no clear evidence that the coverage of treatment as currently offered was achieving a significant measure of success in the wider context of bringing the global epidemic under control. In 2005, Peter Piot, then head of UNAIDS, emphasized the significance of prevention in HIV/AIDS response as follows: "There are six new infections for every person receiving treatment," and therefore "treatment [alone] is not going to stop this epidemic."[5] This clearly suggests that the scaling-up of treatment has to go hand-in-hand with effective prevention.

In the context of its Global HIV/AIDS Program of Action, the World Bank was in no doubt that: "Preventing new infections should remain the highest priority [in HIV/AIDS response] for all countries—at all prevalence levels."[6] The Bank affirmed that prevention and treatment should be seen as linked and part of a comprehensive response, and not as separate or competing interventions: "The more successful countries are at preventing new infections, the more feasible they will find it to provide treatment and care for those who are infected."[7] Real success of treatment efforts will require that such efforts are part of a comprehensive and carefully planned package of HIV/AIDS interventions, including investments in health systems.

Practical and innovative policies and programs are required to expand and sustain HIV prevention efforts. HIV prevention efforts must address the behaviors and situations that increase the risk of HIV and enhance people's vulnerability, and the situations in which risk and vulnerability converge. In this regard, attention should be paid to the structural and societal factors that increase vulnerability, such as unequal gender norms and relations, cultural values and beliefs, and legal frameworks to combat stigma and discrimination. Effective prevention, in turn, makes treatment more affordable and sustainable by reducing the number of persons who will need treatment in due course.

Stigma and discrimination

The achievement of the goal of universal access in many countries is not likely to be realized without addressing the problems of stigma and discrimination which underlie vulnerability to HIV infection and obstacles to treatment access. In this regard, the integration of legal support into HIV/AIDS programs and attitudinal change may be required as fundamental components of universal access efforts to ensure comprehensive coverage and increased access to basic rights and justice for affected groups and communities.

Stigma and discrimination in the context of HIV/AIDS lead to violations of fundamental human rights and remain an obstacle to expanding the coverage of HIV prevention and treatment. Although the United Nations has moved to protect the rights of those infected with HIV through the incorporation of elements of the Universal Declaration of Human Rights and other major human rights instruments into a rights-based approach to guide the global response, the issue of HIV-related discrimination and violations of human rights worldwide remains a major problem in the response. As noted in Chapter 4, there are those in the international health community who are not convinced about the relevance of a rights-based approach in dealing with a global epidemic of the nature and scale of HIV/AIDS, and argue that public health promotion should take precedence over the protection of human rights in the context of efforts to control the transmission and spread of the virus. There are also deep-rooted societal prejudices against those infected with HIV, often based on ignorance about the disease and its mode of transmission, which stand in the way of action to enact and implement right-based laws and promote practical guidelines. The challenge of stigma and discrimination in HIV/AIDS response therefore goes beyond the adoption of legislation and its incorporation into the relevant legal and policy frameworks. It should include practical measures, such as advocacy and public education, backed by social mobilization and strong leadership commitment at all levels to address social, cultural, and political factors that contribute to ignorance, silence, and denial about HIV infection.

Vulnerability of women and children

The issue of gender inequality is an important factor in the spread of HIV/AIDS in the developing world, as recognized by the increasing attention given to the "feminization" of the epidemic in the global response by UNAIDS and other key stakeholders in recent years. Yet the issue has so far received only scant attention at national and local levels in Africa and other developing regions where gender roles are defined and influenced by cultural and social norms and practices. Differentiation and imbalance of authority in the relationship between men and women and between boys and girls within households and in local communities increase the vulnerability of women and girls to HIV infection more than men and boys in similar circumstances, and sometimes prevent women and girls from accessing HIV/AIDS prevention and treatment services as equals of men and boys. Furthermore to being more vulnerable and at greater risk of exposure to HIV infection, women and girls in the developing world tend to bear the greater burden of caring for family members who are sick with AIDS, in addition to traditional female domestic chores, or at the expense of their schooling.

There is an urgent need for women and girls in developing countries to be provided with knowledge about the disease and how to protect themselves from infection. They should be empowered and their rights to equality recognized and protected through legal and practical measures. These include the enactment and enforcement of legislation that outlaws gender discrimination and promotes access of women and girls to education, sexual and reproductive health services, and socio-economic opportunities, and also continued support by international organizations and NGOs for actions that create opportunities to challenge and transform social gender norms, practices, and gaps that are disadvantageous and damaging to women and girls.

The effects of HIV/AIDS on children and their vulnerability to the epidemic are manifested in two critical issues in HIV/AIDS response that are still not being properly and adequately addressed. First, there is the relatively high incidence of pediatric HIV transmission in developing countries, which suggests gaps and failings in "Prevention of Mother-to-Child-Transmission" (PMTCT) interventions. Second, there is the existence and precarious situation of millions of children who have been orphaned by HIV/AIDS, most of them in Africa, who have been left to go through life without the guidance and economic support of adults. In developed countries, pediatric HIV infection has been virtually eliminated through successful PMTCT interventions, and transmission rates are typically below 2 percent. In contrast, transmission rates for pediatric HIV are substantially much higher in developing countries, sometimes approaching 50 or 60 percent, due to lack of access to PMTCT interventions. According to UNAIDS and WHO, there were an estimated 420,000 new pediatric infections globally in 2007, with nearly 90 percent of these occurring in sub-Saharan Africa.[8] This compares with fewer than 250 HIV-infected infants born in the United States each year, according to information provided by the U.S. Centers for Disease Control and Prevention (CDC).[9] There is, therefore, an urgent need to scale-up and improve the quality of pediatric HIV care in resource-limiting settings of the developing world.

UNAIDS and UNICEF estimated in 2005 that HIV/AIDS had already orphaned over 15 million children globally, and that number was projected to reach 20 million by 2010.[10] Many more children are vulnerable in terms of the impact of the epidemic on their health, education, safety, and general well-being. In addition to losing out on parental care and socio-economic support including education, children orphaned by AIDS are often stigmatized and discriminated against, and in some cases deprived of access to household assets belonging to their parents, which in turn puts them at greater risk of HIV infection, sexual exploitation, and child labor. Governments in poor developing countries lack the resources and infrastructure to deal comprehensively with the needs of orphans and vulnerable children (OVC) in their HIV/AIDS response programs. According to UNICEF, less than 10 percent of orphans in the context of HIV/AIDS are receiving assistance from government or official agencies beyond their extended family, neighbors, and the local community.[11] Predictable and sustainable financial resources from donor governments and external partners should be directed specifically for the care and support of OVC in the overall context of the global HIV/AIDS response, to ensure sustainable solutions to what is probably the most serious long-term development impact of the epidemic.

The search for a successful HIV vaccine

When the HIV virus was identified in the early 1980s, it was a reasonable expectation in the scientific community that the next step of finding a successful vaccine was just a few years away. Today, a quarter of a century later, the world is no closer to a successful HIV/AIDS vaccine, despite the hundreds of millions of dollars that have gone into scientific research in the developed countries and clinical trials worldwide.[12] With the global HIV/AIDS epidemic still around and showing little sign of being brought under control, the failure to respond with an effective vaccine is a major challenge in the global response.

In February 2008, David Baltimore of Caltech, U.S.A., a Nobel prize-winning biologist and president of the American Association for the Advancement of Science (AAAS), who himself is involved in HIV/ AIDS vaccine research, informed the annual meeting of the AAAS in Boston that attempts to develop a vaccine to control the HIV virus through antibodies have ended in failure. He indicated that the scientific community now has to work on novel techniques involving the use of gene and stem cell therapy, an area of research which is still in its infancy.[13] Baltimore's announcement followed the collapse in 2007 of a massive, global experimental HIV vaccine trial.[14]

Lack of progress and expression of pessimism in some quarters of the scientific community have led to calls for a halt in HIV/AIDS vaccine research. In the United States, for example, the influential AIDS Healthcare Foundation has openly advocated a freeze in public spending on AIDS vaccine, which it sees as very costly and leading nowhere. The head of the AIDS Healthcare Foundation has argued that money should instead be put into providing life-prolonging ARV treatment for more AIDS sufferers, especially now that the cost of treatment has fallen to as low as under $200 per patient per year in Africa and other developing regions.[15]

Others in the scientific community, such as Quentino Sattentan of Oxford University, while acknowledging that a successful vaccine against HIV infection may still be a long shot, argue that research should continue, as in scientific exploration a breakthrough could come at any time.[16] The supporters of the view that research on an HIV/ AIDS must continue point out that it took nearly 50 years to produce a polio vaccine and over 40 years to develop a successful vaccine for chicken pox, and cite the massive strides in AIDS treatment with the advent and continued upgrading of ARV drugs as an example of what can be achieved in science with perseverance. There are over 30 HIV vaccine clinical trials underway in 25 countries around the world, which should be seen as reasons for optimism.[17]

Governments and philanthropic foundations in the developed countries have been providing the support for research and physical infrastructure for vaccine delivery, and are likely to continue to do so. While the search for a successful vaccine for the body against HIV infection continues, it is equally important to intensify prevention efforts, a "vaccine for the mind," vital for controlling the spread of the epidemic worldwide. Attention by the scientific community should also not be diverted from attempts to develop other new vaccines, such as those targeted against TB, which is a co-infection of HIV/AIDS.

TB/HIV co-infection

The UN and WHO estimate that between 12 and 15 million people are infected with both HIV and Tuberculosis (TB), or about a third of all people currently living with HIV. TB is among the leading causes of death among people infected with HIV, and the HIV epidemic poses a massive challenge for the global control of TB. According to the WHO, people living with HIV are up to 50 times more likely to develop active TB compared with HIV-negative individuals.[18] Diagnosis of TB in HIV-positive individuals is difficult, especially in conditions of poor health facilities, often leading to delays in treatment which in turn contributes to higher death rates. Although TB cases in high-HIV-prevalence countries have more than doubled in the past decade, less than 1 percent of all people living with HIV were screened for TB in 2006, according to the WHO.[19]

Despite increasing recognition of the value of combined treatment and care of HIV and TB, the two diseases are still treated separately in many high-HIV-prevalence countries due to limitations of available diagnostic tools and drugs. Treating HIV and TB separately could result in the interaction of different drugs that are not compatible, which makes managing the co-infection difficult. Experts believe that what is needed is an integrated and comprehensive approach which involves combined diagnosis and treatment of the two conditions. The development of TB/HIV co-infection policy and therapy is still evolving, and it is only quite recently that the international health community began giving attention and resources to TB as a co-infection with HIV, including the launching of global initiatives such as the "Stop TB Partnership," which has been endorsed and supported by both the WHO and the Global Fund. There are other deadly diseases such as Hepatitis C, whose virus also co-exists with HIV, implying a higher risk in HIV-infected persons, but are similarly not being treated effectively as a co-infection in the context of the global response to the epidemic.

The spread of HIV/AIDS in large and strategic countries

The idea of a threat posed to international and national security by the spread of HIV/AIDS globally gained currency in the aftermath of the 9/11 terrorist attacks in the United States. In a report published in 2002, cited in Chapter 5, the U.S. National Intelligence Council (NIC) analyzed the impact of the epidemic in large and populous countries that are of strategic economic or political significance to the United

States and the West. The NIC report noted that if the disturbing trends in the spread of HIV in those countries were not halted and reversed, the effects on the demographic structure and the socio-economic consequences could have serious international security implications.

Since the publication of the NIC report seven years ago, the incidence of HIV infection in large and strategic countries such as India, China, Indonesia, Russia, and the Central Asian republics has increased significantly. Some of these countries are at the forefront of the economic globalization process, which involves increasing movements of people and goods and services and the pathogens they carry across national borders and regions and, thus, an increase in the propensity for the spread of HIV/AIDS globally.

The continuing global spread of HIV, with possible shift in the epicenter of the epidemic from Africa to populous and strategically important countries in Asia, could intensify conflict between the interests of national sovereignty and threaten principles of good global governance, which are founded on international cooperation and the interdependence of nations. Against the background of increasing North–South tension, it may become even more difficult to persuade the rich donor governments to continue to fund HIV/AIDS prevention and treatment in the poor developing countries, or to convince them that their contributions to UNAIDS and the Global Fund should be used to benefit everyone—friend and foe alike. This could add to the daunting challenges of responding to a still evolving global HIV/AIDS epidemic in a changing world economic and political order.

Conclusion

This book has provided insights into the role of global institutions in responding to an exceptional global public health crisis whose impact extends beyond the health domain to threaten economic, social, political, and security objectives at global, regional, and national levels. The range of issues covered provides a general framework for contemplating future directions and strategies to improve the effectiveness of the global response to HIV/AIDS, an epidemic which is now recognized as a long-wave event. It has done so, first, by answering critical questions about what we have learnt from the successes and challenges of past efforts, particularly those that revolved around the actions of global institutions. Second, it has provided a better understanding of current developments and trends in the global HIV/AIDS epidemic and the lessons from these for future requirements of the global response. Third, it has shown the importance of the need for cooperation and partnership between donor governments and recipient countries, between the Global North and Global South broadly, for an effective response to HIV/AIDS at all levels. Fourth, it has reaffirmed that both an emergency approach and a long-term view are needed to address a persistent yet evolving epidemic such as HIV/AIDS in a dramatically changing global environment. Finally, it has provided justification as to why HIV/AIDS should remain a priority issue on the international agenda, in the light of new and emerging global concerns such as climate change, water shortage, and food insecurity.

The global response to HIV/AIDS so far has been characterized by a mix of hope and gloom. While great strides have been made in the response, there are still unresolved issues and challenges, and there are lessons to be learned from the global efforts of the past two decades. The different global institutions that are covered in this book, and others, are certain to continue to play an important part in the global response, as are the financial resources which they mobilize and the technical assistance they provide in the longer term. However, in order to achieve the best possible outcomes for the global HIV/AIDS response, the roles and actions of global institutions will have to be modified to address existing imbalances and shortcomings, as well as be adapted to changing needs and circumstances and to new challenges.

In considering the future roles of global institutions in the context of the global HIV/AIDS response, it is necessary to take into account the consequences of their past actions as well as inactions, and to search for innovative policies and actions based on critical analysis and public debate. In this regard, the voices and opinions of major stakeholders—including in particular countries, communities, and people directly affected by the epidemic—should be heard in relevant global institutions and, accordingly, reflected in decision-making and action by those institutions and new partnerships. There should be a change in global governance, in the sense of a clear understanding, and possibly agreement, between global institutions and their constituents in the North and South about what should or could be done differently, and how, in support of an effective global response to HIV/AIDS.

Appendix 1
Memorandum of understanding on UNAIDS

Memorandum of Understanding on a Joint and Co-sponsored United Nations Programme on HIV/AIDS

WHEREAS, the worldwide epidemic of acquired immunodeficiency syndrome (AIDS)——a syndrome caused by the human immunodeficiency virus (HIV)——is one of the major tragedies of our time which poses a threat of great magnitude to mankind, and requires a multi-dimensional response at global and country level;

WHEREAS the United Nations Children's Fund ("UNICEF"), the United Nations Development Programme ("UNDP"), the United Nations Population Fund ("UNFPA"), acting within their respective mandates from the General Assembly and the Economic and Social Council ("ECOSOC") of the United Nations; the United Nations Educational, Scientific and Cultural Organization ("UNESCO"); the World Health Organization ("WHO"); and the International Bank for Reconstruction and Development ("the Bank"), wish to undertake a joint and cosponsored United Nations programme on HIV/AIDS ("the Joint Programme"), to replace all prior arrangements, bilateral or otherwise, between them concerning HIV infection and AIDS ("HIV/AIDS");

WHEREAS the governing bodies of each of the organizations and ECOSOC, through its resolutions 1994/24 and E/1995/L.24/Rev.1[1], have endorsed the establishment of the Joint Programme;

NOW THEREFORE, UNICEF, UNDP, UNFPA, UNESCO, WHO and the Bank, collectively referred to as the "Cosponsoring Organizations" have agreed on the structure and operation of the Joint Programme as set forth below:

I Establishment of the Joint United Nations Programme on HIV/AIDS ("UNAIDS")

1.1 There is hereby established a joint and cosponsored United Nations programme on HIV/AIDS, to be known as the Joint United

Nations Programme on HIV/AIDS ("UNAIDS"), to further mobilize the global response to the epidemic and provide means of coordinated action.

1.2 UNAIDS is part of a much broader United Nations system response to HIV/AIDS which also includes:

- The Cosponsoring Organizations' mainstreaming/integration activities;
- The resident coordinator[2] system with its UN Theme Groups on HIV/AIDS, or any alternate arrangements, established at country level;
- The Cosponsoring Organizations' respective activities at country level in support to national programmes;
- The Cosponsoring Organizations' respective intercountry/regional activities, within the context of the global workplan of UNAIDS;
- The HIV/AIDS activities undertaken by other United Nations system organizations in such areas as humanitarian aid, assistance to refugees, peace-keeping and human rights; and
- Activities undertaken by other United Nations system organizations in cooperation with bilateral aid agencies.

II *Objectives*

2.1 The objectives of UNAIDS are to:

(a) Provide global leadership in response to the epidemic;

(b) Achieve and promote global consensus on policy and programmatic approaches;

(c) Strengthen the capacity of the United Nations system to monitor trends and ensure that appropriate as well as effective policies and strategies are implemented at country level;

(d) Strengthen the capacity of national Governments to develop comprehensive national strategies, and implement effective HIV/AIDS activities at country level;

(e) Promote broad-based political and social mobilization to prevent and respond to HIV/AIDS within countries, ensuring that national responses involve a wide range of sectors and institutions, including nongovernmental organizations; and

(f) Advocate greater political commitment in responding to the epidemic at global and country level, including the mobilization and allocation of adequate resources for HIV/AIDS-related activities.

III Cosponsorship

3.1 The Cosponsoring Organizations are committed to working together and contributing to UNAIDS. UNAIDS will draw upon the
experience and strengths of the Cosponsoring Organizations to
develop its HIV/AIDS-related policies, strategies and technical
guidelines, which will be incorporated by each of them into their
policy and strategy mainstream, subject to their governance processes, and reflected in the activities specific to their own mandates.
3.2 The activities of the Cosponsoring Organizations relating primarily
to HIV/AIDS at global level shall be within the context of the
global workplan of UNAIDS, developed in collaboration with the
Cosponsoring Organizations. HIV/AIDS activities of the Cosponsoring Organizations at country level shall function within the framework of national plans and priorities and the resident
coordinator system, where it exists.

IV Structure and organization of UNAIDS

4.1 At global level, UNAIDS consists of the Programme Coordinating
Board (PCB), the Committee of Cosponsoring Organizations
(CCO) and the Secretariat.
4.2 At country level, UNAIDS will operate through a "UN Theme Group
on HIV/AIDS" and will have Secretariat staff in selected countries.

V Programme Coordinating Board

5.1 The Programme Coordinating Board (PCB) shall act as the governing body on all programmatic issues concerning policy, strategy,
finance, monitoring and evaluation of UNAIDS. Its composition
and functions shall be determined by ECOSOC as well as the
appropriate governing bodies of the Cosponsoring Organizations.

VI Committee of Cosponsoring Organizations

6.1 The Committee of Cosponsoring Organizations (CCO) shall serve
as the forum for the Cosponsoring Organizations to meet on a
regular basis to consider matters concerning UNAIDS, and shall
provide the input of the Cosponsoring organizations into the policies
and strategies of UNAIDS.
6.2 The CCO shall be comprised of the executive head, or his/her
designated representative, of each of the Cosponsoring Organizations.

Members of the CCO may be accompanied by a limited number of advisers.

6.3 The CCO shall have the following functions:

(i) To review workplans and the proposed programme budget for each coming financial period, prepared by the Executive Director and reviewed by any appropriate committee established for the purpose, in time for presentation to the PCB;

(ii) To review proposals to the PCB for the financing of UNAIDS for the coming financial period;

(iii) To review technical reports, as well as financial statements of UNAIDS and audited financial reports, submitted by the Executive Director, and to transmit these with comments as appropriate to the PCB;

(iv) To make recommendations to the PCB on matters relating to UNAIDS;

(v) To review the activities of each Cosponsoring Organization for consistency and coordination with, as well as appropriate support to, the activities and strategies of UNAIDS;

(vi) To report to the PCB on the efforts of the Cosponsoring Organizations to bring UNAIDS's policy as well as strategic and technical guidance into the policies and strategies of their respective organizations and to reflect them in activities specific to their mandates; and

(vii) To decide, on behalf of the PCB, on issues referred to it for this purpose by the PCB.

6.4 The CCO may establish such advisory committees as it deems necessary for the accomplishment of its work.

VII UNAIDS Secretariat

7.1 An Executive Director shall head the UNAIDS Secretariat. The Executive Director shall be appointed by the Secretary-General of the United Nations, upon the consensus recommendation of the Cosponsoring Organizations. The appointment shall be implemented by the agency providing administration of UNAIDS. The Executive Director shall be responsible for the overall management of UNAIDS. The Executive Director may establish such policy and technical advisory committees as may be required.

7.2 The Executive Director shall prepare a biennial workplan and budget for UNAIDS, which shall be submitted to the PCB for approval, following review by the CCO.

7.3 The Executive Director shall report to the PCB, after consultation with the CCO, on all major programme, budget and operational issues of UNAIDS.

7.4 The Executive Director shall be Secretary of the PCB and of the CCO.

VIII Global level

8.1 At global level, UNAIDS will provide support in policy formulation, strategic planning, technical guidance, research and development, advocacy and external relations. Working closely with the appropriate organizations, UNAIDS will also support normative activities relating to HIV/AIDS in areas such as social and economic planning, population, culture, education, health, community development and social mobilization, sexual and reproductive health, and women and adolescents.

IX Country level

9.1 It is recognized that national Governments have the ultimate responsibility for the coordination of HIV/AIDS issues at country level. To this end, the arrangements of UNAIDS for coordinating HIV/AIDS activities will complement and support Government efforts for national development planning. The Cosponsoring Organizations shall incorporate the normative work undertaken by UNAIDS at global level on policy, strategy and technical matters into their HIV/AIDS activities and related activities undertaken at country level, consistent with national plans and priorities of the countries concerned. An important function of UNAIDS will be to strengthen national capacities to plan, coordinate, implement and monitor the overall response to HIV/AIDS. The participation in UNAIDS of six organizations of the United Nations system will ensure the provision of technical and financial assistance to national activities in a coordinated multisectoral manner. This will strengthen intersectoral coordination of HIV/AIDS activities and will facilitate further incorporation of these activities in national programme and planning processes.

9.2 Within the framework of General Assembly resolutions 44/211 and 47/199, the resident coordinator shall establish a UN Theme Group on HIV/AIDS in countries for carrying out HIV/AIDS and related activities, and designate a chairperson from among the members of the Theme Group, bearing in mind the desirability of making a selection reflecting the consensus views of the Cosponsoring Organizations present in the country concerned. In countries where the resident coordinator system does not exist or where only one of the Cosponsoring Organizations is present, alternate arrangements shall be made, in agreement with the national authorities, to facilitate the support to the national response to HIV/AIDS.

9.3 UNAIDS will facilitate coordination among the Cosponsoring Organizations at country level and may decide to station staff of the Secretariat in selected countries to support the chairperson of the UN Theme Group on HIV/AIDS.

X Flow of UNAIDS funds

10.1 Funds for UNAIDS activities at global level will be obtained through appropriate common global means, including a Global Appeal.

10.2 Funding for country-level HIV/AIDS-related activities will be obtained primarily through existing fund-raising mechanisms of the Cosponsoring Organizations.

XI Administration of UNAIDS

11.1 WHO shall provide administration of UNAIDS. It shall establish a separate trust fund (entitled "UNAIDS Trust Fund"), under its Financial Regulations and Rules, for the receipt and disbursement of financial contributions to UNAIDS

11.2 Financial contributions to the UNAIDS Trust Fund may consist of voluntary cash contributions received from Cosponsoring Organizations, from Governments of Member States of any of the Cosponsoring Organizations, from intergovernmental and non-governmental organizations, as well as from commercial enterprises and individuals. In addition, WHO may also receive, in trust for UNAIDS, contributions in kind, e.g., staff, equipment, facilities or services. The resources of UNAIDS shall consist of the aforesaid cash and in-kind contributions.

11.3 All expenditures under UNAIDS shall be authorized by the Executive Director against funds received or committed, in accordance with the WHO's Financial Regulations and Rules.

11.4 The Executive Director shall be responsible for the selection, supervision, promotion and termination of all Secretariat staff, acting within the staff regulations and rules of WHO which will be adjusted, as necessary, to take into account special needs of

UNAIDS. The appointment, promotion and termination of the Secretariat staff shall be implemented by WHO.

11.5 All Secretariat staff shall be recruited for service with UNAIDS only. WHO shall be responsible for administrative matters of their employment.

11.6 Subject to the possible need to make special arrangements to take into account the particular operational needs of UNAIDS, the operation of UNAIDS shall be carried out in accordance with the administrative and financial regulations, rules and procedures of WHO. WHO shall, in agreement with the Executive Director, elaborate such further details of the administration of UNAIDS as are necessary for its proper functioning.

11.7 WHO shall be entitled to apply a charge covering its costs in providing administration of UNAIDS.

XII Final provisions

12.1 This Memorandum of Understanding shall enter into force upon signature of the executive heads of all six Cosponsoring Organizations listed in the Preamble to this Memorandum of Understanding.

12.2 After the first anniversary of the entry into force of this Memorandum of Understanding and with the unanimous agreement of the existing Cosponsoring Organizations, other United Nations system organizations may become Cosponsoring Organizations by signature of the Memorandum of Understanding.

12.3 At the time of the second anniversary of the entry into force of this Memorandum of Understanding, the Cosponsoring Organizations agree to review the Memorandum of Understanding in order to determine whether it should be amended to further improve the operation of UNAIDS. Amendments to the Memorandum of Understanding shall be made by agreement among the Cosponsoring Organizations.

12.4 The Cosponsoring Organizations assume no liability for the acts or omissions of the Executive Director or his/her staff. *(Signed)* Carol Bellamy, Executive Director, United Nations Children's Fund, *(Signed)* James Gustave Speth, Administrator, United Nations Development Programme, *(Signed)* Nafis Sadik, Executive Director, United Nations Population Fund, *(Signed)* Federico Mayor, Director-General, United Nations Educational, Scientific and Cultural Organization, *(Signed)* Hiroshi Nakajima, Director-General. World Health Organization *(Signed)* James D. Wolfensohn, President, The World Bank, *Done on 1 January 1996.*

Memorandum of Understanding on a Joint and Cosponsored United Nations Programme on HIV/AIDS

In accordance with Article XII, Section 12.2 of the Memorandum of Understanding on a Joint and Cosponsored United Nations Programme on HIV/AIDS, signed by the Executive Heads of the United Nations Children's Fund, the United Nations Development Programme, the United Nations Population Fund, the United Nations Educational, Scientific and Cultural Organization, the World Health Organization and the World Bank, the signature below shall be appended to the aforementioned Memorandum of Understanding.

Done at Vienna on 12 March 1999. *(Signed)* Pino Arlacchi, Executive Director, United Nations Drug Control Programme.

Memorandum of Understanding on a Joint and Cosponsored United Nations Programme on HIV/AIDS

In accordance with Article XII, Section 12.2 of the Memorandum of Understanding on a Joint and Cosponsored United Nations Programme on HIV/AIDS, signed by the Executive Heads of the United Nations Children's Fund, the United Nations Development Programme, the United Nations Population Fund, the United Nations Drug Control Programme, the United Nations Educational, Scientific and Cultural Organization, the World Health Organization and the World Bank, the signature below shall be appended to the aforementioned Memorandum of Understanding. Geneva, 25 October 2001. *(Signed)* Juan Somavia, Director-General, International Labour Organization, ***

Appendix 2
"Resolution on Joint and Co-Sponsored Programme on Human Immunodeficiency Virus/Acquired Immunodeficiency Syndrome, HIV/AIDS," United Nations ECOSOC resolution 1994/24, 29 July 1994

Economic and Social Council

44th plenary meeting, 26 July 1994

1994/24. Joint and co-sponsored United Nations programme on human immunodeficiency virus/acquired immunodeficiency syndrome (HIV/AIDS)

The Economic and Social Council,

Recalling its resolution 1993/51 on the coordination of United Nations activities related to HIV/AIDS,

Taking note of the decisions of the United Nations Development Programme, the United Nations Children's Fund, the United Nations Population Fund, the World Health Organization the United Nations Educational, Scientific and Cultural Organization and the World Bank to undertake a joint and co-sponsored United Nations programme on HIV/AIDS, on the basis of co-ownership, collaborative planning and execution, and an equitable sharing of responsibility,

Noting that the World Health Organization is to be responsible for the administration in support of the programme, including during the transition period,

Emphasizing that the global HIV/AIDS epidemic affects every country of the world and that its magnitude and impact are greatest in developing countries,

Emphasizing also the urgent need to mobilize fully all United Nations system organizations and other development partners in the global response to HIV/AIDS, in a coordinated manner and according to the comparative advantages of each organization,

1 Endorses the establishment of a joint and co-sponsored United Nations programme on HIV/AIDS, as outlined in the annex to the present resolution, subject to further review by April 1995 of progress made towards its implementation;
2 Calls for the full implementation of the programme by January 1996, and requests that a report confirming its implementation be submitted to the Economic and Social Council at its organizational session for 1996;
3 Notes that further details of the programme are being developed by the Inter-Agency Working Group that has been established by the six co-sponsors;
4 Invites the six co-sponsors to take immediate steps to transform the Inter-Agency Working Group into a formally constituted Committee of Co-sponsoring Organizations, comprising the heads of those organizations or their specifically designated representatives, which would function under a rotational chairmanship, establish a transition team and assume interim responsibility, inter alia, for overseeing the transition process leading to the full implementation of the programme;
5 Also invites the six co-sponsors, through the Committee, to initiate action to fill the position of director of the joint and co-sponsored programme as soon as possible, through an open, wide-ranging search process, including consultation with Governments and other concerned parties, and to submit their nominee to the Secretary-General, who will make the appointment;
6 Urges the six co-sponsors, through the Committee, to initiate, as soon as possible, programme activities at the country level, as well as any other programme elements on which there is already full consensus;
7 Stresses that priority should be given to the programme's activities at the country level, where the response to the urgent needs and problems posed by HIV/AIDS should be focused, and underlines the importance of the programme's country-level operations' functioning within the framework of national plans and priorities and a strengthened resident coordinator system, in accordance with General Assembly resolution 47/199;
8 Also stresses that during the transition process, the ongoing HIV/AIDS activities of each of the six co-sponsors should be maintained and/or enhanced, bearing in mind the need for these activities to fit

within national AIDS programmes and the general framework of the joint and co-sponsored programme;

9 Requests the six co-sponsors, through the Committee, to produce the following by January 1995, for the consideration of the Economic and Social Council and other concerned parties: a comprehensive proposal specifying the programme's mission statement and the terms and conditions of co-ownership, and detailing the programme's organizational, programmatic, staffing, administrative and financial elements, including proposed budgetary allocations, and to attach to this proposal an annex containing the proposed legal document that the six co-sponsors will sign to establish the programme formally;

10 Encourages the active involvement of the Task Force on HIV/AIDS Coordination during the programme's detailed development phase, through the direct provision of assistance to the Committee, in accordance with the Committee's requirements;

11 Requests the President of the Economic and Social Council to organize, in cooperation with the Committee of Co-sponsoring Organizations, informal open-ended consultations to be held as soon as possible for the purpose of deciding on the specific composition of the programme coordinating board that will govern the programme, interacting periodically with the Committee during the transition period to facilitate progress towards programme implementation, and reviewing the detailed programme proposal after it is received from the Committee, with a view to making appropriate recommendations on the proposal not later than April 1995.

44th plenary meeting, 26 July 1994

Annex

I. PROGRAMME OUTLINE

1. The co-sponsored United Nations programme on HIV/AIDS represents an internationally coordinated response to the HIV/AIDS pandemic. The programme comprises the following United Nations system organizations: the United Nations Development Programme, the United Nations Children's Fund, the United Nations Population Fund, the World Health Organization, the United Nations Educational, Scientific and Cultural Organization and the World Bank. The programme has been formally endorsed by the Executive Boards of the World Health Organization

(resolution EB93.R5) and the United Nations Educational, Scientific and Cultural Organization (resolution 144EX-5.1.5); the other four co-sponsors have also committed themselves to full participation.

2. The fundamental characteristics that define the programme are set out below.

II. OBJECTIVES

3. The objectives of the programme are to:
   (a) Provide global leadership in response to the epidemic;
   (b) Achieve and promote global consensus on policy and programmatic approaches;
   (c) Strengthen the capacity of the United Nations system to monitor trends and ensure that appropriate and effective policies and strategies are implemented at the country level;
   (d) Strengthen the capacity of national Governments to develop comprehensive national strategies and implement effective HIV/AIDS activities at the country level;
   (e) Promote broad-based political and social mobilization to prevent and respond to HIV/AIDS within countries, ensuring that national responses involve a wide range of sectors and institutions;
   (f) Advocate greater political commitment in responding to the epidemic at the global and country levels, including the mobilization and allocation of adequate resources for HIV/AIDS-related activities.

4.7 In fulfilling these objectives, the programme will collaborate with national Governments, intergovernmental organizations, non-governmental organizations, groups of people living with HIV/AIDS, and United Nations system organizations.

III. CO-SPONSORSHIP

5. The HIV/AIDS epidemic is a global concern. Inter-agency cooperation is vital for ensuring the mobilization of resources and the effective implementation of a coordinated programme of activities throughout the United Nations system.

6. The programme will draw upon the experience and strengths of the six co-sponsors to develop its strategies and policies, which will be incorporated in turn into their programmes and activities. The co-sponsors will share responsibility for the development of the programme, contribute equally to its strategic direction and receive

from it policy and technical guidance relating to the implementation of their HIV/AIDS activities. In this way, the programme will also serve to harmonize the HIV/AIDS activities of the co-sponsors.

7. The programme will be managed by a director, who will focus on the programme's overall strategy, technical guidance, research and development, and the global budget. The co-sponsors will contribute to the resource needs of the programme at levels to be determined. The World Health Organization will be responsible for the administration in support of the programme.

8. Other United Nations system organizations concerned with the HIV/AIDS epidemic may be encouraged to join the programme as co-sponsors in the future.

IV. FUNCTIONAL RESPONSIBILITIES

9. The programme will build on the capacities and comparative advantages of the co-sponsors. At the global level, the programme will provide support in policy formulation, strategic planning, technical guidance, research and development, advocacy and external relations. This will include normative activities relating to HIV/AIDS in areas such as social and economic planning, population, culture, education, community development and social mobilization, sexual and reproductive health, and women and adolescents.

10. At the country level, the programme will provide support to the resident coordinator system. Co-sponsors will incorporate the normative work undertaken at the global level on policy, strategy and technical matters into their HIV/AIDS activities, consistent with national plans and priorities. An important function of the programme will be to strengthen national capacities to plan, coordinate, implement and monitor the overall response to HIV/AIDS. The participation in the programme of six organizations of the United Nations system will ensure the provision of technical and financial assistance to national activities in a coordinated multisectoral manner. This will strengthen intersectoral coordination of HIV/AIDS activities and will facilitate further incorporation of these activities in national programme and planning processes.

11. While the programme will not have a uniform regional structure, it will support intercountry or regional activities that may be required in response to the epidemic, utilizing regional mechanisms of the co-sponsors where appropriate.

V. FLOW OF PROGRAMME FUNDS

12. Funds for programme activities at the global level will be obtained through appropriate common global means. Contributions to the programme will be channelled in accordance with the global budget and work plan.
13. Funding for country-level activities will be obtained primarily through the existing fund-raising mechanisms of the co-sponsors. These funds will be channelled through the disbursement mechanisms and procedures of each organization.

VI. FIELD-LEVEL COORDINATION

14. It is recognized that national Governments have the ultimate responsibility for the coordination of HIV/AIDS issues at the country level. To this end, the arrangements of the programme for coordinating HIV/AIDS activities will complement and support national development planning.
15. The coordination of field-level activities will be undertaken through the United Nations resident coordinator system within the framework of General Assembly resolutions 44/211 and 47/199. This will involve a theme group on HIV/AIDS established by the resident coordinator and comprising representatives of the six co-sponsors and other United Nations system organizations. The chairperson of the theme group will be selected by consensus from among the United Nations system representatives. It is intended that the theme group will help the United Nations system integrate more effectively its efforts with national coordination mechanisms. To support the coordination process, in a number of countries the programme will recruit a country staff member, who will assist the chairperson of the theme group in carrying out his or her functions.

VII. ORGANIZATIONAL STRUCTURE

16. A programme director will be appointed by the Secretary-General upon the recommendation of the co-sponsors. This will follow a search process undertaken by the co-sponsors which will include consultation with Governments and other interested parties. The director will report directly to the programme coordinating board, which will serve as the governance structure for the programme. Annual reports prepared by the director will be submitted to the board and will also be made available to the governing body of each of the co-sponsors.

17. The composition of the programme coordinating board will be determined on the basis of open-ended consultations, as outlined in operative paragraph 11 of the present resolution. In exercising its governance role, the board will have ultimate responsibility for all policy and budgetary matters. It will also review and decide upon the planning and execution of the programme. Its detailed responsibilities and meeting schedule will be specified in a document containing its terms of reference, which is currently being prepared.

18. The programme will also have a committee of co-sponsoring organizations, which will serve as a standing committee of the board. It will comprise one representative from each of the co-sponsors. The committee will meet regularly and will facilitate the input of the co-sponsors into the strategy, policies and operations of the programme.

19. Through consultation with interested non-governmental organizations, a mechanism will be established to ensure their meaningful participation in the programme, so that they can provide information, perspectives and advice to the board, based on their experience and involvement with HIV/AIDS issues.

Appendix 3
Division of responsibility among
UNAIDS co-sponsors

Technical support areas	Lead Organizations	Main Partners
1. STRATEGIC PLANNING, GOVERNANCE AND FINANCIAL MANAGEMENT		
HIV/AIDS, development, governance and mainstreaming, including instruments such as PRSPs, and enabling legislation, human rights and gender	UNDP	ILO, UNAIDS Secretariat, UNESCO, UNICEF, WHO, World Bank, UNFPA; UNHCR
Support to strategic, prioritized and costed national plans; financial management; human resources; capacity and infrastructure development; impact alleviation and sectoral work	World Bank	ILO, UNAIDS Secretariat, UNDP, UNESCO, UNICEF, WHO
Procurement and supply management, including training	UNICEF	UNDP, UNFPA, WHO, World Bank
HIV/AIDS workplace policy and programmes, private-sector mobilization	ILO	UNESCO, UNDP
2. SCALING UP INTERVENTIONS		
Prevention		
Prevention of HIV transmission in healthcare settings, blood safety, counselling and testing, sexually-transmitted infection diagnosis and treatment, and linkage of HIV prevention with AIDS treatment services	WHO	UNICEF, UNFPA, ILO
Provision of information and education, condom programming, prevention for young people outside schools and prevention efforts targeting vulnerable groups (except injecting drug users, prisoners and refugee populations)	UNFPA	ILO, UNAIDS Secretariat, UNESCO, UNICEF, UNODC, WHO
Prevention of mother-to-child transmission (PMTCT)	UNICEF, WHO	UNFPA, WFP
Prevention for young people in education institutions	UNESCO	ILO, UNFPA, UNICEF, WHO, WFP
Prevention of transmission of HIV among injecting drug users and in prisons	UNODC	UNDP, UNICEF, WHO, ILO
Overall policy, monitoring and coordination on prevention	UNAIDS Secretariat	All Cosponsors
Treatment, care and support		
Antiretroviral treatment and monitoring, prophylaxis and treatment for opportunistic infections (adults and children)	WHO	UNICEF
Care and support for people living with HIV, orphans and vulnerable children, and affected households	UNICEF	WFP, WHO, ILO
Dietary/nutrition support	WFP	UNESCO, UNICEF, WHO
Addressing HIV in emergency, reconstruction and security settings		
Strengthening HIV/AIDS response in context of security, uniformed services and humanitarian crises	UNAIDS Secretariat	UNHCR, UNICEF, WFP, WHO, UNFPA
Addressing HIV among displaced populations (refugees and IDPs)	UNHCR	UNESCO, UNFPA, UNICEF, WFP, WHO, UNDP
3. MONITORING AND EVALUATION, STRATEGIC INFORMATION, KNOWLEDGE SHARING AND ACCOUNTABILITY		
Strategic information, knowledge sharing and accountability, coordination of national efforts, partnership building, advocacy, and monitoring and evaluation, including estimation of national prevalence and projection of demographic impact	UNAIDS Secretariat	ILO, UNDP, UNESCO, UNFPA, UNHCR, UNICEF, UNODC, WFP, WHO, World Bank
Establishment and implementation of surveillance for HIV, through sentinel/population-based surveys	WHO	UNAIDS Secretariat

Figure A3

Notes

Introduction

1 UNAIDS and WHO, *AIDS Epidemic Update: December 2007* (Geneva, Switzerland: UNAIDS and WHO, December 2007). Advances in the methodology used by UNAIDS and the WHO for estimations of HIV/AIDS epidemics worldwide in 2007 resulted in substantial reductions in the estimates of the numbers of persons living with HIV in the world. The previous annual *AIDS Epidemic Update* reported that in 2006 an estimated 39.5 million people were infected with HIV worldwide, 4.3 million people were newly infected, and 2.9 million died from AIDS-related illnesses.

2 Sub-Saharan Africa with just over 10 percent of the world's population accounts for about two-thirds of the total global HIV infections.

3 Good accounts of these past plagues are found in Arno Karlen, *Man and Microbes: Disease and Plagues in History and Modern Times* (New York: Simon and Schuster Paperbacks, 1995); Michael Oldstone, *Viruses, Plagues and History* (Oxford: Oxford University Press, 1998); Alfred Crosby, *America's Forgotten Pandemic: The Influenza of 1918* (Cambridge: Cambridge University Press, new edition, 2003); John M. Barry, *The Great Influenza: The Epic Story of the Deadliest Plague in History* (New York and London: Viking and Penguin Books, 2004).

4 For details on these and other recent epidemics see Thomas Abraham, *Twenty-first Century Plague: The Story of SARS* (Baltimore, Md.: Johns Hopkins University Press, 2007); Grattan Woodson, *The Bird Flu* (Deerfield Beach, Fla.: Health Communications Inc., 2005); Laurie Garrett, *The Coming Plague: Newly Emerging Diseases in a World out of Balance* (New York: Penguin Books, 1995); Paul Farmer, *Infections and Inequalities: The Modern Plagues* (Berkeley, Cal.: University of California Press, 2001).

5 Peter Piot, "Why AIDS Is Exceptional," speech given at the London School of Economics, 8 February 2005.

6 See Tony Barnett, "HIV/AIDS, a Long-Wave Event: Sundering the Intergenerational Bond," in *AIDS and Governance*, ed. Nana Poku, Alan Whiteside, and Bjorg Sandkjaer (Aldershot: Ashgate, 2007), 29–47; also Tony Barnett and Alan Whiteside, *AIDS in the Twenty-First century: Disease and Globalisation* (Basingstoke: Palgrave Macmillan, 2002).

7 According to UNAIDS, less than 5 percent of those in need of anti-retroviral treatment for AIDS in SSA are receiving treatment.

8 ILO Programme on HIV/AIDS and the World of Work (ILO/AIDS), *HIV/ AIDS and Work in a Globalizing World* (Geneva, Switzerland: ILO, 2006).

9 For more information on gender inequalities and disparities in the context of HIV/AIDS, see Sofia Gruskin, "Negotiating the Relationship between HIV/AIDS to Reproductive Health and Reproductive Rights," *American University Law Review* 44, (1995): 1191–205; Julie L. Andreff, "The Power and Imbalance between Men and Women and its Effects on the Rampant Spread of HIV/AIDS among Women," *Human Rights Brief* 9, no. 24 (2001), available at http:www.wcl.american.edu.hrbrief/09/hiv.cfm

10 See Franklyn Lisk, "The Labour Market and Employment Implications of HIV/AIDS," ILO/AIDS Working Paper no. 1 (Geneva, Switzerland: ILO, 2002); Desmond Cohen, "Human Capital and the HIV Epidemic in Sub-Saharan Africa," ILO/AIDS Working Paper no. 2 (Geneva, Switzerland: ILO, 2002); Ibrahima Coulibaly, "The Macroeconomic Impact of HIV/ AIDS: A Cross-Country Analysis," ILO/AIDS Research and Policy Paper (Geneva, Switzerland: ILO, 2006).

11 The MDG's are derived from the Millennium Declaration, which was adopted by the United Nations General Assembly at a special summit in September 2000; they are time-bound targets for key aspects of well-being aimed broadly at eradicating extreme poverty and achieving sustainable development by 2015. One of the eight MDGs is aimed at controlling and reversing the spread of HIV. See Sakiko Fukada-Parr, *Millennium Development Goals (MDGs): For a People-Centered Development Agenda?* (London: Routledge, forthcoming).

12 See Desmond Cohen, "Poverty and HIV/AIDS in Sub-Saharan Africa," UNDP Issues Paper no. 27 (New York: UNDP, 1998); and Franklyn Lisk and Desmond Cohen, "Regional Responses to HIV/AIDS: A Global Public Goods Approach," in *AIDS and Governance*, ed. Nana Poku, Alan Whiteside, and Bjorg Sandkjaer (Aldershot: Ashgate, 2007), 237–58.

13 The private sector has been contributing to HIV/AIDS efforts through business coalitions at global, regional and national levels and through collaboration with global institutions such as UNSAIDS, WHO, UNICEF, ILO and the Global Fund. For example, in January 2008 the Global Fund announced the launch of a new program, Global Fund Corporate Champions, with Chevron Corporation making an inaugural contribution of $30 million over three years for Global Fund-supported programs in Africa and Asia.

14 The "Declaration of Commitment on HIV/AIDS," which was adopted by the United Nations General Assembly Special Session on HIV/AIDS held in New York, 25–27 June 2001.

1 The evolution of HIV/AIDS as a global epidemic and early global response

1 See John Iliffe, *A History of the African AIDS Epidemic* (Oxford: James Currey, 2006) for a useful account of the earliest convincing evidence of HIV.

2 One "theory" was that the virus had originated from African monkeys and transferred to humans (apparently through consumption of monkey meat); another was that it was linked to the accidental "escape" of virus during

experimentation on chimpanzees by American scientists working on an oral polio vaccine project in Zaire. For more on conspiracy theories on the origin of AIDS, see Lawrence Altman, "Scientists say African Chimpanzee Species has Similar Non-Fatal Virus," *New York Times,* 1 February 1999; Jan Kuby and Susanne Leb, *Biology 330 Lecture Guide: AIDS: The Biology of a Modern Epidemic* (San Francisco, Cal.: California State University, 1999). WHO eventually agreed in 1987 to link the cause of AIDS to "one or more naturally-occurring retroviruses of undetermined origin." For the official determination of the cause of AIDS by the WHO, see World Health Assembly resolution of May 1987 in WHO Handbook, *Resolutions and Decisions of the World Health Assembly and the Executive Board,* 3rd edition, 1985–92 (Geneva, Switzerland: WHO, 1992). The scientific magazine, *Nature,* carried an article in October 2008 in which it was reported that researchers in 1998 had isolated the HIV-1 sequences from a blood sample taken in 1959 from an African woman in Leopoldville – now Kinshasa, the capital of the Democratic Republic of the Congo, suggesting that HIV has been infecting humans for nearly 50 years, see Heidi Ledford, "Tissue Sample Suggests that HIV has been Infecting Humans for a Century: 48-year-old Lymph Node Biopsy Reveals the History of the Deadly Virus," *Nature News,* published online 1 October 2008 at www.nature.com/news/2008/081001/full/new.2008.1143.html

3 Centers for Disease Control and Prevention (CDC), "Pneumocystis Pneumonia," *Morbidity and Mortality Week Report (MMWR)* 30, no. 21 (5 June 1981): 250.

4 Centers for Disease Control and Prevention, "First Report of AIDS," *MMWR* 50, no. 21 (2001): 429.

5 Iliffe, *A History of the African AIDS Epidemic,* 12.

6 John Cohen, "The Rise and Fall of Project SIDA," *Science Magazine* 278, no. 5343 (28 November 1997): 1565–68.

7 At its peak, Projet Sida had over 300 staff and experimented with new equipment to test blood for HIV, including among women in antenatal clinics; the project also identified the means of transmission as sexual intercourse and bidirectional exchange of blood by injection or transfusion, and infection from mother to child.

8 See Jonathan Mann, Daniel J. Tarantola, and Thomas Netter, *A Global Report: AIDS in the World* (Cambridge, Mass.: Harvard University Press, 1992), 567–70.

9 Mann, Tarantola, and Netter, *A Global Report, AIDS in the World,* 568.

10 Cited in report by Thomas Netter, "UN Agency Announces Steps to Coordinate Fight against AIDS," *New York Times,* 23 September 1985.

11 Cited in Iliffe, *A History of the African AIDS Epidemic,* 68.

12 *Times of Zambia,* 11 September 1985, cited in Iliffe, *A History of the African AIDS Epidemic,* 68.

13 Mahler was later to admit that denials about the heterosexual basis of the HIV/AIDS epidemic and its potential to become a global problem had contributed to the delay in WHO's response to the epidemic: "I know that many people at first refused to believe that a crisis was upon us. I know because I was one of them" (speech to the plenary session of the Fourth International conference on AIDS, Stockholm: WHO, July 1988).

14 Netter, "UN Agency Announces Steps to Coordinate Fight against AIDS."

2 The rise and fall of the WHO's Global Programme on AIDS (GPA)

1 UNAIDS is discussed in the next chapter.
2 In Lawrence K. Altman, "Global Program to Combat AIDS 'Disaster,'" *New York Times*, 21 November 1986; and Halfden Mahler, "Statement by Dr. H. Mahler at an Informal Briefing on AIDS to the 42nd Session of the United Nations General Assembly," (Geneva, Switzerland: World Health Organization (WHO), 1987); and Jonathan Mann, "Statement at an Informal Briefing on AIDS to the 42nd Session of the United Nations General Assembly" (Geneva, Switzerland: WHO, 1987), both also referenced in Elizabeth Fee and Manon Parry, "Jonathan Mann, HIV/AIDS, and Human Rights," *Journal of Public Health Policy* 29, no. 1 (2008): 54–71.
3 Within four years (1986–90), the budget of the GPA increased from about US$1 million to nearly US$100 million. See the Budget on GPA reported to the WHO Executive Board.
4 WHO Fortieth World Health Assembly, *Global Strategy for the Prevention and Control of AIDS*, May 1978, WHA40/26.
5 Halfden Mahler, "Statement by Dr. H. Mahler at an Informal Briefing on AIDS to the 42nd Session of the United Nations General Assembly" (Geneva, Switzerland: World Health Organization, 1987).
6 United Nations General Assembly resolution 42, 26 October 1987.
7 WHO Forty-Fifth World Health Assembly, *Global Strategy for the Prevention and Control of AIDS: 1992, update*, 28 February 1992, WHA45/29.
8 World Health Organization in association with International Labour Office, "Statement from the Consultation on AIDS and the Workplace," 27–29 June 1988, WHO/GPA/88.7 Rev. 1.
9 A rights-based approach addresses HIV-related discrimination as a violation of basic human rights, and is based on the fundamental principle of non-discrimination and all people's equality as enshrined in the 1948 UN Universal Declaration of Human Rights and other international human rights conventions and legally binding instruments. Discrimination on a basis of presumed or known HIV-positive status is therefore prohibited by a rights-based approach.
10 WHO, "Statement on the Consultation on Testing and Counseling for HIV Infection," 16–18 November 1992, WHO/GPA/INF.93.2.
11 Jonathan Mann, "Human Rights and AIDS: The Future of the Pandemic," POPLINE Document no. 12762, *Gaceta Medica de Mexico* 132, supplement 1 (1996): 13–20.
12 WHO, World Summit of Health Ministers, "The London Declaration on AIDS Prevention," POPLINE Document no. 10976 (unpublished, January 1988).
13 Daniel Tarantola, "The International AIDS Control Effort in Africa: The Big Picture and the Little Details," *Le Journal du Sida* 86–87 (June-July 1996): 109–16.
14 UNAIDS, *10th Anniversary Chronicles*, draft, (Geneva, Switzerland: UNAIDS, unpublished and undated).
15 By 1996, UNICEF had expanded its programs in AIDS awareness, prevention, and assistance to families and children in need of support for AIDS-related resources, and the Voices of Youth, a website where children can share information and insights on AIDS and other topics of interest

had been launched. See www.faqs.org/nutrition/Smi-Z/United-Nations-Children-s-Fund-UNICEF.html; last accessed 1 April 2008.

16 The World Bank launched the Multi-Country Aids Program (MAP) in 2000, but had started funding national AIDS programs since 1989 and to date has committed over US$2 billion to support national efforts.

17 United Nations ECOSOC resolution 42/8, 26 October 1987 and ECOSOC resolution 43/15, 27 July 1988.

18 WHO, "Report of the External Review of the World Health Organization's Global Programme on AIDS," January 1992, WHO/GPA/GMC/8.92.4.

19 WHO, "Report of the External Review of the World Health Organization's Global Programme on AIDS."

3 The birth of the Joint United Nations Programme on HIV/AIDS (UNAIDS)

1 WHO, "Annual Report of the World Health Assembly," 14 May 1993, WHA 46.37.

2 "Resolution on Joint and Co-Sponsored Programme on Human Immuno-deficiency Virus/ Acquired Immunodeficiency Syndrome, HIV/AIDS," United Nations ECOSOC resolution 1994/24, 29 July 1994. This resolution is reproduced in Appendix 2.

3 In addition to the co-sponsors of UNAIDS, the membership of IAAG includes other UN agencies outside the UNAIDS partnership. Later, following the establishment of UNAIDS, the UNAIDS secretariat assumed the responsibility for organizing IAAG meetings.

4 ECOSOC, 19 May 1995, E/1995/71: paras. 20–21.

5 "Resolution on the Management and Governance of the New Joint Co-sponsored UN Programme on HIV/AIDS," ECOSOC resolution 1995/5591, 3 July 1995.

6 Interview with Peter Piot, May 2007.

7 UNAIDS, "The Memorandum of Understanding on a Joint and Cosponsored United Nations Program on HIV/AIDS" (Geneva, Switzerland: UNAIDS, October 1995).

8 By 1995, the World Bank had already committed US$450 million toward HIV/AIDS response in low-income countries.

9 See UNAIDS, *UNAIDS Partnership: Working together on AIDS* (Geneva, Switzerland: UNAIDS, June 2004), for a summary of the various roles and sectors of activity of the co-sponsors.

10 See UNAIDS, *Full Matrix of the Division of Responsibility*, available at www.unaids.org/Resources/UNAIDS/images/Cosponsor/FullMatrix.gif. This is reproduced in Appendix 3.

11 For more information on the UNAIDS structure, see UNAIDS, www.unaids.org/en/AboutUNAIDS/default.asp (last accessed 18 September 2008).

12 UNAIDS Programme Coordinating Board, "Five Year Evaluation of UNAIDS, Report of the Ninth Meeting of the Programme Coordinating Board," 6 October 2000, PCB, (9)00.8.

13 United Nations, UN General Assembly Special Session (UNGASS) on HIV/AIDS, "Declaration of Commitment on HIV/AIDS," 25–27 June 2001. The UNGASS Declaration of Commitment established time-bound performance targets for key elements in the fight against HIV/AIDS with specific benchmarks for accountability.

14 "Examining Implications of HIV/AIDS on UN Peacekeeping Operations," UN Security Council resolution 2001/1308, 28 June 2001.
15 "Political Declaration on HIV/AIDS," United Nations General Assembly resolution 60/26, 22 June 2006.

4 HIV/AIDS and human rights

1 See Peter Aggleton, Kate Wood, Anne Malcolm, and Richard Parker, *HIV-related Stigma, Discrimination and Human Rights Violations* (Geneva, Switzerland: UNAIDS, 2005); Marie-Claude Chartier, "Legal Initiatives to Address HIV/AIDS in the World of Work," ILO/AIDS Research and Policy Analysis Working Paper 1, (Geneva, Switzerland: ILO/*AIDS*, February 2005).
2 Such as the "International Covenant of Civil and Political Rights," UN General Assembly resolution 2200A, 16 December 1966; "International Covenant of Economic, Social and Cultural Rights," UN General Assembly resolution 2200A, 16 December 1996; "Convention on the Elimination of All Forms of Discrimination against Women," UN General Assembly resolution 34/180, 1979; "ILO Declaration on Fundamental Principles and Rights at Work," International Labour Conference Session 86, June 1998.
3 See WHO, *Macroeconomics and Health: Investing in Health for Economic Development*, Report of the Commission on Macroeconomics and Health (Geneva, Switzerland: WHO, 2001); WHO, *World Health Report* (Geneva, Switzerland: WHO, 2003); Bertrand G. Ramcharan, *Contemporary Human Rights Ideas* (London: Routledge, 2008); Julie A. Mertus, *The United Nations and Human Rights: A Guide for a New Era*, 2nd edition (London: Routledge, 2009); Bertrand G. Ramcharan, *Preventive Human Rights Strategies in a World of New Threats and Challenges* (London: Routledge, forthcoming).
4 UNAIDS, "14th Meeting Report of the Executive Director UNAIDS Programme Coordination Board," 26–27 June 2003, PCB (14)03.2; UNAIDS, *Handbook for Legislators on HIV/AIDS Law and Human Rights: Action to Combat HIV/AIDS in View of its Devastating Human, Economic and Social Impact* (Geneva, Switzerland: UNAIDS, 1999).
5 UN General Assembly resolution 26/2, 27 June 2001.
6 UN General Assembly resolution 55/2, 8 September 2000.
7 UN General Assembly resolution 60/262, 2 June 2006.
8 World Health Assembly, "Paris AIDS Summit 1995," 1–12 May, 1995, WHA48.27.
9 UNAIDS, *From Principle to Practice: Greater Involvement of People Living With and Affected by HIV/AIDS (GIPA)* (Geneva, Switzerland: UNAIDS, 1999); UNAIDS, *Greater Involvement of People Living with HIV/AIDS: Report of UNAIDS Nairobi Consultation* (Geneva, Switzerland: UNAIDS, 2000).
10 See, for example, UNAIDS, *GIPA-based interventions to Reduce Stigma and Discrimination in the Healthcare Sector and the World of Work: A Case Study from Delhi* (New Delhi, India: UNAIDS India, March 2004).
11 OHCHR, "Report of an International Consultation on AIDS and Human Rights," 26–28 July 1989, HR/PUB/90/2.

12 UN Commission for Human Rights resolution 21, 24 February 1995.

13 UN Commission on Human Rights resolution 196/43, 19 April 1996.

14 UN, "Report of the Secretary-General to the Commission on Human Rights," 1997, E/CN.4/1997/37, annex 1. The international guidelines were eventually published by the OHCHR and UNAIDS as OHCHR, "HIV/AIDS and Human Rights: Second International Consultation on HIV/AIDS and Human Rights," 23–25 September 1996, fourth reprint, April 2004.

15 OHCHR and UNAIDS, *International Guidelines on HIV/AIDS and Human Rights, 2006 Consolidated Version* (Geneva, Switzerland: OHCHR and UNAIDS, 2006).

16 "The Protection of Human Rights in the context of HIV and AIDS," UN General Assembly resolution 1999/49, 27 April 1999.

17 "Declaration of Commitment on HIV/AIDS," UN General Assembly resolution S26/2, 27 June 2001.

18 "Annex, Political Declaration on HIV/AIDS," UN General Assembly resolution 60/262, 2 June 2006.

19 WHO, *WHO Constitution* (Geneva, Switzerland: WHO, 1946). www.who. int/governance/eb/who_constitution_en.pdf

20 Jonathan Mann, Lawrence Gostin, Sofia Gruskin, Troyen Brennan, Zita Lazzarini, and Harvey V. Fineberg, "Health and Human Rights," *Health and Human Rights: An International Journal* 1, no. 1 (1994): 6–23; Sofia Gruskin and Daniel Tarantola, "Health and Human Rights," Francois-Xavier Bagnoud Centre for Health and Human Rights Working Paper Series, no. 10 (2000).

21 The "3 by 5" initiative was launched by the then new director-general of the WHO, Lee Jong-Wook, in 2003 as a global strategy to reach the target of treating 3 million people with AIDS by the end of 2005. It was based on simplified and standardized guidelines on ART in resource-constrained settings; provision of HIV and AIDS drugs and diagnostics; standardized monitoring and evaluation tools; and training for professional and lay health workers at national and community levels.

22 A UN General Assembly resolution adopted on 23 December 2005 requested UNAIDS and its co-sponsors to assist in "facilitating ... goal of universal to treatment by 2010 for all those who need it." The "Political Declaration on HIV/AIDS" adopted by the UN General Assembly in June 2006 called on countries to significantly scale-up their response to HIV/AIDS toward universal access to HIV prevention, treatment, care, and support by 2010.

23 Family Health Institute, "Family Planning Choices for Women with HIV," *Population Reports INFO Project* (Baltimore, Md.: Johns Hopkins Bloomberg School of Public Health, September 2007).

24 For example, the UN Convention on the Elimination of All Forms of Discrimination against Women, and the UN Convention on the Rights of the Child.

25 This position was reversed by an executive order of President Barack Obama within a few days of being sworn in as Bush's successor in January 2009.

26 UNFPA, "The ICPD Vision: How Far Has the 11 Year Journey Taken Us?" report from the UNFPA Panel Discussion at the IUSSPXXV

International Population Conference, 19 February 2005, www.unfpa.org/upload/lib_pub_file594_filename_IUSSP%20icpd-vision.pdf

27 Smith Gordon and Naim Moises, *Altered States: Globalization, Sovereignty and Governance* (Ottawa, Canada: IDRC, 2000), 40.

28 UNAIDS, *2006 Report on the Global AIDS Epidemic* (Geneva, Switzerland: UNAIDS, 2006).

29 UNICEF, UNAIDS and USAID, *Children on the Brink, 2004: A Joint Report of New Orphan Estimates and a Framework of Action* (New York: USAID, 2004).

30 WHO Global Programme on AIDS and ILO, "Statement from the Consultation on AIDS and the Workplace," 27–29 June 1988, WHO/GPA/INF/88.7.

31 See, ILO, *The ILO Code of Practice on HIV/AIDS and the World of Work* (Geneva, Switzerland: ILO, May 2001); Franklyn Lisk, "A Rights-based Approach to HIV/AIDS in the Workplace: The Role of the ILO and Its Constituents," *Law, Social Justice and Global Development Journal*, no. 1 (2007), available at www.go.warwick.ac.uk/elj/lgd/2007_1/lisk; Marie-Claude Chartier, "Legal Initiatives to Address HIV/AIDS in the World of Work," ILO/AIDS Research and Policy Analysis Working Paper 1 (Geneva, Switzerland: ILO/*AIDS*, February 2005).

32 "Convention Concerning Discrimination in Respect of Employment," ILO Convention no. 111, 1958; "Convention Concerning Termination of Employment," ILO Convention no. 158, 22 June 1982); "Convention Concerning Occupational Health and Safety," ILO Convention no. 155, 22 June 1981).

33 ILO, *An ILO Code of Practice on HIV/AIDS and the World of Work* (Geneva, Switzerland: ILO, 2001).

34 "Declaration of Commitment," UN General Assembly Special Session on HIV/AIDS (UNGASS), June 2001.

35 UNGASS, "Declaration of Commitment."

36 UNGASS, "Declaration of Commitment."

37 UN General Assembly resolution 60/262, 2 June 2006.

5 HIV/AIDS as a security threat

1 The literature is extensive on the subject. See, for example, Kanti Bajpai, *Human Security: Concept and Measurement*, Occasional Paper no. 19 (Notre Dame, Ind.: Kroc Institute for International Peace Studies, 2000); Amartya Sen, "Why Human Security?", paper presented at the International Symposium on Human Security (Tokyo, Japan: Ministry of Foreign Affairs, 28 July 2000); Rob McRae and Don Hubert, eds., *Human Security and the New Diplomacy: Protecting People, Promoting Peace* (Montreal and Kingston, Canada: McGill-Queen's University Press, 2001); Lincoln Chen, Sakiko Fukuda-Parr, and Ellen Seidensticker, eds., *Human Insecurity in a Global World* (Cambridge, Mass.: Global Equity Initiative, Asia Center, Harvard University Press, 2003); Neil MacFarlane and Yuen Foong Khong, *Human Security and the UN: A Critical History* (Bloomington, Ind.: Indiana University Press, 2006); Don Hubert, *Human Security* (London: Routledge, forthcoming).

2 UNAIDS, *2006 Global Report* (Geneva, Switzerland: UNAIDS, June 2007).

3 Stefan Elbe, "HIV/AIDS and the Changing Landscape of War in Africa," *International Security* 27, no. 2 (2002): 159.

4 See Tony Barnett, "A Long-Wave Event: HIV/AIDS, Politics, Governance and Security: Sundering the Intergenerational Bond?" *International Affairs* 82, no. 2 (2006): 297–313; Paul Spiegel, "HIV/AIDS among Conflict-Affected and Displaced Populations: Dispelling the Myths and Taking Action," *Disaster* 28, no. 3 (2004): 322–29; Alex De Waal and Alan Whiteside, "New Variant Famine: AIDS and Food Crisis in Southern Africa," *Lancet* 362 (October 2003): 1234–37.

5 World Bank, *The World Development Report 2000/2001* (New York: Oxford University Press, 2001); World Bank, *The World Development Report: Attacking Poverty 2001/2002* (New York: Oxford University Press, 2002). See also, World Bank Post-conflict Unit, *Security, Poverty Reduction and Sustainable Development: Challenges for the New Millennium* (Washington, D.C.: World Bank, 1999).

6 UNDP, *Human Development Report 1994* (New York: Oxford University Press, 1994).

7 For example, agreement on the establishment of the Global Fund to Fight HIV/AIDS, Tuberculosis and Malaria (Global Fund); also the convening of special sessions of the UN General Assembly on the global HIV/AIDS epidemic in 2001 and 2006.

8 See for example, Laurie Garrett, *HIV and National Security: Where Are the Links?* (New York: Council on Foreign Relations, 2005); Peter Chalk, "Infectious Diseases and the Threat to National Security," *Jane's Intelligence Review*, no. 13 (2001): 48–51; Colin McInnes, "HIV/AIDS and National Security," in *AIDS and Governance*, ed. Nana K. Poku, Alan Whiteside, and Bjorg Sandkjaer (Aldershot: Ashgate, 2007), 93–113; Robert Ostergard, "Politics in the Hot Zone: AIDS and National Security," *Third World Quarterly* 23, no. 2 (2002): 333–50.

9 Kondwani Chirambo, "AIDS, Politics and Governance: The Impact of HIV/AIDS on the Electoral Process in Namibia, Malawi, Senegal, South Africa, Tanzania and Zambia," in *Governance of HIV/AIDS: Making Participation and Accountability Count*, ed. Sophie Harman and Franklyn Lisk (London: Routledge, forthcoming).

10 See, for example, Elbe, "HIV/AIDS and the Changing Landscape of War in Africa"; "Session on HIV/AIDS in Africa," UN Security Council, 10 January 2000; Roxanne Bazergan "UN Peacekeepers and HIV/AIDS," *World Today* 57, no. 5 (May 2001): 6–8; Greg Mills, "AIDS and the South African Military: Timeworn Cliché or Time Bomb?" in *HIV/AIDS: A Threat to the African Renaissance?* Occasional paper (Johannesburg, South Africa: Konrad Adenauer Foundation, 2000); Lindy Heinecken, "Facing a Merciless Enemy: HIV/AIDS and the South African Armed Forces," *Armed Forces and Society* 29, no. 2 (2003): 281–300.

11 "Security Council Holds Debate on Impact of AIDS on Peace and Security in Africa," UNSC press release SC/6781, 10 January 2000. www.un.org/News/Press/docs/2000/20000110.sc6781.doc.html

12 National Intelligence Council, *National Security Estimate: The Global Infectious Disease Threat and Its Implications for the United States* (Washington, D.C.: National Intelligence Council, January 2000).

13 "Security Council Holds Debate on Impact of AIDS on Peace and Security in Africa," UN press release UNIS/SC/1173, 11 January 2000.

14 Al Gore, "Statement on AIDS in Africa," U.S. Mission to the UN (New York: UN Security Council, 10 January 2000).

15 See United Nations Security Council resolution 1308 (SC/6890), 17 January 2000.

16 "Security Council Presidential Statement Recognises Significant Progress Addressing HIV/AIDS Among Peacekeepers but Says Many Challenges Remain," UN Security Council 5228th meeting (S/8450), press release, 18 July 2005.

17 United Nations, *Report of the Secretary General's High Level Panel on Threats, Challenges and Change* (New York: United Nations, 2004), available at www.un.org/secureworld/

18 The 2004 Democratic presidential candidate, Senator John Kerry, is documented in Laurie Garrett, *HIV and National Security: Where Are the Links?* (New York: Council on Foreign Relations, 2005), 23; see also, The White House, *The National Security Strategy of the United States of America* (Washington, D.C.: U.S. Government, 2002).

19 National Intelligence Council, *The Next Wave of HIV/AIDS: Nigeria, Ethiopia, Russia, India and China* (Washington, D.C.: NIC, 2002). This report was also discussed at a meeting organized by the influential U.S. think tank, the Center for Strategic and International Studies, in Washington in October 2002.

20 See, for example, UNDP, *Human Development Report 1994: New Dimensions of Human Security* (New York: Oxford University Press, 1994); see also, Roland Paris, "Human Security: Paradigm Shift or Hot Air?" *International Security* 26, no. 2 (2001): 87–102; and Elbe, "HIV/AIDS and the Changing Landscape of War in Africa."

21 See Inter-Agency Standing Committee 2004, *Guidelines for HIV/AIDS in Emergency Settings*, http://data.unaids.org/Publications/External-Documents/IASC_Guidelines-Emergency-Settings_en.pdf

22 UN Inter-Agency Standing Committee (IASC) 2004, *Guidelines for HIV/AIDS in Emergency Settings.*

23 See IASC, "The need for HIV/AIDS Interventions in Emergency Settings" (Geneva, Switzerland: UN IASC, undated), http://data.unaids.org/Publications/External-Documents/IASC_EmergencyBrochure_en.pdf; Ulf Kristoffersson, "HIV/AIDS Among the Most Vulnerable," statement to ECOSOC Humanitarian Segment, UNAIDS, UNFPA, IFRC, WHO briefing (New York: UN AIDS Humanitarian Unit, 15 July 2002).

24 These were reported in a paper presented by UNAIDS to its governing body in December 2006, UNAIDS 19th meeting of the UNAIDS Programme Coordinating Board, "AIDS, Security and Humanitarian Response," Provisional agenda item 6 (Lusaka, Zambia, 6–8 December); see also UNAIDS Humanitarian Unit, *Quarterly Reports* (Copenhagen: UN Nordic Office, various issues, 2002–4); UNHCR, *HIV/AIDS Policies and Programmes 2005–2007* (Geneva, Switzerland: UNHCR, 2004).

25 See UNAIDS, *On the Frontline: A Review of the Policies and Programmes to Address HIV/AIDS Among Peacekeepers and Uniformed Personnel* (Geneva, Switzerland: UNAIDS, 2005).

26 At the end of 2006, there were nearly 100,000 international peacekeepers involved in about 30 UN missions worldwide. In addition, the UN was providing some support to peacekeeping operations of regional organizations such as the African Union. See Alan Whiteside, Alex De Waal, and T. Gerbre-Tensae, "AIDS, Security and the Military in Africa: A Sober Appraisal," *African Affairs*, no. 105 (April 2006): 10–41; Tony Barnett and Gwyn Prins, *HIV/AIDS and Security: Fact, Fiction and Evidence: A Report to UNAIDS: India Case Study* (London: LSE/*AIDS*, 2005); W. Soeprapto, S. Ertono, H. Hudoyo, J. Mascola, K. Porter, S. Gunawan, and A. L. Corwin, "HIV and Peacekeeping Operations in Cambodia," *Lancet* 346 (11 November 1995): 1304–5.

6 HIV/AIDS as a development challenge

1 See Martha Ainsworth and Mead Over, "AIDS and African Development," *The World Bank Research Observer* 9, no. 2 (1994): 203–40; Rene Bonnel, "HIV/AIDS: Does it Increase or Decrease Growth? What makes an Economy HIV-resistant?", paper presented at the International AIDS Network Symposium (Durban, South Africa, 2000); Alan Whiteside, "HIV/AIDS and Development; Failures of Vision and Imagination" in *AIDS and Governance,* ed. Nana Poku, Alan Whiteside and Bjorg Sandkjaer (Aldershot: Ashgate, 2007), 115–132.
2 An estimated 90 percent of those infected with HIV worldwide live in developing countries and about 70 percent in sub-Saharan Africa.
3 According to the ILO, over four-fifths of people living with HIV and AIDS globally are aged between 15 and 49 years, many in the prime of their productive lives, ILO, *HIV/AIDS and Work: Global Estimates, Impact and Responses* (Geneva, Switzerland: ILO/*AIDS*, 2004).
4 UN General Assembly Special Session on HIV/AIDS (UNGASS), "Declaration of Commitment on HIV/AIDS," New York, 25–27 June 2001.
5 UNGASS, "Declaration of Commitment on HIV/AIDS."
6 UNGASS, "Declaration of Commitment on HIV/AIDS."
7 WHO, *Macroeconomic and Health: Investing in Health for Development: The Report on the Commission on Macroeconomics and Health* (Geneva, Switzerland: WHO, 20 December 2001); also, WHO, "Macroeconomic and Health: An Update. Increasing Investments in Health Outcomes for the Poor," Second Consultation on Macroeconomics and Health (Geneva, Switzerland: WHO, October 2003).
8 UNGASS, "Declaration of Commitment on HIV/AIDS."
9 See for example, David Bloom and Ajay Mahal, "Does the AIDS Epidemic Threaten Economic Growth?" *Journal of Econometrics* 77, no. 1 (1997): 105–24; C. Arndt and J. D. Lewis, "The Macro Implications of HIV/AIDS in South Africa: A Preliminary Assessment," *The South African Journal of Economics* 68, no. 5 (December 2000): 856–87.
10 Robert Greener, Keith Jefferis and Happy Siphambe, "The Impact of HIV/ AIDS on Poverty and Inequality in Botswana," *The South African Journal of Economics* 68, no. 5 (December 2000): 888–915; N. Bechu, "The Impact of AIDS on the Economy of Families in Cote d'Ivoire: Changes in Consumption among AIDS-Affected Households," *AIDS Analysis Africa* 8, no.

1 (1998): 2–3; Alan Whiteside, "AIDS in Africa: Facts, Figures and the Extent of the Problem" in *Ethics and AIDS in Africa: The Challenge of Our Thinking,* ed. Anton A van Niekerk and Loretta M. Kopelman (Claremont, South Africa: David Philip Publishers, 2005), ch. 1, 15–38.

11 The Global Fund was conceived as a multilateral mechanism for funding HIV/AIDS, tuberculosis and malaria. Just five years after its establishment on the initiative of the G7/8, it has grown to become the largest funding agency of health programs globally with approved proposals worth nearly $6 billion for about 520 programs in over 130 countries, and over $3 billion already disbursed.

12 UN General Assembly resolution A/RES/55/2, 18 September 2000.

13 UN General Assembly High-level Meeting, New York, 2 June 2005.

14 The IMF coordinated the publication of a volume on HIV/AIDS which explored the economic, social and fiscal effects of the epidemic and the macroeconomic consequences, to mark World AIDS Day (December 1) in 2004; see Markus Haacker, *The Macroeconomics of HIV/AIDS* (Washington, D.C.: IMF, 2004). In the preface to the volume, the then IMF managing director, Rodrigo de Rato, observed that "the HIV/AIDS epidemic is a matter of serious concern—adversely affecting the development prospects of many of our member countries—that it calls for unprecedented actions," and concluded that because "the effects of the epidemic touch on virtually all aspects of a country's social, economic, demographic, and political development ... HIV/AIDS must be major issue of concern to the IMF" (p. ix). This was the first IMF book-length publication to focus exclusively on a public health issue. Earlier in 2000, the IMF had included a piece on "The Economic Impact of HIV/AIDS in Southern Africa" in its annual economic forecast, IMF, *World Economic Outlook* (Washington, D.C.: IMF, September 2000), 66–69.

15 "Statement by Marika Fahlen, Director, UNAIDS," at the International Conference on Financing for Development (Monterrey, Mexico, 19 March 2002), www.un.org/ffd/statements/unaidsE.htm

16 United Nations, *The Monterrey Consensus,* www.un.org/esa/ffd

17 United Nations World Summit on Sustainable Development, *The Johannesburg Plan of Implementation* (New York: United Nations, 2002), www.un.org/esa/susdev/documents/wssd

18 Commission for Africa, *Our Common Interest: Report of the Commission for Africa* (London: March 2005). The Commission for Africa was set up and chaired by Prime Minister Tony Blair and its membership included heads of government, ministers, international diplomats, eminent economists and policy-makers from both developed and developing countries.

19 G8, "The Gleneagles Communiqué," www.britishembassy.gov.uk/Files/kfile/PostG8_Gleneagles_Communique,0.pdf

20 Mead Over, "The Macroeconomic Impact of AIDS in Sub-Saharan Africa," Technical Working Paper no. 3 (Africa Regional Department, Population, Health and Nutrition Division, World Bank, 1993); John T. Cuddington, "Modeling the Macroeconomic Effects of AIDS with an Application to Tanzania," *The World Bank Economic Review,* 7, no. 2 (1993): 173–89; René Bonnel, "HIV/AIDS and Economic Growth: A Global Perspective," *The South African Journal of Economics* 68, no. 5 (December 2000): 820–55.

21 World Bank, *Confronting AIDS: Public Priorities in a Global Epidemic* (Washington, D.C.: World Bank, 1997).

22 World Bank Africa Region, *Intensifying Action Against HIV/AIDS in Africa: Responding to a Development Crisis* (Washington, D.C.: World Bank, 2007).

23 World Bank, *The World Bank's Global HIV/AIDS Program of Action* (Washington, D.C.: World Bank, August 2005).

24 MAP has funded nearly 50,000 NGO, faith- and community-based activities mostly at grassroots level, in the context of MAP-approved country projects.

25 World Bank website, www.worldbank.org

26 This collaboration involved the organization between 2005 and 2007 of inter-agency country assistance missions and a series of sub-regional workshops on the integration of HIV/AIDS into poverty reduction strategy papers (PRSPs).

27 Financing of the global HIV/AIDS response through World Bank programs are discussed in detail in Chapter 9.

28 See Desmond Cohen, "Responding to the Socio-Economic Impact of the HIV Epidemic in Sub-Saharan Africa: Why a Systems Approach is Needed," UNDP Working Paper (New York: UNDP, 1999).

29 UNDP, *Mainstreaming HIV and AIDS in Sectors and Programmes: An Implementation Guide for National Responses* (New York: UNDP, September 2005).

30 See, for example, UNDP, *Botswana Human Development Report 2000: Towards an AIDS-Free Generation* (Gaborone, Botswana: UNDP, 2000); UNDP, *Uganda Human Development Report 2002; The Challenge of HIV/AIDS: Maintaining the Momentum of Success* (Kampala, Uganda: UNDP, 2002); UNDP, *Zimbabwe Human Development Report 2003: Redirecting our Responses to HIV and AIDS* (Harare, Zimbabwe: UNDP, 2003); UNDP, *Zambia Human Development Report 2007: Enhancing Household Capacity to Respond to HIV and AIDS* (Lusaka, Zambia: UNDP, 2007).

31 The HDI was introduced by the UNDP in 1990 to emphasize the paradigm shift in the conceptualization of development from just economic growth to a more people-centered approach focusing on human well-being. See UNDP, *Human Development Report 1990* (New York: UNDP, 1990); UNDP, "HIV/AIDS and Human Development: Thematic Guidance Note," Human Development Report Office, National Human Development Report Series (New York: UNDP, 2005).

32 UN Economic Commission for Africa (ECA), "AIDS and Development," Theme Paper for the African Development Forum 2000 (Addis Ababa, Ethiopia: ECA, 3–7 December 2000); ECA, "AIDS: The Greatest Leadership Challenge," Africa Development Forum Conference Paper, (Addis Ababa, Ethiopia: ECA, December 2000).

33 CHGA commissioners included specialists like Peter Piot, head of UNAIDS, Richard Feachem, head of the Global Fund, and Paulo Teixeira from the Brazilian national AIDS program, in addition to African policy-makers and administrators such as the prime minister of Mozambique and the executive secretary of the ECA and the president of the African Development Bank.

34 Economic Commission on Africa, *Securing Our Future: Report of the Commission on HIV/AIDS and Governance in Africa* (Addis Ababa, Ethiopia: UN, 2008), www.uneca.org/chga/Report/CHGAReport.pdf

7 HIV/AIDS and human resource capacity

1 ILO Governing Body, "HIV/AIDS and Employment," Committee on Employment and Social Policy, March 2005, GB.292/ESP/5; ILO, *HIV/AIDS and Work: Global Estimates, Impact and Response 2004* (Geneva, Switzerland: ILO, 2005).
2 UNAIDS and WHO, *AIDS Epidemic Update* (Geneva, Switzerland: UNAIDS/WHO, various years).
3 UNAIDS, UNFPA, UNIFEM, "Confronting the Crisis," (Geneva, Switzerland and New York: UNAIDS, UNFPA, 2004), www.unfpa.org/hiv/women/report
4 These relate to the promotion of productive, decent, and remunerative employment and the protection of workers' rights, to support improvements in living standards and to contribute toward poverty reduction and sustainable social and economic development. See ILO, "Declaration of Fundamental Principles and Rights at Work" (Geneva, Switzerland: ILO, 1998); ILO Governing Body, "The Labour Market and Employment Implications of the HIV/AIDS Epidemic," Committee on Employment and Social Policy, March 2001, GB.280/ESP/5; ILO Governing Body, "HIV/AIDS and Employment," Employment and Social Policy Committee, March 2005, GB292/ESP/5.
5 ILO, *HIV/AIDS and Work: Global Estimates: Impact and Response 2004* (Geneva, Switzerland: ILO, 2005); ILO, *Global Estimates* (Geneva, Switzerland: ILO, 2005 and 2006); also Desmond Cohen, "Human Capital and the HIV Epidemic in Sub-Saharan Africa," ILO/*AIDS* Working Paper 2 (Geneva, Switzerland: ILO, June 2002).
6 Some of these losses are due to the direct effect of AIDS on labor supply through deaths and illnesses, but there are also losses due to labor migration from countries that are experiencing economic decline and social problems that are precipitated in part by the development impact of HIV/AIDS.
7 Desmond Cohen, "The impact of HIV/AIDS on Human Capital in Sub-Saharan Africa," ILO/AIDS Working Paper 2 (Geneva, Switzerland: ILO, 2002).
8 Paul Bennell, Karin Hyde, and Nicola Swainson, "The Impact of the HIV/AIDS Epidemic on the Education Sector in Sub-Saharan Africa: A Synthesis of Findings and Recommendations of Three Country Studies," working paper (Brighton, U.K.: University of Sussex, 2002); Dramane Oulai and Roy Carr-Hill, "Impact of HIV/AIDS on Education," International Institute for Educational Planning (IIEP), (Paris: UNESCO, September 2000); Michael J. Kelly, "Planning for Education in the Context of AIDS," IIEP (Paris: UNESCO, 2000).
9 See Institute for Democracy in South Africa (IDASA), "AIDS and Governance in Southern Africa: Emerging Theories and Perspectives," a report on the IDASA/UNDP Regional Governance and AIDS Forum, 2–4 April 2003 (Pretoria, South Africa: IDASA, 2003); Per Strand and Kondwani Chirambo, eds., *HIV/AIDS and Democratic Governance in South Africa: Illustrating the Impact on Electoral Processes* (Pretoria, South Africa: IDASA, 2005); Kondwani Chirambo, "AIDS, Politics and Governance: The Impact of HIV/AIDS on the Electoral Processes in Namibia, Malawi,

Senegal, South Africa, Tanzania and Zambia," paper presented at the University of Warwick/UNDP conference on Governance of HIV/AIDS Responses: Making Participation and Accountability Count, University of Warwick, U.K., November 2007.

10 Cited in Desmond Cohen, "The Impact of HIV/AIDS on the Workplace," unpublished paper prepared for ILO/*AIDS* (Geneva, Switzerland: ILO, 6 October 2004).

11 WHO, "Managing Exits from the Workforce" in *World Health Report 2006* (Geneva, Switzerland: WHO, 2006); WHO, *Migration of Health Professionals in Six Countries: A Synthesis Report* (Brazzaville, Congo: WHO Regional Office for Africa, 2004).

12 World Bank, *Health Workers Needed: Poor Left without Care in Africa's Rural Areas* (Washington, D.C.: World Bank, March 2008).

13 Michael A. Clemens and Gunilla Pettersson, "New Data on African Health Professionals Abroad," *Human Resources for Health* 6, no. 1 (2008): 1–11, www.human-resources-health.com/content/6/1/1. The study examined census data collected between 199 and 2000, and it focused on the employment of health workers originally from other countries in Australia, Belgium, Canada, France, Portugal, Spain, the U.K., and the U.S.A. The study counted health professionals who were born in Africa rather than those trained in the continent; the researchers felt that place of birth was a more accurate indication of the extent and effect of the problem, rather than training location, which can substantially underestimate the effect of shortages on a country's health system. See also Center for Global Development, "New Data on African Health Professionals Abroad," www.cgdev. org/doc/data/africa_health_emigration.xls

14 WHO and UNAIDS, *"3×5" Progress Report, December 2004* (Geneva, Switzerland: WHO, 2005).

15 WHO estimates that training a doctor in African countries could cost as much as $100,000 in public funds.

16 Quotation by Dr. Edward Mills of the British Columbia Centre for Excellence in HIV/AIDS, Vancouver, in a commentary (on an article by F. Omaswa, "Human Resources for Global Health: Time for Action Is Now") in *Lancet*, 371, no. 9613 (23–29 February 2008): 623–25. Mills is the lead author of the commentary/piece in the *Lancet* written with colleagues from Uganda, South Africa, Argentina, Ireland and the past and current presidents of the International AIDS Society (William Schabas, Jimmy Volmink, Roderick Walker, Nathan Ford, Aranka Anema, et al.). The Mills et al. piece and the quotation was reported in a piece by AFP (Paris) on 21 February 2008, "Poaching of Doctors from Africa Is 'International Crime': Lancet" (http:// afp.google.com/article/ALeqM5he6tg9Hg1NP-AdLSdz1VtGvcs3w, accessed 3/6/2008). The quotation appeared in the AFP piece as "The practice should therefore be viewed as an international crime." It was also reported by Reuters online on 21 February 2008 as "Recruiting African Health Workers a Crime—Lancet" by Maggie Fox, Health and Science Editor, Reuters, posted Thursday 21 February 2008, 6:30 p.m. EST.

17 Statement by James Johnson, BMA Chair of Council at its annual meeting on 27 June 2005, commenting on the decision of the U.K.'s National Health Service to end active recruitment of staff from sub-Saharan Africa, www.bma.org.uk/ap.nsf/content

18 Even in instances where domestic funds or external financial assistance may be available for improving pay and other conditions for these professionals, externally imposed constraints such as IMF "conditionalities" that put ceilings on public sector spending may stand in the way.

19 According to Jean-Philippe Chauzy, spokesman for IOM, Reuters wire report from Nairobi posted 27 April 2006, 1718 GMT; also, IOM, "Managing the Migration of Health Workers," *MHD/MHCW-05*, 08, April 2008; International Hospital Federation (IHF), Health Research and Educational Trust (HRET) and Health Services Research (HSR), "A Call for Action: Ensuring Global Human Resources for Health," proceedings report, International Conference Centre, Geneva, 2008.

20 WHO, *Taking Stock: Task Shifting to Tackle Health Worker Shortages*, December 2007, WHO/HSS/2007.2.

21 WHO, *Taking Stock: Health Worker Shortages and the Response to AIDS*, December 2007, WHO/HSS/2007.2. The huge difference between the two estimates is the result of two alternative analyses of costs—one assumes a doubling of health workers' salaries and the other a five-fold increase—and variations in health expenses between countries.

22 WHO, *Taking Stock: Task Shifting to Tackle Health Worker Shortages*.

23 The Global Health Workforce Alliance (GHWA) and WHO, "Working Together to Overcome the Crisis in Human Resources for Health: Business Plan," (Geneva, Switzerland: GHWA, 2006).

24 World Bank, *Health Workers Needed: Poor Left without Care in Africa's Rural Areas*.

8 Financing the global HIV/AIDS response

1 See Jonathan Mann, Daniel Tarantola, and Thomas Netter, eds., *AIDS in the World* (Cambridge, Mass.: Harvard University Press, 1992), for a useful account of the early period of the international financing of the global HIV/AIDS response.

2 UNAIDS, "Resource Needs for an Expanded Response to AIDS in Low and Middle Income Countries," in discussion paper, "Making the Money Work: The Three Ones in Action," (Geneva, Switzerland: UNAIDS, March 2005); UNAIDS, *2006 Report on the global AIDS Epidemic* (Geneva, Switzerland: UNAIDS, 2006).

3 108th Congress, "An Act to Provide Assistance to Foreign Countries to Combat HIV/AIDS, Tuberculosis and Malaria, and for Other Purposes," Public Law (P.L.) 108–25.

4 108th Congress, "An Act to Provide Assistance to Foreign Countries to Combat HIV/AIDS, Tuberculosis and Malaria, and for Other Purposes."

5 PEPFAR, "About PEPFAR," (Washington, D.C.: PEPFAR, 2007) www.pepfar.gov/about

6 These are Botswana, Côte d'Ivoire, Ethiopia, Kenya, Mozambique, Namibia, Nigeria, Rwanda, South Africa, Tanzania, Uganda, and Zambia in Africa; Guyana and Haiti in the Caribbean; and Vietnam in Asia.

7 108th Congress, "An Act to Provide Assistance to Foreign Countries to Combat HIV/AIDS, Tuberculosis and Malaria, and for Other Purposes."

8 Interview with Peter Piot, Geneva, July 2007.

9 Kakaire A. Kirunda, "Uganda Gets One Third of Global Fund Money in 5 Years," *Daily Monitor*, 15 September 2008, www.monitor.co.ug/artman/publish/news/Uganda

10 Kirunda, "Uganda Gets One Third of Global Fund Money in 5 Years."

11 There have so far been nine funding rounds for Global Fund grant approvals between April 2002 and October 2008. A tenth round was tentatively scheduled for April 2009, but because of the global economic downturn this may be postponed or scaled down according to a statement issued in December 2008 by the executive head of the Fund, Michel Kazatchkine.

12 Global Fund website, data based on disbursements to principal recipients of all grants so far, www.globalfund.org

13 Global Fund website, www.globalfund.org

14 The largest contributors to the Global Fund are the United States, France, United Kingdom, Germany, and Japan.

15 Statement by the executive director of the Global Fund, Michel Kazatchkine, Sunday 4 May, 2008, in Moscow at a regional meeting of the fund, www.reuters.com/article.

16 See Gorik Ooms, Wim Van Damme, Brook K, Baker, Paul Zeltz, and Ted Shrecker, "The 'Diagonal' Approach to Global Fund Financing a Cure for the Broader Malaise of a Healthy System," *Globalization and Health* 4, no. 6 (2008): 1–7.

17 Julia Dayton, *World Bank HIV Interventions Ex Ante and Ex Post Evaluation* (Geneva, Switzerland: World Bank, 1998), www.worldbank/org/aidsecon/interven.pdf

18 IDA members, which include some of the poorest countries in the world, are eligible to borrow from the World Bank on concessionary terms involving interest-free loans with longer grace and repayment periods and grants.

19 World Bank, Project Database on HIV/AIDS Projects, http://web.worldbank.org

20 World Bank, *The Africa Multi-Country AIDS Program: Results of the World Bank's Response to a Development Crisis* (Washington, D.C.: World Bank, 2007).

21 World Bank, *Our Commitment: The World Bank's Africa Region HIV/AIDS Agenda for Action 2007–2011* (Washington, D.C.: World Bank, 2007).

22 UNAIDS, "Unified Budget and Work Plan 2008–9," http://data.unaids.org/pub/BaseDocument/2007/2008_2009_ubw_en.pdf

23 UNAIDS, *2006 Report on the Global AIDS Epidemic* (Geneva, Switzerland: UNAIDS, 2006); and UNAIDS, *2008 Report on the Global AIDS Epidemic* (Geneva, Switzerland: UNAIDS, 2008).

24 Funders Concerned about AIDS (FCAA), *US Philanthropic Commitments for HIV/AIDS* (New York: FCAA, March 2005); Jennifer Kates, *Financing the Responses to HIV/AIDS in Low and Middle-Income Countries* (Washington, D.C.: The Henry J. Kaiser Family Foundation, July 2005).

25 UNAIDS, *2006 Report on the Global AIDS Epidemic* (Geneva, Switzerland: UNAIDS, 2006).

26 Ibid.

27 Organization of African Unity (OAU), "Abuja Declaration on HIV/AIDS, Tuberculosis and Other Related Infectious Diseases" (Addis Ababa, Ethiopia: OAU, April 2001).

28 UNAIDS, *2006 Report on the Global AIDS Epidemic.*
29 Henry J. Kaiser Family Foundation, *Financing the Response to HIV/AIDS in Low and Middle Income Counties: Funding for HIV/AIDS from the G7 and the European Commission* (Washington, D.C.: Henry J. Kaiser Family Foundation, July 2005).
30 Henry J. Kaiser Family Foundation and UNAIDS, *Financing the Response to HIV/AIDS in Low and Middle Income Countries* (Washington, D.C.: Henry J. Kaiser Family Foundation, July 2008).
31 UNAIDS, *Financial Resources Required to Achieve Universal Access to HIV Prevention, Treatment, Care and Support* (Geneva, Switzerland: UNAIDS, October 2007).
32 The commitment to scale-up toward universal access was made by countries at the High-level Meeting on HIV/AIDS at the UN in New York in June 2006.
33 The commitment to scale-up toward universal access was made by countries at the High-level Meeting on HIV/AIDS at the UN in New York in June 2006.
34 The International Council for AIDS Service Organisations (ICASO) 2007, "Global Fund Advocacy Alert," prepared for the Global Fund Replenishment Conference, Berlin, www.icaso.org/AdvocacyGlobalFund.pdf
35 See, for example, Roger England, "Are We Spending too Much on HIV?" *British Medical Journal* 334 (17 February 2007): 334–44; Laurie Garrett, "The Challenge of Global Health," *Foreign Affairs* 86, no. 1 (2007): 14–38.
36 See Roger England, "We are Spending too much on AIDS" (*Financial Times*, 14 August 2006); England, "Are we spending too much on HIV?"; Roger England, "The Dangers of Disease Specific Programmes for Developing Countries," *British Medical Journal* 334 (17 February 2007): 335–565; Roger England, "Coordinating HIV Control Efforts: What to Do with the National AIDS Commissions," *Lancet* 367 (2006): 1786–789; also, James Chin, *The Myth of a General AIDS Pandemic: How Billions Are Wasted on AIDS Prevention*, distributed by the International Policy Network (London: Campaign for Fighting Diseases, January 2008).
37 Roger England, "The Writing is on the Wall for UNAIDS," *British Medical Journal* 336 (10 May 2008): 1072; Roger England, "Author's Reply to UNAIDS," 14 May 2008, available at www.bmj.com/cgi/eletters/336/7652/1072#195345
38 Laurie Garrett, "The Global Health Challenge," *Foreign Affairs* 86, no. 1 (January/February 2007): 14–38.
39 James Chin, "Myths Behind AIDS Might Lead to Billions in Misspending," *China Post*, 18 May 2008, www.chinapost.com.tw/commentary/; Chin, *The Myth of a General AIDS Pandemic: How Billions Are Wasted on AIDS Prevention.*
40 Elizabeth Pisani, *The Wisdom of Whores: Bureaucrats, Brothels and the Business of AIDS* (New York: Granta Books, 2008).
41 Paul De Lay, "AIDS Remains an Exceptional Issue," response to Roger England, 14 May 2008, available at www.bmj.com/cgi/eletters/336/7652/1072#195345; also, Alan Whiteside, "England Needs Nuance," response to Roger England, 14 May 2008, available at www.bmj.com/cgi/eletters/336/7652/1072#195345.
42 See Paul de Lay, Robert Greener, and Jose Antonio Izazola, "Are We Spending too Much on HIV?" *British Medical Journal* 334 (17 February

2007): 334–45; UNAIDS, *2006 Report on the Global AIDS Epidemic* (Geneva, Switzerland: UNAIDS, 2006).

43 See, for example, UNAIDS, "Making the Money Work: UNAIDS Technical Support to Countries 2008," www.data.unaids.org-jc1388-makingthemoneywork_en.pdf

9 Global governance and HIV/AIDS response

1 See for example, Commission on Global Governance, *Our Global Neighbourhood* (Oxford: Oxford University Press, 1995); Lawrence Finkelstein, "What is Global Governance?" *Global Governance* 1, no. 3 (1995): 367–72; David Held, Anthony McGrew, David Goldblatt, and Jonathan Perraton, *Global Transformations: Politics, Economics and Culture* (Stanford, Cal.: Stanford University Press, 1999); Thomas Weiss, "Governance, Good Governance and Global Governance: Conceptual and Actual Challenges," in Rorden Wilkinson, *The Global Governance Reader* (London: Routledge, 2005), 68–88.

2 Within the UN system, it is the World Intellectual Property Organization (WIPO) that has primary responsibility for the promotion and protection of intellectual property worldwide through cooperation among states, and the World Trade Organization (WTO) serves as the legal and institutional framework of the multilateral trading system, and monitors and enforces multilateral trade agreements. WTO agreements include protection of intellectual property rights in the wider context of the trade agenda of the organization.

3 WTO agreements on the protection of pharmaceutical patents on ARV are central to the issue of "access," and the key question then was whether such agreements should be strictly applied in all countries, or should the well-being of AIDS sufferers in low-income and poor countries constitute a basis for exception and for modifying the rules of international trade.

4 For example, UNAIDS, WHO, UNICEF, UNFPA, and the World Bank joined forces in 2000 to launch the Accelerated Access Initiative (AAI), involving the participation of five (and later seven) global pharmaceutical companies including Abbot Laboratories, Bristol-Myers Squib, GlaxoSmithKline, Merck, Gilead, and Hoffman La Roche, with the aim of making HIV/AIDS treatment and care affordable for a significantly greater number of people by lowering the price of patented HIV/AIDS drugs in low-income countries. About 400,000 AIDS patients were receiving ARV treatment under the AAI by 2005. See WHO, *International Trade and Health* (Geneva, Switzerland: UNAIDS, 2005); International Federation of Pharmaceutical Manufacturing Associations (IFPMA), "Industry Lands Accelerated Access Initiative: Progress in Expanding Access to AIDS Drugs," press release, 26 January 2005. It is important to note that these programs have not been wholly effective; the AAI for instance has provided drugs to only 0.02 percent of the people who need them.

5 The fact that matters pertaining to the intellectual property rights for pharmaceutical products were being handled by WTO, rather than WIPO which would seem to be the appropriate international institution on the basis of its mandate, has been attributed to the influence by governments of the North, led by the U.S.A., with major interest in the pharmaceutical

industry; they used their comparative strength in the international community to ensure that the intellectual property of pharmaceutical products was put on the trade agenda of GATT and its successor the WTO where decisions are made on the basis of consensus, unlike WIPO which has a more "democratic" governance structure, with each member state having one vote and decisions taken on the basis of a simple majority which gives the developing countries as a bloc an automatic majority. The stricter intellectual property protection obtained for pharmaceutical products under the original TRIPS would have been more difficult to obtain though negotiations at WIPO and would certainly have been defeated by the voting strength of the developing countries in that organization. See Yves Beigbeder, *International Public Health: Patients' Rights vs. Protection of Patents* (Aldershot: Ashgate, 2004); James Orbinski, "Health, Equity and Trade: A Failure in Global Governance" in Gary P. Sampson, *The Role of the WTO in Global Governance* (Tokyo and New York: UN University Press, 2001), 223–42; and Caroline Thomas, "Trade Policy and the Politics of Access to Drugs," *Third World Quarterly* 23, no. 2 (2004): 251–64.

6 Article 31, TRIPS Agreement 1995.

7 Article 31, TRIPS Agreement 1995.

8 See Association of the British Pharmaceutical Industry (ABPI), *Global Health and the Pharmaceutical Industry* (London: ABPI, July 2007).

9 ILO, *A Fair Globalization: Creating Opportunities for All.*

10 WHO has only ad hoc observer status on the WTO's Council for TRIPS which means that it can attend only by invitation, and the health agency has still not been able to secure regular observer status in the influential WTO General Council.

11 Oxfam, *Debt Relief and HIV/AIDS Crisis*, Oxfam Briefing Paper 25, June 2002.

12 See for, example, Oxfam, Briefing Paper 25, June 2002; Action Aid, *Changing Course: Alternative Approaches to Achieve the Millennium Development Goals and Fight HIV/AIDS* (Action Aid International, U.S.A., September 2005); ILO, *HIV/AIDS and Work in a Globalizing World* (Geneva, Switzerland: ILO Global Programme on HIV/AIDS and the World of Work, 2006).

13 Zdravka Todorova, "HIV/AIDS in Heavily Indebted Countries and Global Finance, *Oeconomicus* 6 (2003): 101–12.

14 Robert Hecht, Olusoji Adeyi, and Iris Semini, "Making AIDS Part of the Global Development Agenda," *Finance and Development* 39, no. 1 (2003): 36–39.

15 The PRSP initiative was adopted by the executive boards of the World Bank and the IMF in September 1999 as a new approach by the two IFIs to the provision of external assistance to poor countries; it is based on an analysis of poverty in a country and the definition of a national strategy for reducing it. The PRSP document for a country is drafted by the national government, usually led by the ministry of finance, and usually with consultation and advice from the IFIs, other donors, and civil society.

16 Based on my own observations as an external consultant on a joint World Bank-UNDP project, "The Integration of HIV/AIDS into PRSPs," in 2006 and 2007.

17 See, for example, Oxfam, Briefing Paper 25, June 2002; Action Aid, *Changing course: Alternative Approaches to Achieve the Millennium Development*

for example, David Goldsbrough, "Addressing the Challenge of HIV/ AIDS: Macroeconomic, Fiscal and Institutional Issues," Center for Global Development Working Paper 58 (Washington, D.C.: CGD, 2008).

19 Center for Global Development, *Does the IMF Constrain Health Spending in Poor Countries? Evidence and Agenda for Action* (Washington, D.C.: CGD, June 2007).

20 To date, only a handful of developing countries like China, India, and some ASEAN states are showing evidence of the potential of economic liberalization and globalization to promote growth and reduce poverty. See Raphael Kaplinsky, *Globalization, Poverty and Equality* (Cambridge: Polity Press, 2005).

21 This is elaborated in Franklyn Lisk and Desmond Cohen, "Regional Responses to HIV/AIDS in Sub-Saharan Africa: A Global Public Goods Approach," in *AIDS and Governance*, ed. Nana Poku, Alan Whiteside, and Bjorg Sandkjaer (Aldershot: Ashgate, 2007), 237–58.

22 See Giovanni Andrea Cornia, "Globalization and Health: Results and Options," *WHO Bulletin* 79, no. 9 (2001): 834–41; Tony Barnett and Alan Whiteside, *AIDS in the Twenty-First Century: Disease and Globalization* (Basingstoke: Palgrave Macmillan, 2002); and Sue Holden, *AIDS on the Agenda: Adapting Development and Humanitarian Programmes to Meet the Challenge of HIV/AIDS* (Oxford: Oxfam, 2003).

23 The governance structures of the IMF and the World Bank were determined over 60 years ago when those institutions were created and when the world was significantly different, yet these structures have remained more or less the same.

24 See ILO, *World Commission on the Social Dimension of Globalization*. The report called for a more equitable pattern of international development in terms of the distribution of the benefits of globalization between rich and poor countries. This, according to the report, required a reform of global economic governance, including changes in the rules and norms of global institutions to create flexible conditions needed to facilitate the full participation of poor and hitherto marginalized countries in the global economy.

25 See John J. Kirton and Jenevieve Mannell, "The G8 and Global Health Governance," in *Governing Global Health: Challenge, Response, Innovation*, ed. Andrew F. Cooper, John J. Kirton, and Ted Schrecker (Aldershot: Ashgate, 2007), 115–46.

26 See Joseph E. Stiglitz and Stephany Griffith-Jones, "Growth with Responsibility in a Globalized World: Findings of the Shadow G-8," Friedrich-Ebert-Stiftung, Dialogue on Globalization, Occasional Paper no. 31 (New York, May 2007). The proposed reform of the UN system in the area of global development policy similarly suggests the establishment of a forum of world leaders that has more equitable geographical representation within the system, see UN, *Delivering as One*, Report of the Secretary-General's High-level Panel on UN System-wide Coherence in the Areas of Development, Humanitarian Assistance, and the Environment, Final Draft to Co-Chairs (New York: United Nations, October 2006).

27 The G20 comprises the G8 nations and the European Union, plus the rapidly emerging economies of China, India, Brazil, Mexico, and South

Africa, and the systematically significant countries of Argentina, Australia, Indonesia, Saudi Arabia, South Korea, and Turkey.

28 This argument has been widely addressed in the literature, see Jagdish Bhagwati, "Globalization and Appropriate Governance," in *WIDER Perspectives on Global Development*, UN University-World Institute for Development Economics Research (WIDER), ed. Anthony Shorrocks, Giovanni Andrea Cornia, and Matti Pohjola (Basingstoke: Palgrave Macmillan, 2005), 74–100; Joseph Stiglitz, *Globalization and Its Discontents* (London: Penguin Books, 2002); and several contributions in Morten Boås and Desmond McNeill, eds, *Global Institutions and Development: Framing the World?* (London: Routledge, 2004); Deepak Nayar, ed., *Governing Globalization: Issues and Institutions* (Oxford: Oxford University Press, 2002); and Rorden Wilkinson, ed., *The Global Governance Reader* (London: Routledge, 2005).

29 See UN, *Delivering as One*; See also Kermal Dervis with Ceren Ozer, *A Better Globalization: Legitimacy, Governance and Reform* (Washington, D.C.: Center for Global Development, 2005), which advocates a more effective United Nations in terms of global governance and global public policy.

30 See Sonia Smith, "Global Crisis: AIDS and International Law," dissertation submitted for the Diplome d'études supérieures en relations internationals (Geneva, Switzerland: University of Geneva, Graduate Institute for International Studies, October 2006), for a discussion of these two types of global institutions in relation to AIDS governance.

10 Critical and emerging issues in HIV/AIDS response

1 For example, food insecurity and climate change can affect the effectiveness of HIV/AIDS programs and responses, and vulnerability to the epidemic among affected population groups.

2 See UNAIDS, *Making the Money Work through Greater UN Support for AIDS Responses: The 2006–2007 Consolidated UN Technical Support Plan for AIDS* (Geneva, Switzerland: UNAIDS, August 2005).

3 The "Three Ones" principles refer to: "One Agreed AIDS Action Framework" as the basis for coordinating the efforts of all partners; "One National AIDS Coordinating Authority," with broad multi-sectoral mandate; and "One Agreed Country-Level Monitoring and Evaluation System."

4 African Union, 4th Summit of Heads of State and Government, Abuja, Nigeria, January 2005.

5 Cited in article by Sabin Russell, "Politics Worries U.N. AIDS Officials as much as Virus," *San Francisco Chronicle*, 9 May 2007.

6 World Bank, *Global HIV/AIDS Program of Action* (Washington, D.C.: World Bank, August 2005).

7 World Bank, *Global HIV/AIDS Program of Action*, 11.

8 UNAIDS and WHO, *AIDS Epidemic Update 2007* (Geneva, Switzerland: UNAIDS, December 2007).

9 CDC, "Achievements in Public Health: Reduction in Perinatal Transmission of HIV Infection—United States," *Morbidity and Mortality Weekly Report*, no. 55 (Atlanta, Ga.: CDC, 2006).

10 UNICEF, *A Call for Action: Children, the Missing Face of AIDS* (New York: UNICEF, 2005).

11 UNICEF, *A Call for Action: Children, the Missing Face of AIDS.*
12 See, HIV Vaccines and Microbicides Resource Tracking Working Group, *Sustaining the HIV Prevention Research Agenda: Funding for Research and Development of HIV Vaccines, Microbicides and other New Prevention Options, 2000–2007* (HIV Vaccines and Microbicides Resource Tracking Working Group, August 2008); also Global HIV Vaccine Enterprise, *Promoting Innovation and Collaboration to Speed the Search for an HIV Vaccine* (Seattle, Wash.: Bill and Melinda Gates Foundation, 2007).
13 BBC News Service, 15 February 2008, 10.23 GMT, at http://news.bbc.co.uk/2/hi/science/nature/7246117.stm
14 See International AIDS Vaccine Initiative (IAVI), "AIDS Vaccine Blue Print 2008: A Challenge to the Field, a Roadmap for Progress," (New York: IAVI, 2008).
15 Article by Michael Weinstein, "Stop AIDS Vaccine Research," *Los Angeles Times*, 4 April 2008.
16 BBC News Service, http://newsnote.bbc.co.uk/2/hi/health/724696
17 AIDS Vaccine Advocacy Coalition (AVAC), *The Search Must Continue: AVAC Report 2008* (New York: AVAC, 2008).
18 WHO, "Frequently Asked Questions about TB and HIV," (Geneva, Switzerland: WHO, 2007).
19 WHO, "Facts on HIV-TB, HIV-TB Global Leaders Forum," 9 June 2008.

Appendix 1 Memorandum of understanmding on UNAIDS

1 Pending allocation of the final resolution number.
2 Abbreviation for "the resident coordinator of the United Nations system's operational activities for development".
*** (*Source*: Official Bulletin of the ILO, vol. LXXXIV, 2001, series A, no. 1)

Select bibliography

Tony Barnett and Alan Whiteside, *AIDS in the Twenty-First Century: Disease and Globalization*, 2nd ed.—fully revised and updated 2008 (Basingstoke: Palgrave Macmillan, 2002). This is an incisive analysis of HIV/AIDS as a long-wave epidemic whose impact not only affects people and society but, according to the authors, would also influence international political, economic, and social relations in the first decades of this century. It shows, for example, that the trajectory of the epidemic can be directly linked to adverse consequences for developing countries of the process of globalization.

John Iliffe, *The African AIDS Epidemic: A History* (Oxford: James Currey, 2006). This is a handy and scholarly analysis of the evolution and challenges of the HIV/AIDS epidemic, which addresses key issues such as the origins and nature of the virus; the progress of the epidemic across the African continent; the devastating effects on households, social systems, and economies; the circumstances that have made its impact exceptional and so severe; the responses of governments, international bodies, and NGOs; the moral and political controversies; and the search for remedies and vaccines.

International Labour Office, *An ILO Code of Practice on HIV/AIDS and the World of Work* (Geneva, Switzerland: ILO, 2001). The Code, which is the result of collaboration between the secretariat of the ILO and the tripartite constituents of the organization and which was unanimously adopted by the ILO governing body and conference, provides practical guidelines for policymakers, employers and workers' organizations for formulating and implementing workplace HIV/AIDS policies and programs.

——*HIV/AIDS and Work: Global Estimates, Impact and Responses* (Geneva, Switzerland: ILO, 2004). This book provides the first global estimates of the impact of HIV/AIDS in the world of work, based on quantitative and qualitative data and information on the effects of the epidemic on the labor force, production, social protection, and economic growth, including analysis and policy advice.

Markus Haacker, ed., *The Macroeconomics of HIV/AIDS* (Washington, D.C.: International Monetary Fund, 2004). A collection of essays by specialists from the IMF and various other institutions, which focus on the public finance, economic growth, human capital, poverty, social security, and public services implications of the epidemic, all of which add up to a comprehensive resource for public policy-makers addressing the economic and fiscal consequences of the global AIDS crisis.

Sue Holden, *AIDS on the Agenda* (Oxford: Oxfam GB in association with ActionAid and Save the Children, 2003). A user-friendly guidance for policy-makers and HIV/AIDS program managers and staff, based on case studies drawn from the experience of three major international NGOs involved in adapting development and humanitarian programs to meet the challenge of the global HIV/AIDS response.

Jonathan Mann, Daniel Tarantola, and Thomas Netter, eds., *AIDS in the World: A Global Report* (Cambridge, Mass.: Harvard University Press, 1992). When it was published, this massive volume (over 1,000 pages) was the most comprehensive technical account and synthesis of best possible information on the evolution of the global HIV/AIDS epidemic during its first decade, and its effects and worldwide response. Its contributors were a team of experts assembled by Jonathan Mann, founding director of the WHO's Global Programme on AIDS (GPA), and coordinated from Harvard University, to where Mann moved after leaving the GPA. It was intended to be the first in a series of biennial global reports aimed at governments, international organizations, policy-makers, scientists, and healthcare workers, which did not eventuate; but the original edition is still useful as a reference source and as a benchmark for assessing changes over time in important dimensions of the global response to the epidemic.

Office of the United Nations High Commissioner for Human Rights (OHCHR) and UNAIDS, *International Guidelines on HIV/AIDS and Human Rights, 2006 Consolidated Version* (Geneva, Switzerland: OHCHR/UNAIDS, 2006). This is a consolidated version of the International Guidelines on HIV/AIDS and Human Rights adopted by the Second and Third International Consultations (experts meetings) on the subject, organized jointly by OHCHR and UNAIDS in Geneva in 1996 and 2002 respectively; the guidelines are aimed at governments, NGOs, the UN system, regional organizations, and others concerned about the protection of human rights in the context of HIV/AIDS.

Elizabeth Pisani, *The Wisdom of Whores: Bureaucrats, Brothels and the Business of AIDS* (New York and London: W. W. Norton, 2008). A blunt and controversial insider's account of failures in the global response to the HIV/AIDS epidemic, narrated at times in an hilarious manner, highlighting the adverse consequences for those affected by wrong public policy and the prioritizing of politics and "spin" over science and common sense about disease transmission.

Nana Poku, Alan Whiteside, and Bjorg Sandkjaer, eds., *AIDS and Governance* (Aldershot: Ashgate, 2008). Chapters by individual authors covering different dimensions of the impacts and challenges of HIV/AIDS, including development, national security, politics, financing and governance, and the threat posed by the epidemic to the organization of economic, social, and political life—used as the analytical framework to show how HIV/AIDS affects governance and conversely how governance affects the course of the epidemic.

Hakan Seckinelgin, *The International Politics of HIV/AIDS: Global Disease— Local Pain* (London: Routledge, 2007). A lively and well written book on the governance of the global response to the HIV/AIDS epidemic and related policy issues, including an analysis of the political environment in which the response by the international system is pursued.

Alex de Waal, *AIDS and Power: Why there is No Political Crisis—Yet* (London and New York: Zed Books, 2006). A well written and insightful analysis which raises difficult questions and skepticism about the adequacy of the present approach to HIV/AIDS, particularly regarding how the epidemic is managed by African governments, and the question of why such a deadly and devastating epidemic has had only a limited political impact in Africa, or has not been accorded a high priority in African public policy, given the scale of its impact in the region.

Alice Welbourn with Joanna Hoare, eds., *HIV and AIDS* (Oxford: Oxfam GB, 2008). A collection of case studies from around the world, which explores the links between HIV/AIDS, poverty and gender equality and is aimed at development practitioners, policy-makers and researchers.

Alan Whiteside, *HIV/AIDS: A Very Short Introduction* (Oxford: Oxford University Press, 2009). This is a useful and easy to read introduction to the subject, published under OUP's popular "Very Short Introduction" series; it explores the biomedical characteristics and catastrophic impact of the HIV/ AIDS epidemic, and the role of governments, the international system, and big pharmaceutical companies in the response.

World Bank, *Confronting AIDS: Public Priorities in a Global Epidemic* (Oxford: Oxford University Press, 1999). A World Bank policy research report on HIV/AIDS prepared by staff of that institution, with the support of UNAIDS and the European Commission, which focuses on the valuable contribution of public policy and the potential benefits of international cooperation in the global response to the epidemic.

UNAIDS and WHO, *AIDS Epidemic Update* (Geneva, Switzerland: UNAIDS/WHO, various years). Annual publication published on World AIDS Day (1 December) each year, which details global and regional trends and important developments in the surveillance (numbers infected and AIDS deaths by age and sex, etc.) and response to the epidemic worldwide.

United Nations General Assembly, Special Session on HIV/AIDS (UNGASS), *Declaration of Commitment on HIV/AIDS* (New York: United Nations, June 2001). This is the first global Declaration adopted by the United Nations at the UNGASS, 25–27 June 2001, which reaffirmed the commitment of over one hundred world leaders, with the support of business and civil society, to tackle HIV/AIDS in a coordinated manner at the global level and on the basis of a time-bound action plan. Routledge Global Institutions. Edited by Thomas G. Weiss. The CUNY Graduate Center, New York, U.S.A. and Rorden Wilkinson University of Manchester, U.K.

Index